The Harcourt Brace Guide to Teaching First-Year Composition

Kathryn Rosser Raign
University of North Texas

HARCOURT
BRACE

HARCOURT BRACE COLLEGE PUBLISHERS

Fort Worth   Philadelphia   San Diego   New York   Orlando   Austin   San Antonio
Toronto   Montreal   London   Sydney   Tokyo

ISBN: 0-15-508161-6

Address for orders:
Harcourt Brace College Publishers
6277 Sea Harbor Drive
Orlando, Florida 32887-6777
1-800-782-4479

Address for editorial correspondence:
Harcourt Brace College Publishers
301 Commerce Street, Suite 3700
Fort Worth, Texas 76102

Web site address:
http://www.harbrace.com/english

Printed in the United States of America.
7890123456 023 987654321

Preface

The Harcourt Brace Guide to Teaching First-Year Composition is designed for teachers of writing at all levels, but particularly for those brave souls who are teaching for the first time, and for those teachers, such as myself, who are responsible for mentoring and guiding those first-time teachers. This book has three parts:

The Basics of Teaching Writing: eight chapters that discuss the basic principles of teaching writing such as designing a class, evaluating papers, and writing effective assignments.

Selected Essays: essays by first-year writers; essays by graduate students; and multiple drafts of graduate student essays.

Bibliography: a listing of useful books and articles that discuss the process and theory of teaching writing.

I hope this book will lend itself to being used in a variety of ways, but below I suggest some possibilities for those teachers who might elect to use this book when teaching the course my college calls, "Methods of Teaching Freshman Composition."

Using This Book

As I explain in the introduction to this book, I believe it is important for graduate students who are learning to teach writing to be reminded of what it is like to be a writing student and to actually engage in the activities in which they expect their own students to engage. Consequently, I have included exercises at the end of each chapter: writing exercises and collaborative activities. The *writing exercises* ask students to do three things: write assignments that they can use when teaching; write essays based on the communities of discourse assignment, which I provide in Chapter Six and suggest that new teachers use their first semester; and write essays that explore aspects of writing and how they write. It is probably not realistic to expect busy graduate students to complete each of the assignments, but each teacher can choose those that he or she considers most useful or have students do some assignments collaboratively. The collaborative activities follow the writing exercises and ask students to evaluate the exercises and assignments that they have written, try the assignments out, and engage in activities such as peer editing. When graduate students experience the problems and difficulties of activities, such as peer editing, from the student's perspective, they have a much better understanding of how to use those activities in the classroom. By exchanging the exercises that they write, student teachers also have an opportunity to begin creating a library of activities and assignments that they can use in class. Again, each teacher can use as many or as few of these exercises as he or she considers appropriate. I recommend using as many as possible.

Part two includes three types of essays: first-year student essays, graduate student essays, and graduate student essays with multiple drafts—an early and a revised draft. The essays are on a variety of topics, but all represent some version of the six papers included in the communities of discourse assignment. These essays can be used to foster discussion of teaching methods or writing techniques, to generate ideas for future papers or activities, or to serve as models. Students can also use the papers for practice in evaluating student writing or responding to multiple drafts. These are just suggestions, but I find it helpful to occasionally use writing to which no one in a class feels strongly attached because such an attitude fosters honesty. I hope that you find these suggestions helpful.

The book concludes with a bibliography. This bibliography is not comprehensive, but it does include a useful list of many of the most important essays and books on the teaching of writing.

When I began teaching composition, I searched for a book such as this one and found none. When I began teaching others how to teach composition, I renewed my search—again with no results. I felt compelled to write this book so that other teachers, such as myself, have a resource that they can go to when they need advice. I hope this book provides that.

I would like to acknowledge the many people whose help and support made this book possible. First, my thanks goes to all the Teaching Fellows at the University of North Texas who have shared their ideas and their inspiration with me. Their enthusiasm is what made this book worth writing. Special thanks goes to those of you (Sandra, Trey, Priscilla, and Kate) who read my rough drafts and encouraged me to keep going. Thank you to Priscilla Reiser and Dennis Evans, my invaluable assistants and good friends. My gratitude extends to those teachers who taught me a love for my craft and a belief in what I was doing: Win Horner, Gary Tate, and Jim Corder. Finally, I would like to thank my husband Jerry and my daughter Erin. They have taught me the most important lessons of all.

Contents

Introduction

Why Write?

I stood in front of them seven times this week, and I have to say it wasn't bad. I came away feeling that I had juggled my way through it, but at least I didn't drop anything. (An entry from Trey Colvin's teaching journal)

Music is what occurs between the notes, and frankly, that scares me. I feel that a segue from one topic into another isn't really a segue at all but a locomotive that comes to a screeching halt only to begin the slow move backwards. There is nothing smooth about it. My students scare me because, despite all those placating articles that claim I have the power, that I am in control, I know the opposite to be the case, and I fear they will figure this out. (Tom Connelly)

Every fall I teach "Methods of Teaching Composition." I know from my own experience as a student that such courses tend to be popular for a number of reasons:

- You get to have fun telling stories and laughing about your students.
- You learn some things you really need to know, such as how to comment on papers effectively.
- They're easy; everyone already knows how to write, even if he or she hasn't taught before.

In my class two of these things are true. My students and I do have fun swapping stories. The classroom can become that safe place where we can begin to laugh about our disasters, knowing that everyone else in the room has had his or her own. Suddenly falling off the desk as you lecture (Yes. I did this.) isn't really the end of your teaching career. And you aren't the first teacher to make a student cry or teach a class with your pants unzipped. My students do learn things they need to know, sometimes from me, but usually from each other.

But there is one point on which we disagree—the class is not easy because no writer ever stops learning how to write, and anyone who wants to teach writing effectively must first and always write. So I expect the activity in my class to involve more than swapping stories and exchanging exercises. I expect my students—graduate students, teachers, writers—to write, and I expect to respond to them as a writer.

Seeing the World from the Eyes of a First-Year Writing Student

Each term, I ask my graduate students to write several papers over the course of the semester, and I always give them some of the same writing assignments that I include in the sample first-year composition syllabus that I hand out, the syllabus that most of them will use their first semesters as teachers. I also ask my students to write papers in which they consider how they teach and write. I always evaluate those papers in the same way that I evaluate those of my first-year writers. In other words, I disregard that many of them are accomplished readers and react to their papers as works in progress rather than as finished products. Why do I do this? So my students, who are teachers, can have the experience of being first-year writers as they are teaching first-year writers. I suspect I am not popular.

In Chapter Six of this book, I include an extended assignment called "communities of discourse." This is the assignment that I frequently use when I teach first-year composition courses and the one that I encourage my first-time teachers to use because of its accessibility. The assignment includes six papers:

a proposal,

a place paper,

an interview,

an event paper,

an issue paper,

and a response paper.

I allow my first-year writing students to choose their own communities, but I make my graduate students write about the community of writing teachers to force them to think consciously about how they write and teach. This activity allows them to begin consciously conceptualizing what they have been doing unconsciously. This past fall, I had my graduate students write three of these six papers: the proposal, the event, and the issue.

When I told my graduate students that they would be writing these papers, the response was favorable. I heard comments such as,

"Great, I'll have some samples of good writing to use in class when I discuss these essays."

"This will be fun. I haven't written like a freshman since I was one."

"What a nice break from real writing."

These comments were accurate; however, none of my students anticipated that I wanted them to have the full "first-year" experience.

The First-Year Experience

A large portion of the discussions of the graduate class involved sharing methods of teaching writing as a process, an issue that is discussed later in this book. The class agreed that for most papers the students would engage in the following classroom activities:

- Some form of invention. Normally the students engage in some sort of idea-generating activity such as brainstorming, followed by an activity intended to help them narrow their topics, possibly freewriting or recording in a journal.
- Some form of writing exercise, usually a collaborative activity that allows students to practice a specific writing skill.
- Some form of peer editing.

Once the activities resulted in papers that the students turned in, the teacher would evaluate the papers, attempting to meet the suggested criteria below, criteria my graduate students developed:

- Use supportive commentary. Say something good about every paper.
- Avoid appropriating the students' papers or ideas. Make suggestions not corrections or directions.
- Use provocative comments that suggest further writing rather than closure. "Could you find a way to get more of your own voice into this essay?"
- Rather than giving a grade, suggest that the student continue to revise the paper. "This is a good start. I look forward to reading the next version."

I had my graduate students engage in these same activities after I assigned the proposal paper. In fact, we devoted at least two hours of our three-hour class period to such activities.

I introduced my graduate students to the concept of writing a proposal in the same way that I introduced it to my first-year writing students. The graduate students took notes and told me how helpful they expected their students to find my outline of problem, solution, and plan of action. When we tried an invention exercise in class, the students chuckled their way through a freewriting session. When we spent an afternoon writing group proposals and then developing a list of criteria for good proposals, the graduate students nodded their heads wisely and shared their commitment to trying the exercise with their own students. When I informed them that we would be peer editing, they seemed a bit surprised, but engaged in the activity willingly. When I returned their first papers to them, their faces reflected shock, dismay, anger—and betrayal. They could have been any class of first-year writing students I've ever taught.

What did I do to their papers to cause such consternation? I treated them like the papers of my first-year students.

I found something positive to say about every paper.

"I like the commitment to teaching that you show in this paper."

"I enjoyed the humor—especially in regard to those teaching disasters we all dread."

I avoided appropriating the student's papers.

"Is all of this conversation pertinent to your paper?"

"I feel like something is missing here? Did you tell the whole story?"

I used provocative comments to encourage more writing.

"Could you tell more about the events that preceded your wish to become a teacher?"

"Your description of how you felt when the student was crying is great, but what happened afterward? How did you feel when he left? What did you do the next time you saw him?"

Rather than giving grades, I suggested rewrites—for everyone.

"This is an excellent beginning. I'm anxious to see what you do in the next draft."

"The event you described is very compelling. What happens next?"

They were not happy. When the first hand went up, I told them I would be happy to discuss their papers, but not until twenty-four hours had passed. They left quietly.

The next time class met, a student immediately raised her hand and asked, "Why didn't we get any grades?" Then she looked self-consciously around and said, "Did everyone else get a grade?" Before my students could begin taking a tally of whose paper said what, I quickly interjected and told them that I hadn't given any grades. This time another student raised his hand and simply said, "Why? Were they that bad?" And though his tone implied that he was joking, I knew and the class knew that he was deadly serious. Welcome to the Twilight Zone. How does the world look through the eyes of a composition student?

I responded to that graduate student the same way I've responded to many other students in many other first-year composition classes: I reminded him that writing was a process (that thing they had all agreed with just a week ago) and that I had chosen not to give grades because I wanted to encourage each of them to rewrite. What did the student say? "OK, yeah, for freshmen, but what about us? How about our papers? We don't have time to rewrite." And that is the point of this introduction and, to a large degree, the point of this book. My students were thinking like students; they were not thinking like writers. They were responding in exactly the way their own students would respond when they received their papers back from their teachers. They were resentful, confused, hurt, challenged, and all the other things writing students are when faced with a teacher who is treating them as writers rather than as students and emphasizing content rather than grades.

I had several students come to my office to discuss papers. One student in particular came several times. The first time he came to my office, we shared a conversation very similar to this one:

"Why don't you like my style of writing?"

"What makes you think I don't like your style of writing?"

Very sarcastically, "The fact that you told me to rewrite!"

"I didn't tell you to rewrite; the choice is yours."

"Some choice. Obviously, if I want an A, I have to rewrite. I don't understand the problem. Perhaps you write differently at this university. Why don't you just tell me what you want?"

His implication seemed to be that his teachers and colleagues at his previous college had applauded his excessive use of passive voice in a personal narrative.

"Why don't you explain to me why you chose that particular style. How does it help you achieve your purpose?"

"I chose this style because it is the way I've always written, and I've been told I'm a good writer. I guess in this class I'd better disregard that and do what you want."

"You can write however you choose, but I'm going to continue to respond to what you've written, not to what you've been told is the 'right' way to do things."

He concluded by informing me that he would rewrite, but "only because he was accustomed to receiving A's and would do whatever was necessary to receive one. Was this a first-year writing student?

At our second meeting, this student complained that he was not accustomed to having his writing "savaged" in such a manner. I pointed out that many of the comments were positive. He informed me that he could not see those comments because of the many other negative ones, but allowed that they might exist.

My graduate students, who were learning how to teach writing, had become their own students. When I pointed this out to them in class, there was a moment of stunned silence. And then someone laughed. One of the quiet members of the class, piped up from the back, and said

"Now I know why my students always look like they want to cry. It's hard to see your paper all marked up. It doesn't matter if the comments are supportive, all you see is red, even when the teacher wrote in pencil."

Writing teachers need to write because only a writer can understand what it feels like to have his or her work rejected, and that is how it feels when someone comments on your paper and sends it back with anything less than an A. My graduate students are certainly more experienced writers than a group of composition students, and they tend to have higher levels of self-confidence. This may in fact have made the experience even more painful for them because they had preconceived ideas about the writing I asked them to do. It was a diversion. It was an opportunity to show what they can do; it was a chance to do the kind of writing they couldn't do when they were first-year writing students. They are all experienced graduate students who are accustomed to getting good grades and very much accustomed to a product-oriented system. In fact, they are part of the system that this book tries desperately to break away from. I did not respond to them in a product-oriented manner. I responded to them as one writer to another, and they found the experience very uncomfortable.

So what do I expect graduate students to get from the experience of being treated as I hope they treat their own students? I certainly hope that they get the opportunity to fully explore their own capabilities as writers, but perhaps more importantly I hope that they develop an understanding of what the world looks like through the eyes of their students. I want them to understand and remember several important things:

- Having your writing sent back—even if it is for good reasons—always hurts. No one likes to have his or her writing "savaged."
- Students want answers. They want their teachers to appropriate their papers and turn them into A papers—whatever those might be.
- Students are frustrated by the process of writing because most of them are used to functioning in a product-oriented educational system.
- Writing as process can be a frightening experience. There are no easy answers, and personal risks are required and expected.
- Students want to learn how to write. They just need someone to encourage them to get past the anger and frustration and show them how.
- The process does work. Every writer's work improves if he or she refuses to accept a first attempt. Students (even graduate students) just need to experience this first hand.

What They Learned

The student who visited my office several times has rewritten all of his papers— one paper was rewritten twice. He told me that his experience has given him a much greater empathy for what he has blithely put his own students through. He agrees that passive voice is not the only way to write. We are friends, and I enjoy his visits to my office.

My students took a journey, and none of them returned unaffected. As the semester progressed, and they continued to write, the questions that they asked and the comments that they made changed drastically. All of my students agreed that they could teach an assignment that they had written much more effectively than one that they hadn't. As one student put it, "I asked the same questions they were asking, so I knew how to answer because I knew what kind of help I needed." Another student said that having to do a rewrite of a paper based on a teacher's comments made her much more conscious of the types of things she wrote on her own student's papers.

Conclusion

All the graduate students agreed that the process of conceptualizing their beliefs regarding teaching, even though it had been painful, had also been helpful. "I was so self-conscious about teaching that I couldn't say anything without totally obsessing over whether it was the right thing to say," one student offered. Another explained how self-conscious her writing had become: "I used to just write. Now I have to think things like, did I prewrite enough? Am I using the process? I get so frustrated, and I wish I could just turn myself off." But despite the self-consciousness that all the students felt as both writers and teachers, they all agreed that the result of such introspection was a much clearer under-standing of what was involved in both processes. As one of my students put it:

> "Now that I know I have a writing process, and I can describe it, it is much easier for me to convince my students to believe that they have one too. Because I believe what I'm saying, I have a better chance of making them believe it."

I couldn't have said it better myself.

Exercises

Writing Exercise

1. Describe your writing process in a brief essay. Start by considering these questions:
   - Where do you write?
   - When?
   - Does your process change?
   - Why do you write the way you do?
   - Can you describe your process step by step?

Collaborative Activities

1. Working in groups of three or four, conduct some protocol analyses to compare your writing processes. Try one of the following procedures:

   Method One
   - As a group, develop a brief writing assignment.
   - One by one, take turns writing the assignment while the other group members watch and take notes. Remember to have the writer verbalize his or her thought processes as he or she works.
   - Compare the results and develop some standard elements of all writing processes. What do the differences tell you about how people write?
   - How can what you've learned apply to teaching?
   - Share with the class what you learned.

   Method Two
   - As a group, develop a brief writing assignment.
   - Have each group member take the assignment home and record his or her thought processes as he or she writes the assignment.
   - Compare the results and develop some standard elements of all writing processes. What do the differences tell you about how people write?
   - How can what you've learned apply to teaching?
   - Share with the class what you learned.

2. As a class, develop several ideas for papers that ask you to discuss aspects of your teaching or writing that you perform unconsciously and would benefit from considering more self-consciously. Which paper would you choose to write? Which paper would you ask your students to write? Why?

Part I

The Basics of Teaching Writing

Chapter One
Planning a Course in Writing

What a huge responsibility this is. These kids are paying for an education, and I'm as green as a trash-can punch rookie in the morning. (Michelle Niemczyk)

What is amazing is how calm I was once I had begun to teach. Misgivings never-the-less abound. I am ill-prepared. . . . Yet in spite of all incipient crises, a great calm did descend. And they laughed at my jokes. (Kevin Clay)

As the above testimonials eloquently illustrate, few experiences in life are more terrifying than preparing to go in and teach your first class. I had nightmares for weeks before my first class began. I experienced it all, from the clichéd to the horrifying—I showed up for class in my underwear; I showed up for class wishing I was wearing underwear; I showed up for class only to realize that it had been going on without me for six weeks. I still get a knot in my stomach when I think back to those days before I actually walked into that classroom and faced those twenty-eight blank stares. I had to run to the bathroom and throw up five minutes before my first class began.

Unlike those teachers who have degrees in education, those of us who begin our teaching careers while pursuing graduate degrees in English have little, if any, training in how to get through each day with some semblance of grace—forget actually teaching your students anything worth while! Of course, the picture is not quite that bleak, but you will have days when you may feel lost on an uncharted sea. Realistically, I assume that all of you who are teaching for the first time have received some type of training, but as I know from my own experiences, the type and amount of training varies, and it never seems to come early enough to be of any help. As I was working my way through college, I had several types of training:

- *Presemester workshops:* Workshops that occur before you begin teaching can be helpful, but when the class begins and problems start developing, you have no formal support system.
- *Mentorships:* If you're lucky enough to get a good mentor, these can be wonderful. I spent a semester grading another person's papers for comma splices.

- *Semester-length methods courses*: We covered a great deal of material, but we always seemed to be a step behind.

Any training can be valuable, but every method suffers from one fatal flaw—you never get what you need when you need it. I have learned, while teaching a methods course, that no matter how carefully I organize, I'm always a step behind my students' needs. They need to know everything about teaching, right now, and I can't deliver that. No one can deliver that. However, you can prepare yourself as much as possible by understanding how to plan a writing course—something that was never covered in any coherent way in any of the training that I received. I'm not sure that I cover this in my own class. Classes on how to teach writing, like writing classes themselves, generate so much energy and activity that the best a teacher can hope to do is stay afloat. I spend so much time throwing out life rafts that I never feel as though we have the luxury to sit back long enough to consider the big picture, so here it is—the calm in the eye of the storm—a plan for developing a course in writing.

Conceptualizing the Course: Making the Classroom Reflect the Basic Principles of Writing As Process

A coherent classroom is one where the exercises, the activities, and the beliefs of the instructor are all consistent. If you ask your students to free write without knowing why and without having a clear understanding of what you want your students to learn from the exercise, they will quickly lose interest in the activity and the class will lose momentum. For instance, one of my new instructors shared the opinion below:

> "My kids don't understand free writing and want rules. I don't know how to teach things that are so alien to what I've been taught. Of course, technically I don't know how to teach anything."

This instructor had used free writing because I had suggested it to her, not because she felt the exercise had any value or was integral to the class. Her students realized this and the exercise was a failure; it was busy work.

There are many different ways to teach, and every teacher has to find a method that fits him or her. However, some basic principles of teaching apply to every writing class, no matter what method the individual uses:

- Writing is a process.
- Class exercises and activities should be clearly integrated with the goal of the class—to improve writing skills.
- Writing is a collaborative activity.
- Students learn most effectively when they teach themselves.
- The primary activity in any writing class should be writing.
- Students should be encouraged to discover their own motives for writing.

Writing is a process.

Students will not be convinced of the value of writing as a process if they do not see a direct link between the structure of the course and the basic principles of writing as process. In other words, simply using exercises that reflect the generally accepted stages of the writing process—prewriting, writing, and rewriting—will not suffice. Consider the following example:

Jason began his first semester of teaching composition convinced of the value of teaching writing as process. He carefully planned a schedule that included three types of activities for each of the six papers that his students were writing:

- His students began each new writing task with an invention exercise: sometimes freewriting, sometimes brainstorming.
- This planning stage was followed by a writing exercise.
- Next, he had his students peer edit and then incorporate the suggestions that they received into the final paper, which they then submitted for a grade before beginning the next assignment.

Jason's two week schedule to help his students write about a place that was significant to them looked like this:

Tuesday	Freewrite for ten minutes on any topic. Discuss the structure of the descriptive essay. Write an outline for the paper, including the elements of the descriptive paper.
Thursday	Discuss descriptive writing techniques. Place students in groups and send them out on campus to observe a place. Have each group write a paragraph describing the place they observed. Read the paragraphs aloud and ask the other students in class to identify the place being described.
Tuesday	Complete the group exercise. With the remaining time, allow students to write in their journals.
Thursday	Peer edit papers based on questions supplied by the teacher. Paper is due on Tuesday.

Jason didn't understand why his students began the semester enthusiastically but became more and more resentful and lethargic as time passed. Rather than scribbling frantically during freewriting, more and more of his students began doodling and whispering. They began leaving the class upset and asking questions like, "Why are we doing this?" The words "busy work" were frequently mumbled.

What was the problem? Jason thought that he was teaching process writing when he was actually teaching a very product-oriented approach while maintaining a teacher-centered classroom dynamic, and his students recognized the inherent hypocrisy in his methods.

Jason believed his class was process-oriented because he used exercises based on the process of writing, but the fundamental structure of his class is not process oriented for the following reasons:

He approaches the writing assignment from the standpoint that there is one correct structure for a descriptive essay—a structure that he indicates exists separately from the students' individual papers: He reinforces this belief by asking his students to create an outline of a structure that they have not yet discovered.

The process-oriented activities he uses in class have no clear connection to the papers that the students are writing: For example, he asks his students to freewrite about anything rather than helping the students recognize freewriting as preparation for the paper on which they are currently working. And again, with the writing exercise, he has his students do an exercise that involves skills that they might use in their own papers, but he doesn't use the exercise to make that connection for his students.

He works from the premise that his role is to impart information to his students rather than facilitate their discovering it for themselves via the process of both learning and writing: Rather than helping his students develop their own peer editing questions, which would allow them to begin developing an understanding of editing, he supplies them with questions, again reinforcing the teacher/product-oriented nature of the assignment.

Finally, he allows the students to turn in the paper for a grade only once, ignoring the process that went into the writing of the paper: He emphasizes the product-oriented nature of the course by not allowing his students to continue working on their papers after he has commented on them.

Jason planned his class with good intentions, but he sabotaged those intentions by neglecting to integrate class exercises with the goals of the process-oriented writing class.

Class exercises and activities should be clearly integrated with the goal of the class—to improve writing skills.

Jason's basic course outline was sound; such a two-week structure works well. However, within that two-week structure, he needs to integrate his exercises with the goal of the class so that the students can begin assimilating an awareness of their writing process into their own work. The following two-week structure is a good starting place for any writing teacher, regardless of the individual content choice he or she may make:

Day One	Introduce a writing topic.
	Guide the students through invention exercises intended to help them begin developing topics and material for their papers.

Day Two | Write and analyze texts.

Give students a text that incorporates skills that they can incorporate into their own papers to analyze. Supplying a writing sample of your own for analysis is an excellent idea.

Give students an opportunity to begin writing their papers or collaborating on shorter papers of a similar nature. Help them analyze the resulting texts to identify effective structures and techniques.

Day Three | Continue writing and analyzing texts. In-class conferences are another option that allow you to speak to individual students.

Day Four | Ask your students to develop a class list of peer-editing concerns, helping them draw on their discoveries of the previous two class periods to draft appropriate questions.

Peer edit.

Papers are due for initial evaluation the following class period, but students have the opportunity to rewrite the papers after they are returned.

This structure, though basically the same as Jason's, is different in several fundamental ways:

- *Rather than having students write on any topic without guidance, the instructor clearly shows the students that the purpose of each exercise is to help them develop material for a paper that will be evaluated.*
- *The instructor uses the students' actual texts as the focus of class discussion, not artificially created texts that have no relationship to the papers that the students will turn in for evaluation:* This also supplies the instructor with the opportunity to write with the students, especially if he or she is writing any of the papers suggested in this book. Such integration will help the students understand how they can use a process approach as writers and begin to conceptualize a process of their own. Rather than mere busy work, classroom exercises become an extension of the students' own work as writers.
- *Because students have the opportunity to continue working on papers after the instructor has evaluated them, they will be able to apply what they are learning to what they write—reinforcing the concept of writing as a process:* Such an approach removes writing from the realm of the merely academic and gives it a real-world application. Certainly allowing revisions requires more work on the part of the instructor, but a writing class that does not include an opportunity for revision cannot be considered

process oriented. Methods of handling the workload will be discussed in Chapter Five.

This two-week structure can be used as the basis for an entire course in writing.

Writing is a collaborative activity.

It was Paris, in the winter. The temperature in my garret apartment hovered in the thirties. The air surrounding my typewriter, that was placed directly under the only source of light in the room, a dim forty-watt bulb, must have been below freezing. I had been huddled over my typewriter for hours, feverishly pecking out the words that made up the story of my life, my fingers, the only part of my body not swathed in old moth-eaten army blankets, growing increasingly stiff. They finally seized up like a wind up toy that had run down. The doctors in the emergency room uttered two words—frost bite. (A true story told to me by a very distinguished gentleman concerning his experiences during World War II.)

I love this story. It appeals to the romantic in me. I visualize the sloping walls of the garret, covered in the colorful doodling and scrawls of the room's previous inhabitants—Hemingway, Fitzgerald, Picasso. I imagine the bare mattress under the skylight, the stuffing coming out of a hole in one corner. A table with three legs supports a half empty jug of red wine and a partially eaten loaf of bread. Rats squeal as they scuttle under the table, fighting for scraps as the writer fights for words. . . .

Forget it. My wonderful image was just destroyed by the rats—romantic squalor, yes; vermin, no. Unfortunately, the rats may be the most accurate aspect of my description. The image of the lonely, inspired, muse-stricken writer is a popular one and this myth has been exploited by writers for decades, but it is just that, a myth. Writing is never a solitary act, even though most writers' processes include sitting alone in a room putting words on a page or a computer screen.

Writing is never a solitary act because communication is never a solitary act. We communicate with others. We write to communicate. Even when we write to ourselves, we are writing to that other person we sometimes are—the friend, the confidante, the cheerleader. But why not allow our students to perpetuate the myth of the solitary writer? Why not perpetuate it in the classroom? For a very simple reason: students who believe that writing is a solitary act will also be likely to believe that writing is a gift that someone is born with or without. Nine times out of ten they will put themselves in the "without" category. The myth of the solitary writers allows writing to remain mysterious, unknowable, and often unattainable. Writing happens in the dark, when no one is watching, and because no one is watching, no one can ever explain what happened. It is that tree that fell all alone in the forest and never got the satisfaction of sounding THUD! Such a view of writing also cuts students off from their own abilities as communicators by effectively divorcing oral communication skills from written communication skills.

The writing classroom should be the clinical examination room where writing is asked to expose itself under the brilliant light of a two-hundred-watt bulb. Rather than huddling in the shadows and hiding in the closets as though it were a shameful secret, writing is laid out for dissection—and everyone participates. By emphasizing the social act of writing, you can help your students in several ways. You can

- Provide an opportunity for students to discuss their writing processes, which will help them to understand that writing does involve techniques that can be learned.
- Allow students to discuss writing in a nonthreatening environment, further demystifying the act of writing.
- Allow those students who have very little understanding of what writing is all about to learn from those students who already have an established sense of themselves as writers, including you, the teacher.
- Help students learn to recognize the value of writing collaboratively by allowing them to experience its benefits.

You can introduce a collaborative environment into your classroom in several ways:

- Allow students to choose one or two of their required papers for the semester to write with another class member.
- Use class time to allow students to discuss ideas for papers, papers they are writing, problems they are experiencing and anything else relating to writing. When possible, allow students to use e-mail to discuss writing, so you can encourage shy class members to participate.
- Give students the opportunity to peer edit each paper that they will submit for evaluations.
- Place students in groups and give them the opportunity to make their own decisions. For example, rather than telling students what peer editing questions to use, allow each group to arrive at its own list, which the group then presents to the class for further discussion.

Not only will activities such as these help students to recognize writing for what it is—another form of communication—but it will help them begin to understand how to teach themselves.

Students learn most effectively when they teach themselves.

It is easy to confuse group work with collaborative work. However, they are different activities, and it is important to distinguish between the two. Group work is students working alone in groups. Collaboration happens when a group of students reach consensus about a subject and share that knowledge with others, and it is an activity that allows students to teach themselves.

What do I mean when I say group work is "students working alone in groups?" I mean that group work is traditionally teacher-centered. The teacher may place students in groups, but he or she does not relinquish control of the classroom to the students. Consider the following exercise given to students following the introduction of a writing assignment that asked them to write about a place significant to them:

> As a group, read the following essay and identify places where the writer uses adverbs or adjectives. After you identify ten such words, write a paragraph that uses them. Be prepared to submit the paragraph at the end of class.

This is an example of group work. The students are in a group working together to complete an activity, but the exercise is teacher-oriented for the following reasons:

- The students are not given the opportunity to make discoveries. The exercise tells them to do something specific, find adverbs and adjectives.
- The students are told to use the words identified in a paragraph, again the assumption being that the students will make the connection and understand that they are writing descriptively.
- The students are not given the opportunity to discuss what they may have discovered. They are simply told to turn in their work, an act that reinforces the teacher-centered nature of the exercise—the teacher has the answer, the job of the group is to find it.
- The students aren't given the opportunity to understand the significance of the exercise, other than that the teacher will evaluate it.

This exercise could become collaborative by incorporating several changes. Here is a modified version:

1. Read the following essay. As a group, discuss the following essay. Begin by asking yourselves the following questions:
   - What did you like about this essay? Can you identify specific passages or words that you thought worked well?
   - What makes this part of the essay stand out from the rest?
   - What do the passages that you identified have in common?
   - What techniques do you think the writer used? Why?

2. After you finish your discussion, complete the following steps:
   - As a group, generate a list of recommendations that someone writing descriptively could follow. Be as specific as possible.
   - Be prepared to share your list with the class and justify your list of recommendations.

The modified version differs from the first, because it meets a number of essential criteria:

- It is student-centered.

- The students are provided with opportunity to discover knowledge and then share it with each other—they are allowed to teach themselves.
- Because the exercise requires the students to develop a list of criteria based on what they learned and then share it with the class, they are given the chance to understand the importance of the activity as something more than just another exercise to be graded.

Finally, the emphasis of such an activity is always writing.

The primary activity in any writing class should be writing.

Not long ago, one of the semester's crop of new teachers came by my office to talk. He was noticeably distressed, and when I asked what was wrong he replied, "Teaching." My expression must have betrayed my confusion because he continued: "I seem to teach everything but writing. I can teach structure, or style, or how to read critically, but I don't know how to teach writing. People just write; it's not something with parts and steps that I can show them. What do I do?"

His frustration is a common one because in many ways he's right. But as the two-week structure presented earlier illustrates, writing and writing-related activities can be the focus of the class. Your students may learn the most when you seem to be teaching the least—when you're sitting by yourself writing, while your students write or peer edit or otherwise teach themselves. Being a good teacher and keeping the focus on writing means giving up the spotlight. You are no longer the main attraction, let writing have the stage. This is a difficult thing to do, but you can do it. Just remember to avoid these pitfalls:

- Don't turn your class into a literature course or a writing about literature course. Having your students read can work well, but reading should be ancillary to writing. Also, the best reading students can do is a reading of their own texts.
- Don't turn your class into a grammar class. Grammar and punctuation and other rules of writing are important, but only as they apply to writing and not as an end in themselves. You may feel like you're really teaching when you give a series of lectures on points of grammar and punctuation, complete with exercises and quizzes. But are your students really learning?
- Don't turn your class into your own one-person show. If you have the gift of humor, use it—to teach writing. If you are passionate about classical rhetoric, let your students know how your interest inspires you to write. Most importantly, don't dominate the class. Your students are there to learn how to write, not to watch you perform.

Students should be encouraged to discover their own motives for writing.

Not long ago, my husband came home and asked me if I would help him write a memo for the next day. It was 10:00 PM, and I was tired. I had just gotten our two-year-old daughter to bed, and the last thing I wanted to do was write a memo about the importance of maintaining accurate records on customer's credit ratings (not that this topic would have thrilled me at anytime). I dragged my feet before I finally helped Jerry write the memo, and the writing was dull and acceptable at best.

Several days later, after a full day of teaching, I picked up my daughter at her day care center. When we were home, sitting on our sofa together, she held out her arm and said, "Ow, bite." I looked down at her arm and was dismayed to see a clear outline of teeth on top of a huge red and purple bruise. Filled with the outrage of a first-time parent, I immediately picked up the phone and called the director of the day care center. "Brenda," I exclaimed, "Erin was bitten! When I picked her up, none of her teachers mentioned anything about a bite. What happened?" The director expressed her concern and said she would call me back after she investigated. Several minutes later, she called and explained that an "incident" had occurred and an accident report had been filled out, but I had not received it because all of the room's four teachers had been too busy and had forgotten to give me the slip. She assured me that they really had been busy, and mentioned that two other children were sick and said I would receive the report the next day. After I hung up, I grew increasingly angry as I thought of the explanation I had received. Apparently my child's bite was less important than the illnesses of other children. What made me most angry was the director's failure to acknowledge or apologize for what was an obvious oversight. Based on the seriousness of the situation, I felt I must write a letter to both Brenda and her supervisor, which I did immediately. I had discovered a motive for writing, and nothing could have kept me from writing that letter, which was an example of some of my finest writing.

The best thing we can do as teachers of writing is help our students find their own reasons to write so that they will leave our classes with a desire to continue writing for their own purposes, not just to get a grade. How do we do this? Most importantly, by allowing students to have some control over what they write and what they write about. No one who is forced to write about a subject that he or she finds completely meaningless will enjoy writing. But if a teacher allows students to write about topics that he or she feels passionate about, that student may find reasons to keep writing. You can do several things in the classroom to achieve this goal:

- Give students assignments that ask them to find motives for writing rather than ones that supply the motive. (See Chapter Six for a more thorough complete discussion of writing assignments.) For example, don't ask your students to write about the injustice of enforcing the speed limit when you're the one who got the ticket and is upset. Write your own paper, and let your students make their own choice about what is injustice, so they can write their own papers.
- Don't force your students' writing into predetermined structures. Just because you imagine that your students' profiles of other people should be in a question-answer format, doesn't mean that they do. Let your students make their own decisions and find their own way to say what they need to say, not what they think you want them to say.

- Don't judge your students' choices by your own criteria. Just because you consider fraternities and sororities a worn-out subject doesn't mean it is to all of your students. Never ignore a student's compelling need to write.

Putting All the Pieces Together

Now that you understand the basic components of the writing class, it is just a matter of arranging those pieces into a working syllabus. In fact, it is only a matter of using the four-day schedule that we discussed earlier and repeating it as often as necessary to make the full syllabus. You simply fill in the details based on the text you may be using, the number of papers you will be assigning, and things of that nature. Every syllabus should contain the following material:

- *Basic information about the teacher:* office location, office hours, phone number, e-mail address, etc. (I would caution against giving out your home phone number.).
- *Course policies:* policies such as those regarding late work and absences. Your department may require you to use certain policies.
- *Day-to-day schedule of activities:* your daily outline of activities. Clearly indicate due dates for papers, peer editing, out of class assignments, conferences, and anything else that requires the students to prepare in advance. Be specific, but leave yourself enough room to make needed adjustments. For example, I like to build in a "catch-up day" toward the middle of the course.

On the following pages I have included two sample syllabi. The syllabi are basically the same, although the second one has been adapted for use in a computerized writing environment. To help make the syllabi clearer, I have included parenthetical discussions of the various activities. You will notice that the parenthetical discussions become fewer as the syllabus progresses. This is because many of the activities can be repeated, and further examples are given in the chapters that follow.

Introduction to Composition

Instructor:

Office Hours:

Text:

Absence Policy

See written statement on the "attendance" handout. If you are absent on the day that the departmental policy is discussed, it is your responsibility to speak to your instructor about the policy.

Rewrite Policy

Writing is a process. What you write will continue to get better as you continue to work on it. I encourage you to rewrite any paper that receives less than an A. When rewriting, follow the guidelines below:

- Turn the rewrite in within a week of the time it was returned to you.
- Include the graded original.
- Address each of the comments made on the original and sincerely attempt to improve the overall quality of the paper.

Late Papers

Papers will lose one letter grade for every calendar day that they are late.

Class Conduct

I encourage you to feel free to voice your opinions when they relate to the subject being discussed; however, as members of this class, we will treat each other with respect and show concern for other's feelings.

Conferences

Scheduled conferences are mandatory. If you do not make an appointment, you will receive an absence—no questions asked.

Open-Door Policy

I welcome and encourage you to visit me whenever you wish to discuss a paper, problem, etc. If you cannot come during my office hours, schedule an appointment with me.

Peer Editing

Peer editing is an essential part of the writing process, so you will be peer editing regularly. Any student who does not have a COMPLETED draft for peer editing (both a hard copy and a disk copy) will receive a zero for the day.

E-mail

With electronic mail you can easily communicate with your instructor and your classmates. You can use e-mail to ask questions, request conferences, check up on assignments, and maintain a dialogue with other students in other composition classes. My e-mail address is RAIGN@twlab.unt.edu. You may use e-mail from any general access lab on campus.

Paper Format
Please follow the guidelines below:
- Include a title page with your name, the title of the paper, and the date.
- Use a printer.
- Use page numbers.
- Double space.
- Use one-inch margins.
- Spell check.

I will not grade papers that do not meet these criteria.

Course Evaluation
Papers	80%
Journals	10%
Participation	10%
	100%

Course Outline
Highly volatile and subject to change!

Week One

Day 1   Course Introduction (reading of the syllabus, introductions, etc.)

Day 2   Diagnostic Essay—"What Is Good about Writing?" (In-class essay, lets you get to know something about your students and their writing abilities.)

Week Two

Day 3   Discuss Writing Assignment—"Communities of Discourse" (This assignment is discussed at length in Chapter Six. Those of you using a different assignment need to make a substitution here.)

Assign peer groups and discuss diagnostic essays (Put students in groups of three to four. Separate friends. I suggest a random mix. Begin letting students get to know each other and start talking about their own writing in productive ways. I suggest that you do a collaborative activity that asks each class to identify some criteria for identifying good writing to present to the class for discussion.)

Day 4   Begin Journals—"What Is a Community?" (See the handout on journals that follows the syllabi.)

Assign Paper 1—The Proposal (Read the assignment with the class to ensure that they understand what they have been asked to do. Save the discussion of structure, etc., for the next class period.)

Brainstorm topics (I suggest a class free-for-all. Write the topics on the board as the class discovers them. See how many you can challenge them to find. An unmotivated class might respond to the "reward" system. I sometimes bring in bubble gum and throw pieces to people who come up with good ideas. It's goofy, but a lot of fun. Simulating a *Jeopardy* game can also be interesting.)

Freewrite (Ask each student to choose three topics and freewrite on those topics for ten minutes or so. Ask each student to choose one sentence to share with the class. Discuss what they have written in terms of possible paper topics.)

Week Three

Day 5   Discuss Proposals and Proposal Writing (Methods for teaching the proposal are discussed in Chapter Six.)

Group Writing Exercise (Place students in groups and have them write a proposal to a problem that they face as students.)

Day 6   Discuss peer editing—how, why, when, etc. (Peer editing is discussed in Chapter Four.)

Discuss group proposals (Have the students collaborate on peer-editing questions pertinent to the proposal and then swap proposals among the group. Ask them to peer edit the proposal that they receive and then be prepared to tell the class what the proposal did well, how it could be improved, and what they learned that they can apply to the writing of their own papers.)

Week Four

Day 7   Peer Edit Essays (Allow students to develop a list of peer-editing questions to use, and reserve time for each group to discuss with the rest of the class what they learned. You may need another class period to complete peer editing.)

Day 8   Assign Paper 2—The Place (Introduce the assignment.)

Invention Exercise (Repeat any of the exercises already suggested or come up with one of your own. Remember to integrate the exercise and the assignment.)

Paper 1 due

Week Five   *(Teacher's Note: Schedule mandatory conferences for this week. May occur during class or replace day 10.)*

Day 9   Discuss Paper 2—Writing about Places (Methods for teaching description are discussed in Chapter Six.)
Writing descriptions—group exercise (Model after group proposal exercise.)

Day 10 Conferences (Allow fifteen minutes per conference. Discuss student's general questions, and both your general perceptions of their writing and specific questions they may have. Let the student direct the conversation when possible.)

Week Six

Day 11   Peer Editing (Same as above.)

Day 12   Assign Paper 3—The People (Introduce the paper.)
Invention Exercise (Be creative.)
Paper 2 due

Week Seven

Day 13   Writing about People (Methods for writing this paper are discussed in Chapter Six.)

In-Class Interviews (I suggest that you allow your groups to interview you. Ask them to develop a specific focus for the interview and then develop appropriate questions. Give each group the opportunity to interview you, then have them pick the set of questions that they found most interesting, and collaborate on writing a paragraph, based on the interview, that you write on the board for them as they work. Discuss the merits of what they write.)

Day 14   In-Class Conferences (Check in with each student as they work on their own papers.)

Week Eight

Day 15   Peer Editing

Day 16   Assign Paper 4—The Event (Methods for teaching this paper are included in Chapter Six.)
Invention Exercise
Paper 3 due

Week Nine   *(Teacher's Note: Schedule mandatory conferences. May take place outside of class or replace day 18.)*

Day 17   Writing about Events—How do you tell a good story? (Methods for writing this paper are discussed in Chapter Six.)

Writing Exercise (Plan an exercise that lets students practice writing narratives. I do an activity, where I ask each group to describe a conflict that occurs between a man and a woman and takes place in a very public place. Emphasize showing, not telling. Let them discuss what is written and how it applies to their own papers.)

Day 18   Conferences

Week Ten

Day 19   Holiday (These days will need to be moved according to the calendar.)

Day 20   Holiday

Week Eleven

Day 21 Peer Editing

Day 22 Assign Paper 5—Persuasion
Invention Exercise
Paper 4 due

Week Twelve

Day 23 "Writing Persuasively" (Methods for writing this paper are discussed in Chapter Six.)

In-Class Writing Exercise

Day 24 Discuss Writing Exercises

In-Class Conferences

Week Thirteen

Day 25 Peer Editing

Day 26 Assign Paper 6—"Reevaluating Your Community" (Methods for writing this paper are discussed in Chapter Six.)

Invention Exercise

Paper 5 due

Week Fourteen   *(Teacher's Note: Schedule mandatory conferences. May take place outside of class or replace day 28.)*

Day 27 What Did You Learn about Your Community? (Methods for writing this paper are discussed in Chapter Six.)

Writing Exercise

Day 28 Conferences

Week Fifteen

Day 29 Peer Editing

Day 30 *Paper 6 due*

Week Sixteen

Day 31 Film (The last week of class is always difficult. All the papers are written, so what do you do? I like to show a film because it is fun, and provides an opportunity for some extra credit work. *Roxanne* is a good choice because it vividly portrays the power of language.)

Extra credit assignment: Write a brief analysis of the use of language in the film.

Day 32 Film Assignment due

Final Be available to return papers and answer questions.

Computer-Assisted Composition

Instructor:
Office Hours:
Text:

Absence Policy
See written statement on the "attendance" handout. If you are absent on the day that the departmental policy is discussed, it is your responsibility to speak to your instructor about the policy.

Rewrite Policy
Writing is a process. What you write will continue to get better as you continue to work on it. I encourage you to rewrite any paper that receives less than an A. When rewriting, follow the guidelines below:
• Turn the rewrite in within a week of the time it was returned to you.
• Include the graded original.
• Address each of the comments made on the original and sincerely attempt to improve the overall quality of the paper.

Late Papers
Papers will lose one letter grade for every calendar day that they are late.

Class Conduct
I encourage you to feel free to voice your opinions when they relate to the subject being discussed; however, as members of this class, we will treat each other with respect and show concern for other's feelings.

Conferences
Scheduled conferences are mandatory. If you do not make an appointment, you will receive an absence—no questions asked.

Open-Door Policy
I welcome and encourage you to visit me whenever you wish to discuss a paper, problem, etc. If you cannot come during my office hours, schedule an appointment with me.

Course Evaluation

Papers	80%
Journals	10%
Participation	10%
	100%

Computer Applications
Peer Editing
Peer editing is an essential part of the writing process, so you will be peer editing regularly. In addition to reading and commenting on printed copies of works, we will also exchange electronic versions of your papers for on-line peer editing. Any student who does not have a COMPLETED draft for peer editing (both a hard copy and a disk copy) will receive a zero for the day.

E-mail
With e-mail you can easily communicate with your instructor and your classmates. You can use e-mail to ask questions, request conferences, check up on assignments, and maintain a dialogue with other students in other composition classes. My e-mail address is RAIGN@twlab.unt.edu.

Computer Courtesy
Anyone typing, clicking, beeping, hacking, or otherwise disrupting the class may be asked to leave. It is not fair for one student to prevent other students from learning.

Paper Format
Please follow the guidelines below:
- Include a title page with your name, the title of the paper, and the date.
- Use a printer.
- Use page numbers.
- Double space.
- Use one-inch margins.
- Spell check.

I will not grade papers that do not meet these criteria.

Course Outline
Highly volatile and subject to change!

Week One
(Annotations from previous syllabus still apply.)

Day 1   Course Introduction

Day 2   Computer Orientation I (Make arrangements with the lab supervisor.)
Diagnostic Essay: What Is Good about Writing?

Week Two

Day 3   Discuss Writing Assignment—Communities of Discourse
         Computer Orientation II: Using Pegasus Mail
         Assign peer groups and discuss essays
Day 4   Begin Journals: E-mail an entry to your instructor
         Assign Paper 1: The Proposal
         Brainstorm topics

Week Three

Day 5   Discuss Proposals and Proposal Writing
         Group exercise—propose a solution to a problem that affects you
Day 6   Watch Peer Editing Video
         Discuss peer editing—how, why, when, etc.
         Discuss group proposals

Week Four

Day 7   Peer Edit Essays
Day 8   Assign Paper 2—The Place
         Invention Exercise
         Paper 1 due

Week Five   *(Teacher's Note: Schedule mandatory conferences for this week. May occur outside of class or replace day 10.)*

Day 9   Discuss Paper 2—Writing about Places
         Writing descriptions—group exercise
Day 10   Conferences

Week Six

Day 11   Peer Editing
Day 12   Assign Paper 3—The People
         Invention Exercise
         Paper 2 due

Week Seven

Day 13   Writing about People
         In-Class Interviews
Day 14   Discuss Interviews
         In-Class Conferences

Week Eight

Day 15 Peer Editing

Day 16 Assign Paper 4—The Event

　　　　Invention Exercise

　　　　Paper 3 due

Week Nine   *(Teacher's Note: Schedule mandatory conferences for this week. May occur outside of class or replace day 18.)*

Day 17 Writing about Events—How do you tell a good story?

　　　　Writing Exercise

Day 18 Conferences

Week Ten

Day 19 Holiday

Day 20 Holiday

Week Eleven

Day 21 Peer Editing

Day 22 Assign Paper 5—Persuasion

　　　　Invention Exercise

　　　　Paper 4 due

Week Twelve

Day 23 Writing Persuasively

　　　　In-Class Writing Exercise

Day 24 Discuss Writing Exercises

　　　　In-Class Conferences

Week Thirteen

Day 25 Peer Editing

Day 26 Assign Paper 6—Reevaluating Your Community

　　　　Invention Exercise

　　　　Paper 5 due

Week Fourteen   *(Teacher's Note: Schedule mandatory conferences for this week. May occur outside of class or replace day 28.)*

Day 27 What Did You Learn about Your Community?

　　　　Writing Exercise

Day 28 Conferences

Week Fifteen

Day 29   Peer Editing

Day 30   *Paper 6 due*

Week Sixteen

Day 31   Film

Extra credit assignment

Day 32   Film

Assignment due

Final   Be available to return papers and answer questions.

Exercises

Writing Exercises

1. Propose a community associated with the teaching of writing that you wish to study. For specifics on the writing of proposals, see Chapter Six.
2. Write a handout for each of the following types of classroom activities: prewriting, writing, and rewriting.

Collaborative Activities

1. After you write your syllabus, prepare copies to share with your group members, then complete the following tasks:
   - Develop a list of criteria for judging syllabi.
   - Evaluate each of your syllabi according to the criteria that you developed.
   - Identify several examples of positive and negative aspects of the syllabi.
   - Share your list with the class.
   - As a class, discuss what you learned from the evaluation process.
2. Complete the exercise below before writing your proposal:
   - As a group, identify a problem that affects all teachers of writing.
   - Write a brief proposal in which you propose a solution to the problem that you identified.
   - Exchange proposals with another group, and determine whether you consider their solutions persuasive.
   - Based on your decision, develop a list of criteria for evaluating proposals.
   - Present your list to the class.
   - As a class, determine a list of useful criteria for judging your students' proposals.

Chapter Two

The Teacher's Role in the Classroom

When I taught freshman English . . . for the first time, I was really concerned with being accepted by the college community. I especially wanted to be accepted as a student by the students. I wanted my students to feel that I was one of them and that I could relate to them. I told my students to call me David. I let my hair grow really long so that I could put it in a pony tail. I wore earrings . . . and I dressed like a hippie. . . . Trying to be one of the students did not work well when I was the instructor. My students were disruptive, disrespectful, and disinterested in what they needed to learn to be good writers. (David Mitchell)

Who you are when you step into the classroom each day depends on many different factors, from your hair, to your demeanor, to the shoes you wear. I vividly remember a remark a student made on one of my teaching evaluations the first semester I taught: "I like her OK but she sits on the desk and swings her feet back and forth, and I really hate the shoes she wears." Now I laugh about this, but at the time I was crushed. All the time and effort I had spent getting ready to teach, and all he could do was obsess about my shoes! When I began teaching, I was so sure that the only thing that mattered was what I said, not how I said it or how I looked when I said it. Actually, I was wrong. All of these things matter, and it is important for you to consider these things when you prepare to teach. In fact, you need to address several basic issues before you ever step into the classroom:

- Making a good impression.
- Ethics.
- Discipline problems.
- Finding your place in the classroom.

Making a Good Impression

Like David, when I began teaching, my colleagues and I spent more time worrying about whether our students liked us than about almost anything else. We talked about how we could dress to look like one of "them." We tried to keep up with current music, so that they would think we were "hip." We considered it important to be friendly and laid back so that they wouldn't think we were unapproachable. As David discovered, all these things sound good in theory, but they don't always work in practice.

One of my good friends was a mid-fortyish man with a goatee. He had a deep, compelling voice. I observed him teach one semester and was impressed by the rapport he had established with his students. He stood at the front of the room in a ratty T-shirt and a pair of jeans looking like he had just rolled out of bed, and his students sat quietly enthralled as he talked about the writing process. I concluded that students felt more rapport with someone who had a more casual persona, so when the new semester started, I decided to abandon my pumps and dresses in favor of my jeans and running shoes—real clothes. Apparently my deductive reasoning was faulty. A small twentyish woman dressed like a slob doesn't have the same effect as a bearded fiftyish man dressed like a slob. On the first day of class, one of the students informed me that I'd better move my stuff off the teacher's desk before he or she got to class. I'm not sure who was more embarrassed when he discovered I was the teacher. Back to square one.

I have since come to realize that students respond not just to how someone looks, but also to his or her level of assurance, confidence, and accessibility—in short, the level of professionalism. Professionalism doesn't always means wearing a suit and a tie. It does mean showing respect for both your own status as a professional and respect for your students. One young woman recently came into my office very distressed because her teacher's shorts were so brief that she was deeply embarrassed and felt uncomfortable when speaking with him. She felt that his attire indicated that he had no respect for her or her sensibilities, and she was right. This young man, who is otherwise a very good teacher, had made a poor choice. Avoid wearing clothing intended to draw attention toward you and away from what you are saying. Avoid wearing anything that might be offensive to your students. No one expects you to spend a month's salary on an expensive suit, but dressing in an appropriate manner shows respect for your profession and your students. I gave up the jeans and the running shoes, but I didn't go back to the pumps and the suit. I was never comfortable in those clothes, and I felt like an imposter. Now I wear khakis and blazers. I'm comfortable and so are my students—that's what it's all about.

Being a professional also means acting professionally. Unfortunately, acting professionally usually means doing what is right rather than doing what is popular. Prepare yourself now for the fact that not all of your students will like you all of the time. Some of them may never like you. However, that doesn't mean that you aren't a great teacher—it may mean that you *are* a great teacher. Not too long ago, I was working registration, and a young man came into my office and asked me to recommend a teacher for him. As you would expect from the director of the writing program, I said that all the teachers were outstanding. He gave me that smile that meant, "OK, preliminaries are out of the way. Let's get down to business," and asked me to recommend a teacher who was less picky. "You know," he said, "some English teachers have this thing about every little comma being in the right place. I need a teacher that's less picky." What I wanted to say to this student would not have been professional. So I bit my tongue and explained to him that the sort of "pickiness" he had described was an attitude we encouraged in all our teachers. By the time he left my office, I was not his favorite person.

On many occasions, you will be tempted to lose your temper or your patience, but no matter how frustrated you get, you never have the right to treat your students unprofessionally. Even if you think you're being funny when you make jokes about all athletes being dumb, your student athletes may not. Not everyone in your class may share your sense of humor. Be sensitive to your students' feelings and let them know that you expect them to be sensitive to yours. If you do not have the right to call a student dumb, neither do you have to sit and listen while a student calls you names, and this may happen. Students get frustrated also, and teachers are frequently in the line of fire, but you may certainly tell angry students that you will speak to them after they have calmed down. In fact, I include what I refer to as the twenty-four-hour rule on my syllabus. I will not discuss any student's grades until he or she has thought about them for twenty-four hours. This rule has helped me avoid confrontations with many angry students.

What do you do when the inevitable happens and you mistakenly do something unprofessional? Sometimes you can use such a situation to your advantage. One of the teaching assistants in my department prepared very carefully for his first day of class. He went shopping for new clothes and bought himself a water bottle to combat nervous drymouth so he wouldn't squeak. When he walked into class that first day in his freshly starched shirt, he felt very professional. Ten minutes into class discussion he felt his throat closing and casually reached for his water bottle, pausing to squirt a stream of water into his mouth. Unfortunately, rather than hitting his mouth, he hosed down his new shirt. As he told me, he realized while he stood there dripping water and feeling like a complete fool that he had two options: become morally outraged and glare at everyone who dared to laugh, or beat them to the punch by laughing at himself. He wisely chose option number two and turned an embarrassing moment to his advantage by letting his class know that he was human and giving them the opportunity to laugh with him, rather than acting defensively and encouraging them to laugh at him.

Ethics in the Classroom

All teachers want their students to like them, but as one of my mentors pointed out to me early in my teaching career—you aren't there to be liked. Frequently, doing what is right means doing what is unpopular. You will always have students whom you like or dislike more than others. Personal feelings aside, you must treat all your students fairly—even when it means giving your favorite student an F on a paper because he or she turned it in late.

Writing classes are sensitive places. Writing, by its very nature, is a personal act, and we are asking our students to take huge personal risks when we ask them to share their writing in class. We further compound this agony by asking them to submit this writing to us for a grade. Imagine the dilemma of the student who gets that first paper back covered with marks and suggestions even though she thought you liked her. It is difficult for students and teachers to separate the personal from the public. This is precisely why it is so important for you to act ethically at all times, and acting ethically means establishing policies intended to ensure fairness and then abiding by those policies, no matter how difficult it might be. Recently, two of my instructors came to me with a dilemma. They took a lunch break together after grading papers all morning, and like most teachers, began discussing the papers they had read. Lisa said to Lindy, "One of my students wrote an interesting paper on the advantages of legalizing marijuana, but I'm concerned because so much of his material came from the Internet and wasn't cited. I'm not sure how to handle the situation." Lisa replied, "That's odd. One of my students wrote on the same topic, and I was going to ask you the same question." As you've probably guessed, both students had turned in the same paper. Lisa and Lindy were both upset because they had caught their students plagiarizing, but each had different ideas concerning how to handle the situation. Our university has a strict plagiarism policy, and these instructors could have failed the students for the entire class if they chose. In this case, Lisa wanted to give her student an F on the paper with no chance to rewrite—a grade that would give him a D in the class— and then report his case to the dean of students so the administration could "throw a scare into him." When I asked Lisa how she developed this plan of action, she told me that the student had been a problem all semester and deserved what he got. Lindy told me she was sure her student was just misguided because he came to her after turning in his first draft (the plagiarized paper) and wanted to know if he could start over with a new topic, which he did. Because of this request, she was sure he hadn't really wanted to plagiarize and she wanted to give him a B for the second paper and forget the first plagiarized paper. This grade would ensure that he received a B in the class.

After speaking to both instructors, my initial reaction was to agree with both plans. I knew how Lindy felt. When a good student makes a mistake, you hate to punish him or her by ruining a whole semester's grade because of one mistake. I also knew how Lisa felt. It's hard not to feel an I-knew-it-all-along kind of satisfaction when a student who obviously never cared anyway really makes a mistake and you catch him or her in the act. But was it fair to treat the two students differently because they had developed different relationships with their teachers? Before I could tell Lindy that I thought she needed to reconsider, she came to me and said "As much as I hate to do it, I realize it's only fair to Lisa's student and all our other students if we give both plagiarists the same punishment." She was right; the ethical decision was to give both students F's and report them to the dean of students, which we did.

These types of decisions are hard to make, but the only hope you have of justifying what will seem to your students to be very subjective decisions regarding their writing is to be as fair in your treatment of them as possible. Never go back on a policy. If you tell your students you will deduct points for late papers, deduct points. Otherwise the number of late papers you receive will grow exponentially, and your students will lose faith in your ability to be fair. After all, why bother to turn a paper in on time if nothing good happens to those who do and nothing bad happens to those who don't?

Finally, because your students may share their private problems and feelings with you in their writing, you may discover that a student has problems that you are not qualified to handle. For instance, students sometimes address issues such as physical abuse, drug problems, and emotional problems in their journals and papers. You are not a therapist, but you should discuss the issue with your director or someone in your program whom you trust so that you can send the student where he or she can receive appropriate help.

Discipline Problems

I hope you'll never have them, but even in the college classroom, it's inevitable that students will sleep, yell, stomp out, plagiarize, refuse to peer edit, work on material for other classes, hack out of your computer lab and explore the net, etc. Things happen, and you need to cope. Much of what I've already said regarding professionalism and ethics applies here. In addition, I would like to emphasize two points: your classroom isn't Romper Room, and you do not have to spend your time policing the area. Students do not have the right to disrupt class for other students.

So what do you do? You can ask students to leave your classroom. You can speak to students privately concerning their behavior and suggest appropriate changes. If things escalate to a level beyond which you feel you cannot cope, for example, if you're being sexually harassed or feel physically threatened, you can ask your director or the chair of your department to intervene—but save this for extreme cases. Calling in reinforcements can damage your ethos. But I always tell my instructors never to suffer in silence. We've all had to deal with discipline problems. Share yours with your colleagues and see what they can suggest.

Finding Your Place in the Classroom

Who will you be when you step into the classroom? Answering this question is what teaching is all about, and if you take your teaching seriously, you will spend a great deal of time considering it. You will remake yourself each semester, each week, each day for each student.

When I first began teaching, my mind was full of the many essays and articles I had read on the art of teaching. Aware of the contrariness I was embracing, I prepared myself to be a coach, a mentor, a fellow writer on the journey toward true expression. I would encourage my students to explore while I effectively wielded the editor's pen, always encouraging, never correcting. I would allow my students to choose the direction of the course as I simultaneously guided our progress. I would be a fellow writer, allowing my ideas to simmer before I shared them in the safe, collaborative environment we had created. By the time the first week of class ended, I fled the classroom, a schizophrenic banshee with ink-stained fingers.

No teacher can be everything to everyone, and you cannot simultaneously practice every theory that you may read. Try different things, read about different approaches, use what works, and throw out the rest. It takes time and patience, and you never finish because what works with one student may not work with another. Most importantly, be yourself. Don't knock yourself out trying to be witty if it doesn't come naturally to you. I couldn't tell a joke if my life depended on it. If you aren't comfortable with Burke's pentad, don't use it. Find something you can talk about with enthusiasm and assurance. If something doesn't work, don't be afraid to change it. I once threw out my entire syllabus six weeks into the semester. My class and I started over, and we were all much happier.

Conclusion

Who am I in the classroom? What is my place? I'm still trying to answer that question. I do know that I am not the strict disciplinarian with the red pen. I'm not a hip story teller in jeans and Birkenstock's either. I'm the small woman in the tailored clothes who has been told that she would look more authoritative in heels yet chooses to wear flats. I can't tell jokes, and I'm known to be sarcastic. I sound tough and melt like a Popsicle in the Texas sun. I love teaching and work at it constantly. I respect my students, and they seem to respect me. I've been told that I teach well, and I know I have a lot to learn. Where is my place in the classroom? Wherever it needs to be.

Exercises

Writing Exercise

1. Write about a role or roles you play in the classroom. You can describe yourself from your own perspective or that of your students—or both. How do you think who they see you as might be different from who you see yourself as? Be prepared to share your paragraphs with your class.

Collaborative Activities

1. After you share your descriptions of the roles you play in the classroom, make two lists: productive roles and destructive roles. Let the groups share their lists and then discuss these questions:
   • What factors determine the roles teachers play in the classroom?
   • Do teachers have any control over the roles they play?
   • How can teachers effectively choose the roles they play?
2. Write a scenario in which a teacher finds himself or herself in a difficult situation. Swap scenarios and do some class role-playing. Take turns playing the teacher and the student, and discuss the approaches used.

Chapter Three
Teaching Writing As Process

Writing as a process is valid, especially as a tool to enfranchise those writers previously excluded from the system. However, I also think that teaching the modes is valid. (Michelle Niemcyzk)

Many of my new teachers frequently bemoan the fact that, while they like the idea of writing as process in principle, they find it difficult to teach. As one young man exclaimed in class one afternoon, "If you take away the form of writing, what's left?" This is the same concern that the quote above mirrors.

Most of my new instructors are products of a modes-oriented approach to writing that emphasizes the product of writing rather than the structure—a view of writing that assumes the existence of [S]tructure rather than the approach that I favor that allows for structures. My students are good writers, and consequently, many of them have an "if it was good enough for me, it's good enough for them" attitude when it comes to teaching writing. In fact, one of my students explained in a paper, "I feel that I have experienced at least limited success in writing. . . . Therefore, I am hesitant to abandon the older method of teaching writing that I felt was successful in teaching me" (David Mitchell). However, as I point out to them, such a viewpoint fails to consider that they probably would have been good writers regardless of what approach they learned in the classroom. That they are pursuing graduate degrees in writing-intensive fields testifies to their skills. They also tend to remember the product approach fondly because it is familiar to them. It is a security blanket that they can take with them into the classroom, and it is large enough to fill up many class periods. However, neither of these arguments stands up under closer scrutiny. For example, look at the two methods side by side:

Product-Oriented Writing	Process-Oriented Writing
Students write in response to assigned topics.	Students write in response to assigned topics.
Little emphasis is placed on the stages of the writing process.	Heavy emphasis is placed on the stages of writing.
Class time is devoted to activities such as the discussion of the structure of different forms of writing, style, coherence, grammar, etc.	Classroom activities include in-class writing, collaborative work, the evaluation of student writing, and the discussion of issues such as grammar, structure, etc.
Students submit only one draft of each paper for evaluation.	Students are required to produce multiple drafts of each paper that they submit for evaluation.
Students submit finished essays for evaluation.	Students submit finished essays for evaluation.

As this list illustrates, although process-oriented writing is fundamentally different from product-oriented writing, using a process-oriented approach does not mean throwing away everything that is good about the product-oriented approach. It means adding to that approach to make it even more accessible.

The product-oriented approach fails because it perpetuates the myth that writing occurs in private and is a natural gift that cannot be taught. The process-oriented approach works because it demystifies the writing process and makes it available to everyone. However, I emphasize again that the new approach is an adding to of the previous approach, not an abandoning of. Structure and grammar still need to be taught and learned but in an environment that allows for error and provides an opportunity for improvement. Despite what many new teachers seem to think, using a process approach in the classroom does not necessarily lead to anarchy and chaos, though the energy generated by a motivated class can certainly be chaotic.

The Process in Action

All writers use some version of the standard writing process: prewriting, writing, rewriting. For example, when I began working on this book, I engaged in all of the following activities:

- I began by throwing around ideas with different people: my assistant, students, colleagues, friends, my husband.

- I started reading articles that related to the teaching of writing and renewed acquaintances with some old favorites by Murray and Elbow.
- I sketched out an outline that included each chapter in as much detail as possible.
- I incorporated the outline for the book into my syllabus for Methods of Teaching Composition, which I was about to teach.
- I asked the students who took the methods course to write teaching journals and began gathering material from them.
- I asked my students to answer a questionnaire that included questions such as "What topics would you like to see included in a book on how to teach writing?"
- I began writing a more extended outline for each chapter.
- I sent copies of the extended outline to several people, including students, colleagues, and book publishers.
- I wrote a formal proposal in response to queries by several publishers.

After the proposal was accepted for publication, and I was ready to begin writing, I used these approaches:

- I read all of the questionnaires that I had received from my students and tried to get a sense of what the book needed to do.
- I shared the outline with several graduate students and then incorporated the changes they suggested.
- I sat down in front of my computer and started writing the introduction. (I'm one of those people who likes to write in order. I have a mental block about the whole project until I get past the opening.)
- After struggling for two weeks, I had a complete draft of the introduction, but the writing of it was messy. I like to work in my office at school because the atmosphere is hectic. Most people find this annoying, but the activity helps me to focus my attention on my writing. My assistant, or one of her friends, or all of them are frequently there with me, and I can read them bits and pieces and get feedback. Also, when I get stuck I can always wander down the hall and find someone to talk to about my difficulties. This type of conversation is essential for me. I am a very collaborative writer.
- I passed out copies of the introduction to as many graduate students as I could and then incorporated their changes into the draft. I also sent copies to several of my colleagues.
- I started this process all over again on the next chapter.

I include this lengthy example of my writing process for several reasons. First, since I am suggesting that you teach writing as process, it is only fair to establish that I use the method that I endorse. Also, I think the sheer messiness of my process illustrates both the awesome complexity and the amazing simplicity of the writing process. Regardless of every writer's individual idiosyncrasies, and whether they do it consciously, most, if not all, writers who are successful, do engage in all three stages of the writing process. In most cases, those writers, such as the students I quoted earlier in this chapter, are not aware they have a writing process. For most experienced writers, their process becomes so ingrained in how they work that they cease to be aware of it. It's like breathing; you never think about how you do it until you suddenly find that you can't. I believe that one of the most effective things writing teachers can do is consciously attempt to study and understand their own writing process so that they can teach writing as process with some semblance of commitment. Otherwise a teacher may find him or herself in the same position as the first time teacher: "I've always been leery of doctrines that promote themselves to the exclusion of every other doctrine, sort of like the denominations who preach that everyone else is going to hell but them" (Michelle Niemcyzk). Until she understood her own relationship to the process of writing and understood that she was already one of the "chosen," she could not effectively convince her students to see writing as a process because she didn't.

Teaching Writing As Process

You can use many different techniques to teach writing as process; however, one thing is essential. You must always actively engage your students in all the steps of the writing process: prewriting, writing, rewriting, or if you prefer, invention, writing, editing. The terminology is less important than the activity. Assuming that your answer to the question "Should you teach writing as process" is an unequivocal, "Yes," the more important question is "How do you do it?"

Teaching writing as a process is a process in itself and involves several steps that you should incorporate into your class structure:

- Allow students to have as much input as possible when you assign writing topics.
- Always include prewriting, writing, and rewriting exercises with every assignment.
- Insist that students produce multiple drafts, and arrange some sort of method for evaluating those drafts as the students produce them.
- Make student-produced writing the focus of the class.
- Consider the students' progress as well as their products when evaluating their class performance.

Allow students to have as much input as possible when you assign writing topics.

If you want your students to write successfully, you will have to help them learn to recognize the potential in any topic, no matter how boring it might initially seem. You can do this in a number of ways, the most important involving an emphasis on invention techniques that will help them discover their own creativity. However, before you can effectively engage your students in invention exercises, you may discover that you have to overcome their initial mistrust of writing assignments and writing in general. Students seem to come to composition classes with a preprogrammed belief that everything that occurs within the context of this class will bore them. How can you convince them otherwise? How can you make them believe that those exercises that you scribble up on the board or the overhead projector really help jump-start a stalled brain? It's simple—you show them by writing.

I had the good fortune to study with Jim Corder when I was in graduate school, and I fondly remember a story he told my class one day. Apparently, students have always been bored, and several decades ago, Professor Corder decided to change the direction of his composition class by proving to his students that no topic was boring. He challenged them to come up with the most boring topics imaginable and then had the class vote on their first choice—Cheerios. He then proceeded to write a witty and entertaining essay, complete with illustrations, on Cheerios. How can any student argue with that type of demonstration? I took Professor Corder's idea and adapted it for my own use.

I let my students choose a boring topic (I make a big event out of this and write all the suggestions on the board.), and then I begin writing the essay while they watch. I always begin with a brainstorming session and then work into an outline and a thesis statement. This evidence of organization when I write impresses my students. After this, I write the introductory paragraph and then I stop and turn the challenge back to my students. I put them in groups and let each group choose a topic. Then I swap the topics and make each group write an introductory paragraph. Last semester some of the winning topics included: blow-drying your hair, watching paint dry, choosing a boring topic to write about, and getting old.

Once you have gotten past your students' initial resistance by demonstrating three important things—you write; you have a writing process; and any topic can be interesting—you're ready to get started with that first paper. I discuss creating successful writing assignments in detail in a later chapter, so now just remember to choose topics that suggest possibilities without being restrictive. For example, choose a topic such as "Is anything OK anymore?" as compared with "Compare the crime rates in 1907 to the crime rates in 1997 in 500 words."

The first topic suggests possibilities, but it doesn't do the work for the student or assume that he or she has anything to say about crime that involves comparing one thing to another. If your goal is to have each of your students write basically the same paper, then choose the second topic and don't bother with any invention exercises. Walk your students through a lecture on the basics of the comparison essay and send them home. However, if your goal is to help your students discover that they have things to say that are worth writing about, choose the first topic and invent, invent, invent.

Always include prewriting, writing, and rewriting exercises with every assignment.

The prewriting exercises you use in class are limited only by your imagination and willingness to invent. However, whether you prefer the term invention or prewriting, exercises that help students generate ideas are essential. A student who doesn't develop a good idea won't develop a good paper, and more importantly will never understand that he or she has the ability to invent interesting topics on which to write. A student who isn't convinced that he or she has something to say will stop writing as soon as your class ends. Because the wealth of introductory writing texts and software currently available contain many prewriting exercises to which you can refer, I will limit the number of examples I provide here, and I will mention them only briefly. However, if those methods that I list here are unfamiliar to you or you would like to know more about them, refer to the bibliography in Part III of this book for further reading on the subject. Standard methods of invention include freewriting, brainstorming, and clustering. Some of the more exotic techniques include the use of tagmemics, the classical topoi, and the use of Burke's pentad. You can consider any technique that asks students to spontaneously generate writing or responses to a topic invention, and whenever possible, the material that students generate should pertain directly to a paper on which they are currently working. Invention exercises that do not help students write the papers that they will submit for evaluation are no more a part of the writing process than the isolated grammar exercises that you may ask them to complete, and they do not reinforce a belief that such techniques will help students become better writers.

Writing exercises are equally important and come in many forms. You may ask students to keep journals or you may have students write in groups. You may even allow students to work on their papers during class while you work with individuals. Again what is essential is that students clearly recognize a connection between what they do in class and their own writing outside of class. The best teachers of writing are the ones whose students need them the least.

Revision exercises allow you to help students learn to recognize the weaknesses in their own papers by learning to read as readers, not writers. The only way they will learn to do this is by practice and imitation. Arrange for your students to review each other's papers as often as possible. Guide them through their first experiences so they can listen to you, a more experienced writer, respond to a text. Give them the opportunity to rewrite their papers after you have evaluated them. Only by actually editing their own work, and then seeing how it improves, can they fully appreciate the value of the writing process.

Insist that students produce multiple drafts and arrange some sort of method for evaluating those drafts as they are produced.

If students are to have faith in the ability of writing as a process to help them improve their writing, they must have constant feedback throughout the phases of each paper they produce. Certainly you want to respond to as many of your students' drafts as possible, but because of time limitations, you may need to develop alternate methods to simply taking home a stack of papers each night:

- Cancel class periodically and have individual conferences.
- Give students class time to work on their papers and go around to each student and spend five minutes working with him or her.

- Give students the chance to evaluate each other's work by requiring peer editing.
- Let your students continue to work on any papers on which they make less than an A. After all, why bother to comment on a student's paper if you aren't going to allow that student to put those comments into effect?

Make student-produced writing the focus of the class.

One of the benefits of writing as process is the way it demystifies writing and its production. The published essay you share with your class might not intimidate them when you also show them the four revisions the editor required you to make. You can also emphasize the students' understanding of how the writing process affects their own writing by making student writing, rather than works by published authors, the focus of your class's outside reading. I'm not suggesting that you never have your students read published essays; however, they will never believe you when you tell them their writing matters if it doesn't matter enough to be worthy of class time.

Consider the students' progress as well as their products when evaluating their class performance.

Every semester as I begin calculating my students' grades, I struggle with an ethical dilemma: How much should a student's effort count? As much as I try to deemphasize grades when I teach writing, ultimately they are a requirement at most universities. Because writing classes that stress the process approach depend so heavily on the need for students to participate, it seems as though participation should count heavily. However, is it fair to give an average writer an A in a writing class? That student may have worked very hard, but not necessarily harder than those students who are above-average writers. I try to solve this dilemma by explaining to my students that, while their grades will reflect the quality of their writing, the harder they work and the more they rewrite, the better their writing will become and the higher their grades will be. So ultimately, an average writer may produce above-average writing if he or she is encouraged and given the opportunity to keep reworking his or her papers. In such a situation the teacher is taking the student's progress into consideration, but only as far as it affects his or her writing ability. Such an approach allows a teacher to consider progress in a way that is fair to all the students in the class, and it prevents the danger of sending false messages to students by giving them grades that do not directly reflect their writing abilities.

Conclusion

Why should you teach writing as a process? First, I guarantee that you have a writing process whether you realize it or not. The exercises that follow will give you a chance to intimately explore that process. Shouldn't you give your students equal access to something that has worked well for you? Second, process writing provides you with a tangible way to demystify writing for your students. Once you turn on the lights and force your students to face the monster in the closet (the one that's really an old shirt) they will have no reason for avoiding writing or abandoning it as a talent they "weren't born with." Make your students take responsibility for the fact that they can all write—and then make them do it!

Exercises

Writing Exercises

1. Read the "Place" portion of the community assignment from Chapter Six. What place do you associate with your community? What is unique about that community? What does it say about you? Write an essay that explores the relationship of place to your community. Refer to Chapter Six for specifics on the place paper.
2. Develop a classroom exercise that will encourage your students to develop an awareness of their writing process. Be prepared to share this process with the class.

Collaborative Activities

1. Evaluate the exercises that you wrote individually. Consider the following issues:
   • What worked?
   • What didn't work?
   • Which exercise would you choose to use? Why?
   • Develop a list of criteria for judging process-oriented exercises.
2. Develop a writing assignment that includes prewriting, writing, and rewriting activities and share it with the class. What qualities do all the best assignments share?

Chapter Four

Encouraging Collaboration in the Classroom

I am in the process of doing a collaborative exercise with my class as I am writing this entry. We are sitting outside, and they all seem to be getting along well and enjoying getting to know each other. They all are also still very aware of me. Everytime I move they glance my way. Occasionally one or two of them will look suspiciously over their shoulders, like they can't believe I am letting them do this. Like it is all some big trick, and pretty soon I am going to leap out at them with a crazed look in my eye brandishing grammar exercises. (From Kate Hickerson's journal)

In Chapter Two we discuss where you belong in the classroom; in this chapter we discuss where you don't belong in the classroom—front and center, all day every day. "What?" you might say. "I'm the teacher; my place is at the podium in front where I deliver my lectures." Wrong answer. Podiums have their purposes. I like to rock mine back and forth when I'm bored. Sometimes I use it to stack papers on. I've been known to retreat behind one when I feel the need to appear more "teacherly." But podiums are not where you stand to give lectures—at least not in writing classes—because you should not be lecturing.

So why not lecture? I have had more arguments with more teachers over this particular issue than over any other one that I can remember, but there are several reasons why you shouldn't lecture. Lectures tend to be boring, and no one pays attention except the person lecturing. The students don't learn anything because they're bored, and they're not paying attention. Most importantly, writing is an activity. You learn it by doing it—not by listening to someone talk about it. You could probably deliver an excellent lecture on the introductory paragraph, complete with examples of what you consider good introductions, but telling your students about introductions is not the same as giving them the opportunity to write introductions and learn for themselves what works and what doesn't. The same is true of any other topic related to writing. Lectures are cold, sterile things. Writing is a messy business. The sooner your students get in there and muck about, the better.

Most new teachers rely on the lecture, not out of a perverse need to control the classroom, but because they simply cannot imagine any other way of effectively filling up all those long empty hours of class that loom before them. However, to effectively teach writing as process, you need to use a workshop approach—and workshopping means collaboration.

What Is Collaboration?

Collaboration seems to be a simple concept: groups of two or more people work together rather than individually. Essentially this definition is correct, but it is important to distinguish between true collaboration and something that is definitely *not* collaboration—group work. Collaboration does involve groups of people working together, but for an activity to be truly collaborative the following activities must occur:

- The teacher must provide each group with a specific task that provides guidelines but does not attempt to elicit a "correct" answer.
- Each member of the group must participate.
- The group must reach a consensus, even if that means agreeing to disagree.
- The group must present its findings to the rest of the class.
- The teacher must help the class understand the relevance of what is shared.

This is different from group work in several essential ways. Primarily, group work doesn't require consensus, and the teacher does not expect the students to share the results of their work. Frequently, group work is done in response to an assignment that seeks to elicit a specific response. Let's look at two examples:

Example One: Your students are writing about a personal experience that changed their perspective on life in some way. You give them an assignment that asks them to get into their assigned groups and write a paragraph about some "first" in their lives: college, senior prom, boy or girl friend, etc. You give them the rest of the class period to write the paragraphs, then you collect them and take them home to grade. The next day you return them to their groups and you begin another activity.

Example Two: Your students are writing about a personal experience that changed their perspective on life in some way. You give them an assignment that asks them to get into their assigned groups and discuss the question, "What is a life-changing event?" You ask them to develop a list of criteria for judging the relevance of such an event and ask them to be prepared to share that list with the class. After each group shares its list, you ask the class as a whole to tell you how those same criteria can be used to help each of them judge the effectiveness of the event that each student has chosen to write about. You then ask them to consider how those criteria can be used to develop the paper.

Example One is group work. It is not an effective exercise because it simply expects the students to guess the "right" answer, the teacher's answer. Also, because it doesn't give the students the opportunity to share what they learned, it reinforces the "busy work" aspect of the assignment. The class never discusses the relevance of the exercise and what they have written, so they probably will not see any relevance to the exercise, and only the best students will connect it to the individual papers on which they are working.

Example Two is different because it provides an opportunity for students to understand—discover in fact—the relevance of the activity. Rather than simply turning their papers into the "teacher void," students are expected to share what they have done. Such sharing should increase their commitment to the exercise. Also, students are expected to consider the relevance of both the activity and its connection to their own papers. Finally, the teacher brings closure to the exercise by leading the class in a discussion aimed at helping the students draw connections between their group discoveries and their own work. Now that's collaboration.

Creating a Collaborative Environment

For collaboration to occur, you have to decenter your classroom, that is, you must give up control of the class, release your grip on that podium, and give the class an opportunity to teach itself. This doesn't mean that you can stop coming to class, but it does mean that you cease to be the center of attention. In a collaborative classroom a good teacher is one who sets up and plans activities and then retires quietly to an unobtrusive place in the room, occasionally moving forward to referee discussions or answer questions. You are the director, not the star, and people observing your class might say, "The students seem very productive and busy, but what's the teacher doing?"

The best teacher is not always the most visible teacher. Frequently you help your students more by sitting at your desk and grading papers while they wrangle over some question you've posed. You are giving your students the opportunity to teach themselves. The ability to think and learn without a teacher is the most valuable gift you can give students because that is the gift that will allow them to keep on thinking and learning long after your class is over. The information contained in a lecture will stay in a student's head until the class ends; the ability to learn independently will last forever.

You can't decenter your class over night, and you may find yourself very uncomfortable and bored with your limited role in classroom activities, but be daring and patient; see what happens. Creating a collaborative classroom involves the use of two essential activities:

- Collaborative exercises.
- Peer editing.

Collaborative Exercises

I sat at the front of the room, trying not to smirk in satisfaction as I slyly watched my neatly grouped students working away, their voices filling the room with a quiet hum. My satisfaction was short lived. Five minutes after they had begun peer editing, the first group quietly clustered around my desk, their various bags and books hanging from their appendages. "We're finished" the self-appointed leader flatly stated, "Can we go?" I opened and shut my mouth a few times like an asphyxiated goldfish, then returned with, "You can't be done. Surely you have something to say about each other's papers." "Yeah," he returned, "We told each other how good they were. Can we go now?" Before I could say no, another group slunk out the front door. "If you're sure you have done everything possible to make your papers all that they can be, then you can go," I said with a challenge in my voice. They went. Fifteen minutes of an eighty minute class period had passed and my class was reduced to half. The other hardy souls lasted a full thirty minutes. When I skulked out after the last group, I swore to myself that I would never peer edit again. (Yours truly, many years ago)

Collaboration can work well; it can also be a dismal failure. If you want your class to get the most out of collaboration, don't let them get away with being lazy. Every semester I have at least one teaching assistant come to me and say, "I put them in groups to work, and they did OK for about twenty minutes, then they said they were done, and they left thirty minutes early. What should I do?" I have much better answers to that question now.

First, make sure your students are collaborating, not doing group work. Usually, when a teacher comes to me with this problem, he or she has asked the students to do group/busy work. When the students realize this, they basically blow the assignment off. For instance, if you gave your class Example One on page 49, most groups would talk sporadically for a few minutes, one person would write the paragraph, and they would all leave early. This sort of scenario is unlikely with Example Two because it is a more demanding exercise. So, if collaboration is failing you, make sure your students are collaborating. It may be your exercise that is at fault, not the students.

Let your students know that you take collaboration seriously and expect them to also. If all your students work for ten minutes and then say they're finished, call their bluff. You'll be surprised how often they decide that they need to do more work when you tell them that they will be reporting to the class—yes them, all alone, front and center. You may also find it necessary to let your students know that there will be consequences if they fail to participate fully. For example, you might deduct points from their participation grade or give students absences. Follow through with collaboration—make sure your students have the opportunity to recognize the relevance of the collaborative work they do. Show them how it applies to them and their own work, and you will convince them to fully collaborate.

Peer Editing

Peer editing is an essential activity in any collaborative classroom because it allows you to provide your students with an audience beyond you, the teacher. Peer editing gives you the opportunity to create a forum in which your students can see and hear other readers respond to their ideas and opinions. This experience will do more to convince your students that they have worthwhile ideas to share than any glowing comments you can write on their papers. Peer editing, like anything else in the classroom, can be the highlight of your semester or a complete failure. It's guaranteed to fail, however, if you don't do several things to prepare your students before they begin peer editing:

- Provide them with a vocabulary for discussing each other's writing.
- Provide them with examples of peer editing.
- Establish peer editing groups.
- Have them write a group constitution that outlines the procedures by which they will govern themselves.

Provide them with a vocabulary for discussing each other's writing.

For your students to have the confidence to effectively discuss each other's writing, you need to help them develop a vocabulary for doing this. Begin by structuring several initial peer editing sessions as whole class discussions. My preferred method is to have students volunteer their papers to be edited. I choose one or two of the solicited essays and make copies for the whole class, which I pass out the class period before we plan to peer edit. Before we actually begin editing, I ask the class to help me develop a list of peer-editing questions that are appropriate for the assignment. For example, assuming that they are writing a narrative of an event, they might ask questions such as:

- Is the purpose of the essay clear? In other words, does it pass the "so what" test?
- Is the essay fully developed?
- Is the essay interesting?
- Is the sequence of events clear and logical?
- Does the writer use descriptive details?
- What part of the essay would you identify as most effective? Why?
- What part of the essay would you define as least effective? Why?

Initially, you will have to prompt your students to create these sorts of questions, but they will gain aptitude with practice. I try to allot time before every peer-editing session for the development of peer-editing questions, though I place increasing responsibility on the students to develop the questions as time passes.

Provide them with examples of peer editing.

I use three methods to accomplish this goal:

- Once the questions are complete, I lead the class through a discussion of the essays, acting as a peer editor rather than an observer. This is important because your participation will provide your students with a model to imitate.

- I have also had good luck inviting peer groups to my office for editing sessions. In these cases, I again participate and provide an example. Sometimes I invite a friend to sit in and participate also.
- Finally, you can try staging a peer session for your class to observe. Ask a group of your colleagues to come to class with essays that they are working on and have them peer edit. When they are finished, let your class ask them questions.

Establish peer-editing groups.

I suggest that you avoid letting your students group themselves—friends will always want to work with friends. I normally create groups using random selection. Beginning with the first person on the left or right of the room, start counting from one to five or six, depending on how many people are in your class. For example, in a class of twenty-four, I would plan on six groups of four each and would count from one to six to end up with six groups of four. After everyone has a number, let the groups meet and get to work. I consider these groups permanent because, if you keep changing the make-up of the groups, your students will spend more time socializing than working. Occasionally, I will let someone change groups, but only under extenuating circumstances. Make it clear to your students from the beginning that autonomy has its price, and they must learn to work out their differences.

Have the groups write a group constitution that outlines the procedures by which they will govern themselves.

If you want your peer groups to function independently, you must force them to create some guidelines by which they will govern themselves. I like to accomplish this by having my students write "constitutions." I give my students a handout that asks them to fill in the blanks on the following document:

> *We the people, of the group _____, in order to form a more perfect peer-editing group, establish justice, ensure domestic tranquility, provide for our common benefit, promote our general welfare and ensure the improvement of our writing for ourselves and our classmates do ordain and establish the following constitution:*

In the space that follows the colon, I expect them to list the rules by which they will govern themselves. For example, I tell them that I don't want them complaining to me because one group member takes more than his share of time or one group member never types her papers or brings extra copies. I state on my syllabus that I will give anyone who is not prepared to peer edit an absence for the day. Beyond that, the groups must monitor themselves. I suggest that you remind them to consider the following issues:

- Will they read papers silently or aloud?
- How much time will they allow per paper?
- Will the editing be on a voluntary basis or is each member required to participate in his or her turn?
- What sort of comments are or are not allowed? For example, has someone participated if she simply says, "I agree," after the previous speaker has finished? Is it enough to give positive comments, or is constructive criticism also necessary? Should specific examples be provided? Is the writer of the paper allowed to interrupt the editors to defend his or her paper? How many defenses or explanations are allowed?
- Does each group member need to provide typed copies of his or her paper for the other members?
- What are the consequences if someone does not follow the rules?

After your class has written their constitutions, you need to ask them to print up a copy that includes a place for each group member's signature as well as yours. As the teacher, you have the right to approve or disapprove each constitution. Encourage your students to take this task seriously and let them know that you will be referring to their constitutions should any problems or complaints arise. I have found that this exercise forces my students to think seriously about peer editing in a positive way. It also cuts down on the amount of time spent arguing over whether to read papers aloud.

Conclusion

Have I convinced you of the evils of the lecture as compared with the glory of collaboration? I hope I have, but only to a certain degree. I don't encourage you to lecture, but I'm not trying to argue that there won't be times when an extended discussion of a specific topic is not necessary. These sorts of discussions allow you to give your students information that they need to collaborate effectively. Remember—keep the discussions short and the class active.

Exercises

Writing Exercises

1. Writing is an event, and as a writing teacher, you will witness many individual events. A conference with a student is an event; a peer-editing session is an event. A thirty-second conversation with a student can be a major event. Write about one such event. How did it affect you? Did it make you question your role as a teacher? What would you do differently? How did you affect the student? Refer to Chapter Six for specifics on the event paper.
2. Write a collaborative exercise. Be prepared to present it in class.

Collaborative Activities

1. After you get into your peer-editing groups, discuss how you want your peer-editing group to collaborate and then write your group's Declaration of Independence. Share your documents with the class and then collaborate as a class on a list of the best criteria from each group's document. What recommendations will you make to your students and why?
2. Collaborate with the class as a whole, and choose a date for peer editing. You and your group will peer edit each other's papers according to the guidelines you established for yourselves. When you have finished peer editing, consider these questions:
   - What aspects of peer editing did you enjoy? How can you emphasize those elements for your students?
   - What aspects of peer editing didn't you like? How can you diminish them for your students?
   - How would you adjust your group constitution to make your next peer-editing session better?

   Be prepared to share your conclusions with the class.

Chapter Five

Responding to Student Writing

At 7:00 on a Wednesday evening, I sat down to grade a stack of twenty essays, determined to pass them back the next morning at 9:30. I had promised my students that I would not keep the papers for more than a week, but, the other six days had been sucked up going to class, teaching, studying for my own classes, preparing for the ones that I taught, reading, and even occasionally eating or sleeping. I think my husband figured in there somewhere, but I'm honestly not sure at this point. By midnight I had eaten an entire bag of Chee-tos (bad choice, I left orange smudges everywhere) and had graded only ten papers—two per hour I realized. At that rate I would be grading until 9:00 the next morning. I sighed, went to the fridge for my third Coke, and swore I would never put off paper grading again. By the time I figured out how many papers I would have to grade per day to stay on schedule, fifteen more minutes had passed, and I was running out of time. By 2:00 in the morning, I had graded three more papers. I had been stumped by a really good paper. I had to do more than just write "great" on the bottom along with a big fat A. My hand was locking up. I was ready to begin automatically assigning every paper a C with a note to "See me in my office for further comments," and I was beginning to hallucinate. I had been beaten by the first-year student essay (Yours truly, several years ago).

You may frequently find all your time in the classroom, no matter how valuable it is, overshadowed by those mountains of papers that seem to continually heap themselves on every available flat surface. Of all the difficult tasks that face new teachers, I found the overwhelming job of trying to keep up with grading more than I could manage. No one ever told me not to try to identify absolutely every error in every paper every time, so that is what I tried to do. No one ever told me that marking errors served little purpose beyond convincing students that they knew nothing and that the teacher knew it all. Not only did I exhaust myself, I also completely demoralized my students. They believed that I had possession of the secret to good writing and was willfully withholding it. On more than one occasion I had an upset student wave a paper in my face and wail, "Just tell me how to fix it!" Given the cryptic nature of many of the comments I wrote, I can now understand why they believed this so fervently.

"Awk." "II.a.3. 1-4." "Frag." Most of us have gotten back papers covered with strange encryptions that covered a huge amount of space, sometimes the entire paper, yet said nothing intelligible. Unfortunately, I have been just as guilty of speaking in tongues as many of my own teachers. I never intentionally tried to prevent my students from learning; I simply had no clue how to share the secret. In fact, I wasn't even sure I knew the secret. Now I realize that there is no secret, just people struggling to learn how to write and how to read, and that is the message I try to share with my students.

Most of what I know about responding to student writing I have learned from my students, but I have also learned from some other notable sources such as Mina Shaughnessy's *Errors and Expectations*[1] and the other articles listed in the annotated bibliography of this book. I have also gathered advice from many other quarters and can tell you with certainty that it is possible to not only grade all those papers you require your students to write, but even achieve some positive results in the process. If you want to respond effectively to your students' writing, you need to follow these guidelines:

- Respond rhetorically.
- Motivate students to continue writing.
- Conference with your students regularly.

Respond Rhetorically

When you read one of your student's essays, you may be confused about how to most effectively respond. Your first instinct may be to start marking errors: punctuation, grammar, spelling, even style and coherence. Responding this way does have some positive aspects. Correcting errors is a very objective way of responding to a paper, so you can be sure that you are being fair. It is also easy to assign a grade based on errors. However, this method of grading requires a huge time commitment on your part, and it will usually have only negative affects on your students' attitude toward writing.

When I was a first-year student in college, I had a teacher who passed out a very lengthy score sheet the first day of class, which he told us would determine our grades on our papers. It looked something like this:

Punctuation
    comma splices: −10
    run-on sentences: −10
    fragments: −10
    misuse of apostrophes: −5
    misuse of colons: −5
    misuse of dashes: −5

[1]Shaughnessy, Mina P. *Errors and Expectations: A Guide for the Teacher of Basic Writing.* New York: Oxford University Press, 1977a.

Grammar
> agreement errors: −10
> pronoun reference errors: −10
> misplaced modifiers: −10
> dangling modifiers: −10

Other Errors
> spelling: −5 per word
> awkwardness: −5
> lack of thesis: −10
> lack of coherence: −10

This is not a complete list. I include only those errors that I found on my own papers when I went back and looked at some of them. Even though many of us discovered that it was possible to make a negative score on an essay, none of us ever argued about our grades. How do you argue with a −30 when a score sheet is attached to your paper? I lost ninety points for comma splices on my first paper. More importantly, we didn't care. We knew that Dr. Grammar (our loving nickname for him) never read what we said. He apparently didn't care about our ideas. You notice that nothing regarding content made the score sheet. I believe I could have written six essays on the making of a peanut butter sandwich and received A's—if I wrote correctly. None of us had any personal involvement in what we wrote; we simply strove to be correct. In many ways this was a very low-pressure way to write, but when that class was over, I was not inspired to keep writing. Had anyone asked, I would have told them that writing was like algebra, something to be avoided at all costs.

Luckily, I was forced to take a creative writing course my next semester, and I had a wonderful instructor who knew how to respond to what her students were saying and encourage them to reach beyond their own limits. I know this sounds trite, but it was because of that teacher that I chose to be an English major with a concentration in writing. She had a way not of disregarding errors, but of focusing on content first and the messages her students were trying to communicate. She always explained that we needed to avoid errors because they prevented us from communicating as effectively as possible. In other words, writing strings of run-on sentences is like speaking too quickly—no one can follow what you're saying, no matter how interesting it is. I never heard her identify her grading technique in this way, but I know now that she was responding rhetorically.

What is a rhetorical response? Most of you probably have a general sense of what rhetoric means: Rhetoric is the art of speaking persuasively. However, the definition also includes the concept of the rhetorical situation: audience, purpose, and occasion. Whenever you begin responding to a student's paper, you must consider the rhetorical situation:

> *audience:* someone who is learning to write and is likely to be insecure about his or her abilities. He or she may or may not be motivated, depending on past writing experiences.

purpose: helping your students overcome their insecurities and develop a belief not only in their ability to write but in the effectiveness of writing as a means of expression.

occasion: a classroom situation in which you are in the difficult position of trying to convince your students that progress is more important than grades and that you are not just their teacher but also their trusted advisor and fellow writer—all of this while knowing that you evaluate papers to give grades.

You also have to convince your students to consider the rhetorical situation of their own papers when they write because they will understand the usefulness of your rhetorical responses only within such a context. For instance, the best way to teach students to avoid grammar and punctuation errors is within a rhetorical context. In other words, you have to show them that errors are not somehow inherently evil; they should be avoided because they damage the effectiveness of the communication act. Consider this sentence: "He promised to take care of her children at her death bed." Or how about this one: "Writing in a journal the words reveal many truths about myself." These sentences don't read that badly. However, we don't know if the man in question is going to care for the children indefinitely or only beside the woman's bed as she dies. And who is learning from the journal? Since words do not write themselves, this is a difficult question to answer.

Students understand this concept in terms of "real life," but they have difficulty applying the same principle to their writing. A wise student would not show up for an interview at a bank dressed in ripped Levi's. A wise communicator realizes that no speaker, no matter how charismatic she might be, will speak persuasively if she doesn't establish her credibility. For example, would a group of teenagers believe a speaker who is trying to convince them of the difficulties of avoiding unsafe sex, or smoking, or even jay walking, if they do not believe that the speaker has personally experienced the difficulty? A wise job candidate will not submit a letter of application that is full of misspelled words. The same is true of any paper, so just as you must convince your students to be aware of the rhetorical situation when they write, you must consider it when responding to your students.

Read the following student paper:

Achievers and Dreamers

As a youngster life had nothing to keep you down except for the occasional unfair grounding, because your sister decided to cry to mom that you looked at her weird or ate an extra piece of candy. Being a kid had its advantages; playing outside with a tennis ball and a raggedy splintering bat to see who had the strongest swing. All too common was the "back porch swing" which involved the slicing swing of a youngster putting too much power into it and sending the defenseless ball into the unchartered territory of another neighbor's backyard. This is just one of the many past times of a youngster as myself indulge in. Other activities that we participated in involved racing bikes, football, and the occasional shoplifting of candy and toys.

The sport that my friends and I always played was basketball, whether it was playing on the cracked, tar covered pavement of elementary school parking lots, or the dusty backyard playgrounds of neighboring kids. The favorite place to play was the recreational center that allowed kids to play on real courts. I remember entering the gym with my eyes wide open; I was in awe to the spacious room before me as I strolled through the heavy double doors I appeared to the other kids jumping on the wooden bleachers like someone who came here to play some big time basket ball. I stepped onto the hardwood floor covered with the purple lettering of the junior high that owned the gym and tried to impress the kids goofing off but unfortunately the other kids didn't care about my attitude or ability because they were watching the big guys play. After I realized that I wasn't any concern of the kids, I too went to the bleachers and watched. How I envied those older guys, shooting three-pointers with hardly any effort. When I tried to copy the shot, I was lucky to get anything other than the floor on the way down. The rim seemed so low to the them, as they jumped and hung on the rim. When I tried to leap towards the rim, the hoop might as well of been at the top of the Empire Statess Building. The result would of been the same, no hang time, no nothing. I was embarrassed to play in the same building as those giants but I was determined to grab some spot light. I wanted to be the man the little kids admired and wanted to be like. I wanted kids to look at me like I looked at the giants shooting and dunking. I would shoot on the goals which weren't occupied and try complicated lay-ups involving snakelike turns and twists which looked good when the big guys did it, but with my small frame and horrible accuracy turned the move into an acrobatic mess of motions. I tried to get attention and sometimes I would get what I wanted, the attention and the opportunity to play with the big guys.

If I didn't play at the recreation center I would be playing for my junior high team at St. Luke. At the end of each season I would always return to the recreation center to showcase my new abilities that I gained over the St. Luke basketball season. Each year I got bigger the gym got smaller the rims got lower and closer, and the kids seemed smaller and less skilled, and yes I did get better each year. Throughout my Bishop Dunne high school years I would continue to go the recreation center to play the older guys. They seemed a little smaller each time I played them. After my junior year I must admit, I was actually better than the people I once held in such high regard and was afraid to play against when I was younger. I felt that I needed to find stronger competition. Almost all the goals that I had set for myself in the beginning of my basketball life had been reached; to play with the giants, to become a giant, and to be respected as a giant by those younger than myself.

I needed to find and set new goals. What was the next level of competition? I succeeded in junior high and high school ball I guess college was next. Where was I to find college competition? I looked around at parks and gyms and finally came across some serious players at a little hid away park surrounded by an auto shop and grocery store. I was mesmerized I felt like a kid again, they looked liked giant leaping monsters. Again I was afraid of going out there and getting embarrassed due to lack of size and talent. These people were a different breed of player altogether, and I wanted to learn how to become part of their superior race. I decided to talk and to mimic these players like I did when I was a basketball baby practicing lay-ups. When I arrived at the park I realized that it was different from what I was accustomed to. The park was out side and crowded with oak trees and old part benches. The court itself was shorter and commonly covered with rocks from the playground area and shattered glass from beer bottles. As unappealing as it may look, ironically it showcased the prettiest plays and best talent in the area. Many guys who had achieved college player status came back to the park to impress the less talented.

As I realized that they used to be in my shoes at one time, that means I had chance to achieve their position. If only I could learn from them and put myself onto that court without fear of embarrassment and once again achieve a higher level of play. I now stay in the park till the street lights come on and continue to practice moves I saw performed with such ease from players earlier in the afternoon. I begin to make my own moves. I feel that the best way to catch up to others is to practice and work hard while others are sleeping.

What was your first reaction? It may have been "F." Admittedly, this paper is a mess, virtually unintelligible in places. But once I recovered from sensory overload, I was very excited about this paper. It was written by a young man named Jason who has aspirations to be a college ball player. And while he is passionate about basketball, he is not passionate about writing, or English in general. He told me on more than one occasion that he had never gotten "this stuff" and that his previous teachers had just given up and let him play ball. From the first minute he opened his mouth in class, which he did frequently, everyone else listened. I won't say he was well-spoken; he wasn't, but he had a way of saying things that were interesting and often humorous. Those same qualities are apparent in his writing, despite the many errors. That phrase, "raggedy splintering old bat" works. And how about "basketball baby?" That is real and powerful stuff. This student presented a challenge to me. I knew there was a writer inside the ball player, and I knew that he cared enough to want to try and find that writer. Despite his previous experiences with writing teachers, he was willing to listen to what I said to him about his writing and voluntarily rewrote his papers two and three times each. I had to prod him, but he did the work. The challenge I faced was finding a way to respond to his papers that would allow me to focus on what was good about his writing, while still helping him to gradually begin conquering his weaknesses. I responded rhetorically. Now look at the same paper, which begins on the next page, with the comments that I wrote in the margins.

Interesting title

Achievers and Dreamers

vivid image— I remember doing that!

As a youngster life had nothing to keep you down
except for the occasional unfair grounding, because
your sister decided to cry to mom that you looked at
her weird or ate an extra piece of candy. Being a kid
had its advantages; playing outside with a tennis ball
and a raggedy splintering bat to see who had the
strongest swing. All too common was the "back porch
swing"which involved the slicing swing of a youngster
putting too much power into it and sending the
defenseless ball into the uncharctered territory of
another neighbor's backyard. This is just one of the
many past times of a youngster as myself indulge in.
Other activities that we participated in involved racing bikes, football, and the occasional shoplifting of
candy and toys.

You've done a nice job of leading into your topic.

The sport that my friends and I always played was
basketball, whether it was playing on the cracked, tar
covered pavement of elementary school parking lots, or
the dusty backyard playgrounds of neighboring kids.
The favorite place to play was the recreational center
that allowed kids to play on real courts. I remember
entering the gym with my eyes wide open; I was in awe
to the spacious room before me as I strolled through
the heavy double doors I appeared to the other kids
jumping on the wooden bleachers like someone who came
here to play some big time basket ball. I stepped onto
the hardwood floor covered with the purple lettering of
the junior high that owned the gym and tried to

Good description

I like the way you appeal to all the senses. You also describe what is going on inside—this sort of emotional description works well.

impress the kids goofing off but unfortunately the other kids didn't care about my attitude or ability
because they were watching the big guys play. After I
realized that I wasn't any concern ofthe kids, I too
went to the bleachers and watched. How I envied those
older guys, shooting three-pointers with hardly any
effort. When I tried to copy the shot, I was lucky to
get anything other than the floor on the way down. The
rim seemed so low to the them, as they jumped and hung
on the rim. When I tried to leap towards the rim, the
hoop might as well of been at the top of the Empire
Statess Building. The result would of been the same,
no hang time, no nothing. I was embarrassed to play in
the same building as those giants but I was determined
to grab some spot light. I wanted to be the man the
little kids admired and wanted to be like. I wanted
kids to look at me like I looked at the giants shooting and dunking. I would shoot on the goals which
weren't occupied and try complicated lay-ups involving
snakelike turns and twists which looked good when the
big guys did it, but with my small frame and horrible
accuracy turned the move into an acrobatic mess of
motions. I tried to get attention and sometimes I
would get what I wanted, the attention and the opportunity to play with the big guys.

nice

You have a nice sense of transition.

If I didn't play at the recreation center I would
be playing for my junior high team at St. Luke. At the
end of each season I would always return to the recre-

ation center to showcase my new abilities that I
gained over the St. Luke basketball season. Each year
I got bigger the gym got smaller the rims got lower
and closer, and the kids seemed smaller and less
skilled, and yes I did get better each year. Throughout my Bishop Dunne high school years I would continue
to go the recreation center to play the older guys.
They seemed a little smaller each time I played them.
After my junior year I must admit, I was actually better than the people I once held in such high regard
and was afraid to play against when I was younger. I
felt that I needed to find stronger competition. Almost
all the goals that I had set for myself in the beginning of my basketball life had been reached; to play
with the giants, to become a giant, and to be respected as a giant by those younger than myself.

How did you get from junior high to high school?

I needed to find and set new goals. What was the
next level of competition? I succeeded in junior high
and high school ball I guess college was next. Where
was I to find college competition? I looked around at
parks and gyms and finally came across some serious
players at a little hid away park surrounded by an
auto shop and grocery store. I was mesmerized I felt
like a kid again, they looked liked giant leaping monsters. Again I was afraid of going out there and getting embarrassed due to lack of size and talent. These
people were a different breed of player altogether,
and I wanted to learn how to become part of their
superior race. I decided to talk and to mimic these
players like I did when I was a basketball baby practicing lay-ups. When I arrived at the park I realized
that it was different from what I was accustomed to.
The park was out side and crowded with oak trees and
old part benches. The court itself was shorter and
commonly covered with rocks from the playground area
and shattered glass from beer bottles. As unappealing
as it may look, ironically it showcased the prettiest
plays and best talent in the area. Many guys who had
achieved college player status came back to the park
to impress the less talented.

Why not try a college rec center?

How did you know they were college players?

Were you planning on going to college? Did you hope to get a scholarship to play basketball?

As I realized that they used to be in my shoes at
one time, that means I had chance to achieve their
position. If only I could learn from them and put
myself onto that court without fear of embarrassment
and once again achieve a higher level of play. I now
stay in the park till the street lights come on and
continue to practice moves I saw performed with such
ease from players earlier in the afternoon. I begin to
make my own moves. I feel that the best way to catch
up to others is to practice and work hard while others
are sleeping.

nice closing image

Jason, as my comments should illustrate, you did many things well in this essay. Your description is excellent; the ideas you express are complex, and the story flows nicely. However, the sophistication of your natural style is hurt by the many punctuation errors. So that is our challenge—to help you understand how punctuation works, so you can use it to improve your writing, rather than letting it hurt your writing. Make an appointments with me, and we'll get started!

You probably immediately noticed the many problems that I didn't identify or discuss when I responded to this paper. If I explain the rhetorical situation, you will understand why I limited my criticism. First, this was the first paper Jason turned in, and I wanted to encourage him, not demoralize him. Second, students can process only a limited number of things at once. I praised several aspects of the paper that he could build upon and then identified one or two errors that he could concentrate on as he began revising. I framed the negative comments rhetorically not by pointing out the errors, but by asking questions when my understanding as a reader was impeded. I expressed my suggestions in terms of questions, not direct commands, because the paper belongs to Jason, and he must decide for himself what works and doesn't work. However, the questions are intended to give him a direction in which to move as he begins reevaluating the paper from the standpoint of the reader, not himself, the writer. Most importantly, I included a fairly lengthy concluding comment. I began this comment by praising the essay as realistically as possible and then trying to point out how his errors were affecting his ability to communicate effectively. In other words, rather than just listing the errors with point deductions beside them, I tried to help him see how the errors function within a rhetorical context—how they affect the audience, purpose, and occasion.

Finally, you may have noticed that I did not assign a grade, and you may be wondering why, given the fact that assigning grades is normally the end result of evaluating a student paper. When students submit their papers to me for the first time, I frequently will not give them grades, but will require a mandatory rewrite instead. I have discovered that delaying the assigning of grades can have several positive benefits:

- Students do not have to recover from the demoralizing effects of a C, D, or F before they can work up enough enthusiasm to rewrite.
- You can send a message to your students that their progress is just as important as their products.
- You can delay assigning a grade to a student's paper until he or she has produced a level of work that will result in a grade that the student can enjoy.
- And sometimes you can slap a bad grade on a student's paper when he or she is expecting a mandatory rewrite and turns in something that doesn't even qualify as a completed draft. You can shake them up a little.

You can't avoid assigning grades, but you can delay the inevitable to give your students a chance to produce work of which you are both proud.

Motivate Students to Continue Writing

"Are you kidding?"

"I'm sorry, but nobody is this stupid."

"Based on the writing skills you've exhibited in this paper, I'd suggest you reconsider your decision to pursue higher education."

Teachers actually write comments such as these on their students' papers and return them. In fact, I was the recipient of one of these comments. That same teacher informed me in front of the entire class that I was much too young (at the age of twenty-one) to be in graduate school and should leave the program. To this day, I'm not completely sure how much my desire to spite him was responsible for my decision to finish his class and pursue a Ph.D. I do not remember him as an inspirational teacher; he did not make me want to write. I do not recommend insulting your students either verbally or in writing as a motivational technique. I am not a proponent of shock treatment.

Rhetorical comments, by their nature, normally serve to encourage students to write, but even they can have a negative effect. For example, you could respond to Jason's paper in this way:

"Despite the numerous errors, which impede your paper's ability to communicate effectively, I encourage you to rewrite. If you would like help correcting your errors, please refer to your handbook. Good job."

Most students would respond to this by saying, "Good job of what? Making mistakes?" Such a student response is not unreasonable considering that the comment does not refer to anything the writer did well. In the comment's defense, it does point out the rhetorical ramifications of writing incorrectly, and it does provide the student with a specific assignment to improve his writing, correct the errors. But it does not encourage the student to write. Now look at this comment:

"Jason, I especially like the way this paper sounds like you. I can't imagine anyone else using a phrase like 'basketball baby.' Your descriptions are also very vivid. I have never played basketball or hung out around ball parks, but I have such a vivid image of the place you described, that I feel I was there. What keeps your paper from being completely compelling is the disjointed nature of the sentences. Because you tend to forget to use punctuation, your thoughts sometimes dribble right off the page. You need to keep working on your ability to identify sentences and punctuate accordingly. Why don't you redo the first page or two and then bring it by my office. Keep up the good work."

This comment does make specific reference to what is "good" about the paper and the student's work. It also makes specific reference to what is wrong and provides the student with a specific task. The hope is that the student will focus on the positive and be motivated to continue working on the paper. Remember, put yourself in your student's place. Don't forget what it feels like to have someone tell you that your ideas aren't worth the effort. If they aren't, why should you make the effort? Never forget to let your students know that they have done something right, even if it was just coming up with a good title or remembering to use multiple paragraphs. Never forget to let your students know that you consider their potential just as important as their actual skill level. See more in their papers than what is actually on the page. Show them how to reach beyond their own expectations.

Conference with Your Students Regularly

Many of the comments that you put on your student's papers will suggest that you participate in the rewriting process. For example, in the comment that I wrote on Jason's paper, I suggested that he come by and get help with his punctuation errors. Another comment suggests that he work on a page or two and then bring it by for me to look at. This sort of individual work is essential to many students. You can spend class time explaining the use of the comma, but such class explanations are not as effective as individual tutorials. Of course conferencing with all your students can be time-consuming. However, you may find it is manageable. I normally make the invitation to the students and then leave the responsibility for making an appointment or coming by during office hours up to these students. Those who do come by are showing their level of commitment, as are those who never find the time.

You can also work with students in groups. I guarantee that students like Jason are rarely alone. In fact, Jason and two of his classmates had similar difficulty identifying and punctuating sentences, so we met several times as a group to work on their skills, and I also put them in a peer group together. Because they all recognized that they shared similar problems, they were comfortable working together and learned to help each other effectively.

In addition to making informal invitations to your students on the papers, I suggest that you schedule at least two mandatory conferences per semester per student. Conferencing is time-consuming, so I suggest that you cancel a class and substitute one fifteen-minute conference per student. During your conferences you can do several things:

- Discuss the student's writing in terms of papers he or she has written or is currently writing.
- Read and evaluate one of the student's papers while he or she watches. I like to read the paper aloud and pause every time some aspect of the paper disrupts the reading. I explain the nature of the disruption and then move on.
- Check in with your students and give them a chance to talk with you in a more informal setting. Encourage them to discuss their concerns or their triumphs.

You can use conference time in many useful ways. Remember that the student, not you, should control the conference; be open and encouraging, but don't go into a conference with a set agenda. Listen to your students and learn.

Conclusion

You may have wondered why I responded to the same student paper in so many ways throughout this chapter, sometimes to illustrate what I consider a positive way to respond and sometimes to illustrate a negative way to respond. I didn't do this to confuse the issue of responding to student writing. On the contrary, I did this to demonstrate that there is always more than one way to respond to any piece of student writing. Different teachers have different styles, and that is to be applauded. However, some styles are more rhetorically effective than others. Don't reread this chapter looking for the one right response to Jason's paper. You won't find it. You will find several suggestions and what I hope are some useful guidelines. Finally, you will probably have already started grading papers by the time you read this chapter. Just remember: keep doing what works, and forget the rest.

Exercises

Writing Exercises

1. Just as everyone has his or her own writing process, every teacher has his or her own method of evaluating student papers. Interview one or several teachers and find out how they handle this difficult task. For specifics on the interview paper, see Chapter Six.
2. Make copies of a student paper that you haven't graded, for the members of your peer group, then grade your own copy. Be prepared to share your response with your group.

Collaborative Activities

1. Get in your peer group and pass out the copies of the papers that you copied. Choose one and spend some time grading it individually. Compare your results and consider these questions:
   - Did you all assign the same grade? Why do you think you disagreed? Whose grade was most appropriate?
   - What types of comments were made? Identify those that you consider most effective and those that you consider inappropriate. What criteria did you use to make your selections?
   - What conclusions can you draw about evaluating student papers? Make a list of what works and what doesn't.
2. Compare the results of your group work with the other groups in the class.
   - Do you all feel as though you have an understanding about how to evaluate papers?
   - Is it OK to disagree on grades sometimes?
   - What advise would you give other new teachers?

Chapter Six

Writing Assignments

I truly believe that if students would stop thinking about writing as a matter of form and structure that you must plug information into, then they might be able to learn something about the way they feel and think by the choices they make when they write. My ploy was to make them think I wanted them to surprise me. By doing this, I hoped that they would be forced to reach within themselves to discover something surprising or unique they could present to me. (Shane Shukis)

Writing assignments are often like legal documents—the more you say, the more confused the reader becomes. A good writing assignment is one that creates a delicate balance between telling the student too much and telling the student so little that he or she is left completely adrift.

How much is enough? How much is too much? At what point have you appropriated the student's writing experience? How often do you need to give your students assignments? Should you give them a new assignment every time they write a paper? These are questions you will have to answer as you begin teaching and throughout your teaching career. Writing assignments are the basis of every writing class and the effectiveness of your assignments will have a direct impact on the effectiveness of your entire class.

When you beginning planning for class each session, you have two choices: extended assignments or individual assignments. Both methods have advantages and disadvantages, and you will have to try both to decide what works best for you. In this chapter, I will begin by suggesting some guidelines that you can follow when writing assignments, extended or individual, for your students. Next, I will give you examples of both types of assignments and will discuss some of the pros and cons of each.

Guidelines for Writing Good Assignments

A writing teacher's primary goal should be preparing his or her students to become good writers, not good students. A good writer is someone who has the necessary skills to write in any situation with or without help or guidance—someone self-motivated and self-sufficient. A good student is someone who is adept at learning what a given teacher expects and meeting those expectations—someone motivated by grades and dependent on a teacher's guidance. A good writing student will not always be a good writer if you have not taught him or her to be self-sufficient. To teach your students self-reliance you need to give them writing assignments that require that they do more than figure out what you want and fill in the blanks appropriately. Look at the following writing assignment:

> **Example One:** *In an essay of no more than four pages, double spaced, describe your favorite place. This essay must contain a clear statement of thesis and at least five paragraphs: an introduction, a conclusion, and three supporting paragraphs. I suggest that you describe the place in terms of physical location. In other words, describe what you see and move through the place in a logical order. Remember to include details that affect each of the five senses. Finally, demonstrate your ability to use metaphors and similes by using at least three of each in the essay. This paper is due in two weeks.*

Most students will love this assignment. It is clear and specific, and they will have very few doubts about what the teacher "wants." Will this assignment result in good writing? Probably not. Students will try to figure out the teacher and fill in the blanks accordingly so that they can take their grade and move on. But is this what we want our students to do: Produce papers that are vapid reflections of what they think teachers want that say nothing about them, their world, or anything that they care about? I hope not, because that is the sort of writing that will effectively reinforce what many of your students may already believe: Writing has nothing to offer them. But you can help your students become writers by giving them assignments that give them something to care about. Now look at this assignment:

> **Example Two**: *Everyone has a place that is special to them. Yours might be a city, such as Santa Fe, New Mexico; the room where you grew up; or a friend's house. A place can even be a psychological space rather than a physical space, such as yourself at age 13, or you when you are dancing or cooking. What is interesting about people's places is what makes them special, because it is different for each of us and says a lot about who we are or were. In this paper, I want you to explore the idea of your favorite place. What can you say about it? What can it say about you? Begin by writing in your journal and go from there. We will peer edit these papers in one week.*

Both of these assignments suggest the same topic—describe a place. But the assignments are fundamentally different. The first assignment is extremely specific. The students know that they will be graded on these criteria: length, development, use of sense description, and use of six figures of speech. Choose a place, write five paragraphs, include the senses, and use some metaphors and similes. Turn it in. Get a grade. Next assignment. Safe, secure, and infinitely boring.

Your students will not know what to do with the second assignment because it doesn't tell them what to do. They will probably claim it doesn't tell them anything, and in many ways they are right. It doesn't tell them how long. It doesn't tell them how many paragraphs. It doesn't require a thesis or a metaphor or a simile. It doesn't even use the word describe. If the first assignment will inspire yawns, this one will probably inspire anxiety and panic. But it will also inspire learning. The second assignment is fundamentally different in terms not of what it doesn't expect or require (such as five paragraphs), but in terms of what it does—learning. Students can usually find a way to turn any assignment into an exercise in mediocrity, but they will have to work hard to do that with assignment two. Assignment Two requires thought. It requires reflection. It requires planning and commitment. The students are not given a topic. They are not given a method of organization. They are not given specific rhetorical strategies for developing the topic. They are given something to think about. The job of discovering how to turn that something into a paper is up to them.

You, of course, will be there along the way giving them ideas and suggestions, but they have to make the connections and the decisions themselves. You can introduce them to metaphor and simile, but you need to let your students figure out how effective they can be when trying to describe something. You can introduce your students to the various rhetorical techniques: description, narration, comparison and contrast, etcetera, but you need to let them figure out when it is appropriate to use each and, more importantly, to understand that things such as description papers and narrative papers are artificial constructions. No one in the real world will ever tell a student to write a description. Someone might tell your students to write a report about the conference he or she attended, a new medical technique, or a mechanism, but they will have to figure out for themselves what rhetorical strategy is appropriate to the task.

A good writing assignment, then, is one that allows learning to take place, not one that presents itself as learning. When you write assignments, you should try to remember these criteria:

- Avoid providing students with a method of organization.
- Avoid providing students with a rhetorical strategy.
- Emphasize the process not the product.
- Suggest possibilities rather than solutions.
- Encourage exploration.
- Let your students write about topics that they care about.

Let's look at both the previous assignment and an alternative assignment in terms of these criteria.

Avoid providing students with a method of organization.

The first assignment clearly presents itself as a five-paragraph theme: introduction with thesis, three body paragraphs, a conclusion. It goes even further and tells the students to describe a place in terms of physical location: now I'm in the kitchen, now I'm in the bedroom, now I'm in the living room. It even includes a required number of similes and metaphors, six. Most students will immediately say, "One for each of the three body paragraphs and maybe one in the introduction for bonus points." This is about as clear a statement of organization as you will ever find. This sort of prescriptive assignment fails to account for an individual student's creative impulse. For example, maybe a student would like to describe a place in terms of the memories that it triggers. Or maybe a student would like to describe a place in terms of how the reality compares to the memory. Neither of these approaches would be likely to earn a student a good grade; consequently, the student would probably choke down his or her own sense of what the assignment means and regurgitate some sort of "teacherese." I hope that is not what teaching writing is all about.

The second assignment, on the other hand, does not suggest an organization. No mention is made of length, number of paragraphs, rhetorical strategies, or use of metaphors and similes. The assignment poses questions and suggests possible topics—even the suggestions sound as though they are coming from another writer rather than a teacher. This assignment puts the burden of learning on the student and the burden of teaching on the instructor—as it should.

Avoid providing students with a rhetorical strategy.

Whether you call them modes of discourse, methods of development, or rhetorical strategies, at some point you have to introduce your students to the techniques available to them when writing. Many writing teachers and writing texts do this systematically, working from expository to argumentative writing (the assumption being that it is somehow easier to write a personal essay), to providing a writing assignment to correspond to each. In such a course, students might be asked to write narration, description, comparison/contrast, definition, cause and effect, and argument papers. I find this approach shortsighted for several reasons.

First, these sorts of assignments do the work for the student. Much of what is difficult about writing is choosing appropriate strategies of development. Second, these sorts of assignments assume the existence of the genre of narration, description, etc. None of these types of papers exists anywhere in the world outside of the classroom. Look at it this way: When you study oil painting, your teacher does not introduce you to the colors one by one from simplest to most complex (which is easier blue or red?). You aren't asked to do a red painting or a blue painting or a green painting. Your teacher introduces you to the color spectrum, showing you each color simultaneously. Rather than demonstrating your ability to use one color, each painting demonstrates your ability to effectively use the full range of colors present on your pallet. A writing teacher should do the same—present each student with a full pallet of strategies at the beginning of the course. Then the instructor can help the students learn to make effective choices that result in rhetorically sound papers.

The first assignment provides the students with a rhetorical strategy—describe your favorite place and appeal to all five of the senses. Most students who read this will assume that this paper should use no method of development other than description. This assumption will lead to papers that sound unnatural and stilted. For example:

> I walk into the hallway of the house. The walls are green paneling with flecks of white in them. I smell mothballs and dust. The floor is covered with brown shag carpet. It feels rough under my feet. . . .

Would you like to read twenty-five or thirty of these papers? If you use Example One, that is likely. Example Two, on the other hand, does not specify a strategy. It does ask some questions that the students can consider that should lead them to make some logical decisions regarding their choices. We want our students to be able to analyze writing situations, determine what their purpose is, and respond accordingly. For example, it is hoped that this assignment will allow students to make a connection between their need to find a way of talking about a place and the use of description as a rhetorical strategy. But the assignment does not just assume this; it leaves the students with the option of making other choices that might be equally appropriate, and most importantly, it forces them to be responsible for their own learning by not doing the work for them.

Emphasize the process, not the product.

If you teach writing as a process, you need to give your students assignments that reflect the process as much as possible. No assignment can do everything, and much of the emphasizing of process will be done by you in your choice of exercises and your approaches to teaching; however, avoid the mistake of giving assignments such as that in Example One, which clearly states that the paper is due in two weeks. No reference is made to any part of the process and the assignment suggests that the student should do nothing above and beyond what is specified. Other than choosing the place and creating the appropriate number of metaphors and similes there is not much to do in the way of invention. Example Two does introduce the expectation of multiple assignments with the reference to peer editing. This same reference also encourages the students to imagine an audience beyond the teacher. Most importantly, the assignment indicates that the teacher has specific expectations regarding how the student will respond—there is room for invention.

Suggest possibilities rather than solutions.

There is no one way to respond to any writing prompt, and teachers do their students a disservice when they imply that there is. The last thing we want to do as teachers of writing is reinforce our student's belief that writing well means nothing more than writing to the teacher's expectations. If they want their students to become self-sufficient writers, instructors must allow, in fact require, their students to learn to test their wings and discover for themselves what constitutes effective writing. Students can do this only by exploring their own capabilities and trying different approaches. They cannot do it by writing what they believe a teacher wants.

Example One gives a very clear message to the student regarding what is correct and what type of writing will be rewarded. Example Two, however, suggests possibilities—you could consider this or this or this or . . . . It does not suggest that there is one correct way to write to the prompt.

Encourage exploration.

My mother is fond of the expression, "There's more than one way to skin a cat." As a cat lover, I've never liked this particular turn of phrase, but my mom manages to use it very effectively because it works for her. Students are the same. They may write things in ways that you don't like, but that doesn't mean that they aren't writing well. Remember, the point of giving your students nonprescriptive assignments is to give them room to explore. Encourage them to make each assignment a reflection of their own personal viewpoints and motives. Encourage them to investigate what they think and feel rather than trying to discover what you, the teacher, think and feel. Encourage them to explore both their world and what they write about that world, and remember to read their attempts with an open mind.

Let your students write about topics that they care about.

The danger with any prescriptive assignment is that the students will be able to muster up any sort of true interest or concern about the topic. I know that I could not get too excited about the prospect of describing some place in detail, for no apparent reason. What's the point? Who cares? At least by failing to prescribe the exact handling of the topic, Example Two does allow students to take that topic and find a way of making it into something that they do care about. If I were given that assignment, I would explore what the common elements in all of the many places I have lived (I was an army brat.) say about me. I had many different bedrooms in many different houses when I was growing up, and I was almost obsessive about ensuring that some things remained the same—particular posters and stuffed animals and the arrangement of my books. I suppose that was my attempt to control what was a very uncontrollable lifestyle. Friends came and went, but I could depend on my books to be there. Example Two lends itself to this sort of personal adjustment because it is open-ended. The assignment puts the burden on the student to invent a good idea. If a student is ultimately bored with the topic, it is his or her own fault, not the fault of the assignment. There are no boring topics, only boring writers.

Next is an extended assignment that I have had very good luck using. In fact, many of the writing assignments I include in this book are from this assignment. It is also the assignment that I suggest each of my first-time teachers use the semester he or she begins teaching. Read the assignment first, then I'll discuss its advantages and disadvantages.

Communities of Discourse

Over the course of this semester you're going to write a series of papers about one topic—a community that you choose. What is a community? That is one of the questions you'll have to ask yourself when you're making your choice, but to start, we'll say a community is any group of people who get together for a common purpose and who share activities, ideas, and goals. Before you groan and say, "Six papers on the same topic! How boring!" remember two things:

- You are choosing your own topic, so it is only as boring as you make it.
- There are no boring topics, only boring writers.

My advice is choose carefully. I do not allow anyone to change topics midsemester.

Paper One: The Introduction

In this paper I want you to explore your topic's feasibility as a choice for this project. Based on your exploration of your topic, your peer group and I will decide whether or not to approve your choice. You might want to consider the following issues:

- Do you have enough interest in the topic to sustain you through six papers.
- How will you answer your questions? What will you learn? Is your community accessible? Are you really interested? Why did you choose this community? Do you have compelling reasons?
- Can you actually write each of the remaining five papers? Can you think of real possibilities for each one of the papers and give examples? What event will you observe? Can you get to your community? Do they have a meeting place? Are there people to talk with? What issue will you write about?
- What are your motives for choosing your topic?
- What do you hope to learn? For example: "I can't decide if animal activists help animals or make things worse." "Do I really want to jump out of an airplane?" "Is being a musician as cool as it seems?"
- Why do you find your community interesting?
- Can you identify any potential problems with your choice? How would you solve them?

Paper Two: The Place

Your community probably has a place where the members meet. Or maybe the place is even more important than people. Either way, there is probably a physical, geographical place associated with your community, and giving your audience a sense of that place is fundamental to helping them understand and appreciate your community. So for this paper, I want you to go to your community's place and write about your experience. You might consider these questions:

- What was the emotional atmosphere?
- What was the physical atmosphere?
- What was most memorable?
- Do you want to go back? Why or why not?
- Did the place have an impact on you? In what way?
- If you had to choose one color, word, or sound to represent your place, what would it be?

In other words, paint a portrait that will make your readers feel as though they were with you, wherever you were.

Paper Three: The People

People are an important part of your community—they *are* the community. So for this paper, I want you to get to know one or two of the members of your community well. How? By talking to them. Don't panic. We'll talk about interviewing techniques in class. Writing this paper will involve:

- Calling and scheduling an interview.
- Sending a thank-you note.
- Writing up the results.

Remember, what you do with the notes you take and the experience you have is up to you. But you might consider these questions. What did you learn from the person? What can other people learn? How is this person like you or different from you?

Paper Four: The Event

Most of you have written research papers and know all about note cards, bibliographies, and the library. For this paper, you'll be doing a different type of research. You could learn about your community by reading, but this time I want you to learn by doing. I want you to choose an event in your community that will actually occur and arrange to attend—talk to the people; observe the activities; be part of all the action. Remember, this isn't a news report; you have to do more than present the facts. Choose some angle, some interesting and telling way of looking at what you observed, and use that as the focus of your essay.

Paper Five: Persuasion

When you write persuasively, you take a stand on an issue that has more than one side. For example, you could argue for or against the benefits of writing on a computer. You could argue against the increased speed limit. You can argue about whether body piercing should be considered an art form. All of these topics are issues because you can argue for or against them. You can't write a persuasive paper about a topic like, I love the opera, because it's not controversy, it's just your personal opinion. See the difference? You might consider how an issue has affected your community's members and their attitudes. How might this issue change their opinions about the community? How does it affect you and your opinions of the community? Do you still want to join this community? Why?

Paper Six: The Response

You've spent over two months with your community, so I want you to look back and reevaluate your original opinions. Have your feelings about your community changed? How? Have you changed? You might want to reread the other essays and your journal, for inspiration. You might consider the following questions:

- What have you learned?
- How have you changed?
- Are you a different person in some way?
- Do you still see your community in the same way?
- If you had to describe your community again, would the description be the same?

Extended vs. Individual Assignments

This assignment has definite advantages and disadvantages, so let's look at the disadvantages first. According to my teaching assistants, they have these problems when they use this assignment:

- The students and their instructors get tired of the topic after three or four papers.
- Sometimes the students choose topics that don't work as well as anticipated.
- The students run out of things to say about their topics.

I agree that these issues can be problematic; however, the weaknesses of the assignment can also be attributes. Your students might get tired of their topics, and they might feel like they have nothing else to say that they haven't already said. But look at it this way: Your students can devote time and energy to coming up with a completely new topic every two weeks, or they can devote their time and energy to finding creative ways of writing about a topic that they have already addressed. For example, it is fairly easy to write six different papers about six different people, but much more difficult to write six papers about one person. Most students could easily write about six different types of entertainment or even six different movies, but writing six papers about one song or one movie would be challenging. I believe that students learn more from the challenge of stretching their imaginations to find new ways of looking at old topics than they do in constantly recreating the wheel.

Sometimes your students' topics may not work as planned. The question is why? Assuming that you have not approved any topics that you felt were destined for failure, the problem may be more practical. For example, one of my students was working with the community of members of Alcoholics Anonymous. He was told that nonmembers were not allowed to attend. He came to me very upset because he couldn't write his paper because he couldn't attend his event. We talked about it, and I asked him how he found out he couldn't attend. He told me that he had spoken to several members to ask them when and where he could attend a meeting, and they had all given him reasons why he could not come. As he began talking about these individual conversations he became very animated, and seemed to recall the brief discussions with great clarity. I pointed out to him that his discovery that he couldn't attend a meeting seemed to have been an event in and of itself. He was startled when I pointed this out and objected that an event had to be some sort of scheduled activity. I asked him if his previous encounters had been eventful and he agreed that they had. I told him that I thought he had already attended a very interesting and significant event.

I give this example to point out again that what students and instructors sometimes perceive as problems are often opportunities to find a new way of looking at an old topic. Students are going to make poor choices, and they will get bored, and they will get frustrated, but I don't think that this is the fault of the assignment. Students in writing classes always get bored and frustrated no matter what the assignment.

So in the end, I have to say that the assignment's weaknesses are also its strengths:

- The repetition allows students to concentrate on writing rather than on figuring out a string of new assignments and different topics.
- Students are pushed to the edges of their creative capacities by the assignment's repetition and are given the opportunity to discover the limits of their own imagination.
- The responsibility for the success or failure of the assignment is the student's because each student makes an individual choice. If a student is unhappy, he or she has to take responsibility for the situation and find a way out because there isn't a new topic coming in two weeks.
- Students are given the chance to investigate a topic interesting to them in a significant way, and then allowed to discover how what they say about that topic might be interesting to others. Students can find a motive for writing.

As I'm sure you can tell, I enjoy using extended assignments. However, individual assignments also have benefits. Read the examples I've included below.

> *"I should have . . . ." There are many ways to complete that phrase:*
> *"I should have said," "I should have done," "I should have never." We*

have all had "should have" experiences. For this paper, I want you to explore one or several of your "should haves." You might consider these questions. How would you finish this statement? Why? Is it even helpful to use such phrases? What does a person's obsession with a "should have" say about him or her? What can we learn from "should haves"? Should I have given you a different topic?

"Is Anything Really Alright Anymore?" This was a title on the cover of a recent issue of Outside *magazine, and it poses an important question. Is anything really alright anymore? Was it ever? When did things change? What exactly isn't alright? Do you even agree with this statement? Explore this statement and what it means to you and your world.*

Thomas Wolfe said, "You can never go home again." Most of us would argue that we go home all the time. But what does going home really mean? Home to your apartment? Home to your parent's house. Home to the town where you grew up? What is "home"? Do we lose it at some point? Can we ever return? Explore what this quote means to you.

You could easily use each of these three assignments in a first-year writing course. However, because they do not require the students to draw upon any material other than their personal experience, you might include them at the first part of the semester. There is no one way to organize a series of writing assignments, but most departments are going to suggest that you introduce students to the major rhetorical strategies and supply them with assignments that encourage them to use each. Specifically, you should cover: narration, description, definition, classification, and argument. Many programs are also beginning to include more multidisciplinary forms such as proposals, reports, feasibility studies, and processes. I recommend that you follow these steps:

- Introduce your students to each of these strategies.
- Give them an opportunity to try each.
- Begin providing the students with assignments that allow them to use these strategies selectively to achieve a particular purpose that they have chosen.

As you introduce each new writing assignment, devote class time to invention exercises that will allow the students to help each other develop ideas, and try to help the students see a connection between the assignments you give. Show them how one builds on another.

Conclusion

Should you use extended assignments or individual assignments? As I have pointed out, each has advantages and disadvantages. I know some teachers who absolutely refuse to use extended assignments, and some teachers like Donald Murray require their students to write on the same topic over and over and over again. You will develop your own preferences, but I suggest you try both methods before you decide. Finally, the writing of, or choosing of, any assignment is a serious endeavor, so take it seriously. After all, you're asking your students to devote at least two weeks to each one. Make the experience a pleasant one, not a visit to the dentist.

The one constant element that will occur each time you teach writing will be the necessity for you to provide your students with writing assignments. As time passes, you'll develop a collection you can choose from, but you will constantly be writing and adding new ones and modifying old ones. I won't say that the success or failure of a class depends on the writing assignments that you choose, but it will certainly set the tone.

Exercises

Writing Exercises

1. The teaching of writing involves many sticky issues: evaluating student writing, building trust, dealing with developmental writers effectively, etc. Choose one and offer an opinion. Refer to Chapter Six for specifics on the persuasion paper.
2. Write an assignment for your students that asks them to write some sort of essay. Make copies for your group members.

Collaborative Activity

1. Get in your groups and evaluate the writing assignments that you wrote. Determine which elements of each were effective or ineffective and then write a new assignment that includes the best of your previous work. Be prepared to share your assignment with the class and justify why you did what you did based on what you identified as effective in your individual assignments.

Chapter Seven

Teaching Grammar and Punctuation

The instructor tells her students: "Please complete the exercises on using commas in chapter four and be prepared to turn them in on Monday. Now let's work on your papers." One student says to another, "I hate punctuation. I'm glad it doesn't have anything to do with writing." (Classroom anecdote)

Studies have repeatedly shown that teaching grammar and punctuation in isolation does little to teach students how to use grammar and punctuation when they write—though students may become masters at completing fill-in-the-blank exercises.[1] Using exercises to teach grammar and punctuation reinforces students' belief that such things have nothing to do with writing or communication because students simply may not know how to apply to their own writing the skills that they practice in exercises. If you think about it, it makes complete sense. Most of our students have excellent oral communication skills, and they tend to think of communication in terms of oral mediums. Our students are right; even those students who might struggle to write a complete sentence usually have no trouble spinning out a long tale, especially if the topic is their excuse for not finishing a paper! And students are again right in believing that grammar and punctuation don't apply to those forms of communication in the same way. A student who has absolutely no idea of how to use punctuation can still do a perfectly good job of telling a story because he or she knows instinctively when to pause and stop. And a subject-verb agreement error or a dangling modifier can be easily clarified in a speech situation where questions can be asked and answered. Our job is to help our students translate those skills that they already have to writing, and then to help them understand how practicing those skills can help them learn to develop a sense of style.

[1]See Braddock, R., R. Lloyd-Jones, and L. Schoer. *Research in Written Composition.* Urbana, IL: National Council of Teachers of English, 1963; Hillocks, George, Jr. *Research in Written Composition.* Urbana, IL: ERIC Clearinghouse on Reading and Communications Skills/National Conference on Research in English, 1986.

Methods for Teaching Grammar and Punctuation

How do you do this difficult thing of teaching grammar, punctuation, and style? I can easily tell you several things *not to do*:

- Do not spend too much time having your students do grammar or punctuation exercises from workbooks or similar formats. They have limited usefulness.
- Do not mark your students' papers with mysterious codes and symbols that indicate errors. Your students will not understand their significance or relation to their own writing.
- Do not emphasize correctness to the exclusion of everything else (like content), but don't completely ignore it either. Students need to understand the rules of writing and how to exploit them for their own stylistic purposes.

More importantly, things that you *should do* are:

- Explain to your students that effective written communication relies on the use of punctuation and grammar because writing must be self-sufficient.
- Integrate your students' own writing into discussions of grammar and punctuation whenever possible.
- Make your students responsible for teaching themselves.
- Integrate your student's oral skills with their writing skills.
- Help your students understand the connection between grammar and punctuation and style.

None of these techniques provide a cure-all for what ails your students, but they can help to introduce your students to the basics they need.

An Opening Apology

Remember, you can't teach each and every one of your students everything he or she needs to know in one semester, so don't be too hard on yourself or your students—set realistic expectations.

Your students will have different levels of knowledge concerning grammar and punctuation. Some of your students may already understand the basics and may be ready to begin considering more sophisticated issues of style such as the intentional use of fragments. Other students may still be unable to identify a complete sentence, much less write one—either intentionally or unintentionally. And what of the international students in your class who may be well-versed in the rules but are unable to successfully use verb tenses? How do you meet the needs of all of these students? Let me share an anecdote with you.

Recently, my department's Undergraduate English Committee met to discuss adding a junior/senior level grammar course to the undergraduate curriculum. Some members of the committee felt that such a course was necessary because "our students needed to learn it somewhere." As you might guess, the nature of what was being taught in first-year composition was questioned, and the age-old question, "Why aren't you teaching them the basics?" was asked. As I pointed out then, and as I want you to remember, how much we can teach our students in one or even two semesters is limited. What each student learns will vary. Some students will master grammar and punctuation, but most will just improve their abilities, possibly learning to write a complete sentence or more consistently avoid subject-verb agreement errors. Students' retention levels are short-lived when they do not continue to practice what they have learned. Unfortunately, many students do very little writing once they leave first-year composition. Some may write in their sophomore-level literature classes, but many won't. How much do you think these students will remember when they are asked to write in their junior or senior years, if they haven't been writing all along? We teach more than just grammar and punctuation in a writing class. Perhaps most importantly we try to make writing an accessible activity for our students by teaching them to discover their own writing process. We also begin teaching them to think critically, write argumentatively, negotiate different writing styles, and critique written texts—wow! And that's only some of what we do in any given semester. We also evaluate our students on the basis of more than grades. Does a student who can't write a complete sentence deserve an A? Probably not, but if that same student has rewritten each of her papers several times, she may certainly deserve a C.

Just remember, you need to do your best to teach all of your students as much as you can, but don't turn a writing course into a grammar course. Writing is a comprehensive activity of which grammar and punctuation are only a part.

Explain to your students that effective written communication relies on the use of punctuation and grammar because writing must be self-sufficient.

When our students talk to each other, they are for the most part engaging in an activity in which they are equally skilled. With the possible exception of a few international students, all of your students are native speakers who have verbal facility with the oral form of English. They instinctively know how to alter speech patterns for different audiences, how to use tone and pitch and gesture. Many of them speak more than one dialect, and most of them are able to sprinkle in the use of some very sophisticated stylistic techniques such as metaphor and simile. How often do you hear your students say things like this: "It was like my face was on fire!" Little do they suspect that they are using a simile. They are probably even facile at using different styles to achieve different effects. They know instinctively that the way they speak to friends at a party is not the way to speak when they are interviewing for a job. If only writing were more like speaking . . . Who needs to use commas? You just draw a breath and move on. Actually some forms of writing are becoming more like speech.

I recently published an article on how the distance imposed by e-mail affects the art of collaboration. One major effect caused by the distance is the lack of physical presence. For instance, many of the techniques on which speakers depend, such as the use of tone, eye contact, gesture, etc. are not available to writers, so they must find ways to duplicate these effects in writing. Because e-mail is an inherently informal mode of communication, writers frequently misuse or even disregard rules of correctness to overcome the imposed distance and often rely on the use of emoticons (typographic symbols, for example, :)) that express emotion. Our students face the same problems, but they cannot rely on the informal techniques used when working in e-mail, and they certainly can't disregard the rules. Our students will certainly use e-mail, maybe even in your classes. However, they ultimately have to learn to function in a more formal writing environment. But how do you convince your students that writing is necessary, and how do you convince them that learning rules of grammar and punctuation are necessary, if they want to communicate effectively? You need to prove to them that people will read what they have written and will not understand what is being said if they haven't followed the standard conventions. After all, a writer can't plan on being present every time someone reads his or her paper to explain things. Rules of writing were developed in the first place so that writing could function independently.

Many of your students may never have been given the opportunity to get direct feedback on anything that they have written, so they may not have a true sense that they are writing for other people. And it's logical that, if you don't feel that what you write is likely to be read by anyone, you are not likely to care whether you are communicating effectively. So you need to begin by convincing your students that they are writing for real people. You can do this in several ways:

Ask students to read their essays aloud in class, or if they prefer, offer to read them aloud yourself. Solicit your volunteers ahead of time and make copies of their papers to pass out to the class. Ask the class to mark any discrepancies between what is read and what is written. Discuss the discrepancies identified by listeners and why such discrepancies occur. Make a point of telling your students that reading aloud is an excellent way to "hear" errors they might not see. Solicit response to the content from the class so that the writer will understand his or her ability to have an impact on others. These activities may make your students uncomfortable, so try to create a supportive atmosphere.

Give your students an assignment that requires them to send their writing to an existing forum. For example, they could write letters to the school or local paper, or to a magazine or journal that they like to read. Encourage them to enter university writing contests, or possibly set one up with the help of your teaching colleagues—"Best First-Year Student Essays of Spring '97."

Ask your students to read their papers out loud to you during confer-ences and read them aloud for the students to hear. They may never have heard their own writing read aloud. Again, discuss discrepancies between what they read and what is actually written. Are they correcting errors as they read?

Make an anthology that includes each student's best paper and make copies for the whole class. Your students will enjoy the experience of being published.

Peer edit, peer edit, peer edit. Let your students read each other's papers. Teach them how to respond. Make them participate.

What will your students gain from all these activities? First, hearing some-thing, because it uses oral skills, is not the same as reading something. Because your students' oral skills will probably be stronger, they will often hear errors that they haven't seen. Also, by watching the reactions of other listeners they can gain a sense of what does and doesn't work about their papers.

Your students need to understand that their writing must stand alone and work and make sense without added help from them, the writers. Your students must realize that the sorts of errors that normally wouldn't obscure the clarity of what they're saying can seriously damage the clarity of what they have written. No one will miss a comma or two in a conversation. You see them; you don't hear them. If you can teach your students to listen for what's missing, perhaps they will learn to look for it as well.

Integrate your students' writing into discussions of grammar and punctuation whenever possible.

You will have to discuss specific grammar and punctuation issues, and to do this you must refer to specific examples. What source should you depend on for your examples? You could take exercises from a textbook, workbook, or handbook. All of these sources are full of grammar and punctuation drills and exercises. However, these sources have one fundamental problem—they are not connected in any concrete way to your students' own writing. Consequently, it is difficult for all but the best students to apply the skills they practice in the exercises to their own writing. For example, if you were trying to learn to paint, how helpful would it be to you to spend time correcting mistakes in someone else's paintings? How much would you learn about painting your own paintings? You need the oppor-tunity to make your own mistakes and to learn to recognize and correct them. Writing is no different. Your students need to make their own errors, learn to recognize them, and learn to correct them. Don't tell your students not to buy a handbook; a good handbook is essential. Expect them to use the handbook as they need it, but concentrate on their writing when you are in class.

Don't ask your students to correct other people's writing; have them correct their own. One good method of doing this is to select one or two sentences from each of your students' papers every time one is submitted. Depending on your students and their abilities, you can concentrate on one or two errors that the entire class is making or select sentences that represent a broader range of errors. I prefer the first method. Once you create this worksheet, you can use it as the basis for class discussion. And because your students are working on their own writing, they will have a much better chance of applying the lesson to their next attempt. Also, because each of your students will have a sentence included in the worksheet, your students who have weaker skills will not feel so singled out, an effect that you will see reflected in their willingness to peer edit.

Grammar lessons of more than ten minutes become tedious and ineffective, so keep your discussions short and use your students' own writing whenever you can. Make things fun. Sometimes I toss mini candy bars to my students when they come up with correct answers. Other times we play a class version of "Jeopardy." Use your imagination and see what happens. Grammar and punctuation do not have to be deadly dull.

Make your students responsible for teaching themselves.

Your students expect you to be the expert who dispenses knowledge—especially in the case of grammar and punctuation. In many ways this is true, but as we've already discussed, let your students discover their own knowledge whenever possible. This is especially true when you are teaching grammar and punctuation for a number of reasons:

- For most of your students, grammar and punctuation represent a great, mysterious, unknowable, unlearnable vast body of material.
- Grammar and punctuation are for many students what math is for me, something they just don't get, don't like, and can never learn.
- The sheer number of errors many of your students make may be enough to convince them that grammar and punctuation is something they can never master.

How do you overcome all of this grammar and punctuation anxiety? First, help your students keep things in perspective. Most of them probably aren't making every possible error. Help your students to identify the errors that they make most consistently, and then tackle them one at a time. You can do this in several ways:

> *The first time that you evaluate one of your student's essays, correct only one or two of the errors that he or she is consistently making.* Don't mark every occurrence of the error; mark just enough so the student can see several examples of the problem. For instance, if a student is having trouble writing run-on sentences or comma splices, mark only these errors in one paragraph, then stop and include a side note explaining what you have done and asking the student to identify the remainder of the errors. Work with the student in class and in conferences until he or she begins to feel that he or she has mastered these two concepts, then move on to something else.

After you identify the errors that each of your students tends to make, put your students in groups according to error and assign each group a chapter from the **Harbrace Handbook** *that discusses the error you have assigned that group.* Tell each group that you expect them to learn the concept explained in their chapter and then present it to the class and give examples and answer questions. Let the students in each group know that all future questions on their concept will be directed to them in the future. I suggest you give your groups time to work in class or meet with you so that you can help them gain an understanding of whatever concept you have assigned them. Continue doing this throughout the semester. Do not use your peer-editing group for this assignment because each member of the group will know the same things and they will be of limited help to each other. You will find that your students with weaker skills will take great pride in being an authority on at least one topic.

Ask your especially skilled students to tutor those students who need additional help, and offer both students extra credit. Students enjoy working together; facilitate this activity.

Integrate your students' oral skills with their writing skills.

We've already talked about the importance of integrating your student's oral skills with their writing skills. According to Walter Ong, "the new secondary orality" (38) has encouraged students to privilege their oral skills rather than their writing skills—a natural development in Ong's view because, while "humans are innately verbal beings, writing is false and artificial construct" (40).[2] The world of secondary orality is the world of radio, television, and film—a world with which your students are intimately connected. However, while these are oral mediums, they require listeners to have some degree of literacy (47), but much less than we wish our students to possess. So how do we help students harness their oral strengths to improve their writing abilities? Thomas Farrell noted that students who move from orality into writing tend to "make assertions that are totally unsupported by reasons, or they make a series of statements which lack connections of the most complex, multi-level sort" (40).[3] These absences are perfectly acceptable in oral communication, where the underlying assumption is that listeners will request further information when they need it. It doesn't work in writing. However, I have developed a method of using Burke's pentad that can aid students in discovering those problems (absences created by students' use of oral communication methods within a literate medium) that formerly remained hidden to them. The pentad allows students to play the role of reader

[2]Ong, Walter. "Literacy and Orality in Our Times." *Writing Teacher's Sourcebook.* Eds. Gary Tate and Edward P.J. Corbett. New York: Oxford University Press, 1981, pp. 38–47.

[3]Farrell, Thomas. J. "Literacy, the Basics and All That Jazz." *College English* 38 (1977): 443–459.

for their own writing. This method may be too simple for some of your students, but those who are still struggling with sentence-level problems will find this very helpful.

The six key terms of Burke's pentad work more successfully than the standard grammatical terms because they represent parts of a drama that have equivalents in oral speech—they identify actions based on units of corresponding meaning rather than arbitrary linguistic codes. However, these elements of the pentad also correspond with grammatical units, as you will see below. So you can use the terms of the pentad while the students acquire an understanding of grammatical terms. Also, when the elements of the pentad are placed within a chart, as in the later example, students are able to see more effectively how the components of the pentad work together. For example, Agent asks, who did it? While Act asks, what happened? Scene asks, where did it happen? Agency asks, what did the actor do it with? And Purpose asks, why? A Co-agent (counter agent) is also frequently included.

Let's say you have a student who wants to write about something that happened to her yesterday. She could use the pentad this way:

Agent (noun): I

Act (verb): hit

Co-agent (object): Marcia

Scene (prepositional phrase): in the face

Agency (prepositional phrase): with my fist

Purpose (dependent clause beginning with "because"): because I was mad at her.

The student has created a good sentence. Now look at the sentence in chart format:

Agent	I
Act	hit
Co-agent	Marcia
Scene	in the face
Agency	with my fist
Purpose	because I was mad at her.

You can begin by giving your students blank charts and then letting them practice filling in the blanks. You can also explain to your students that subjects do not always have to be human or even animate. An emotion can also drive someone to commit an act, so an Actor could be passion or fear. Also, not every sentence must contain every element, though you should insist that they do until your students gain greater verbal facility.

More advanced students can use this same method to construct paragraphs. To do this, the student would supply an appropriate sentence for each element of the pentad. Look at this example:

Agent	Jan got angry during lunch because her friend Leslie said she was fat.
Act	The fight started when Jan flung her mashed potatoes and gravy in Leslie's face with her fork because she was so upset.
Co-agent	Leslie dumped her cottage cheese in Jan's hair after she wiped the potatoes out of her eyes because she had only said Leslie should watch what she ate.
Scene	The cafeteria line supplied the girls with an abundance of ammunition.
Agency	Jan and Leslie fought with food rather than words because they did not know how to communicate effectively.
Purpose	Friends often fight each other because they don't listen to what the other person really says.

Is this a great paragraph? No, but it is made up of complete sentences that bear a relationship to one another. This exercise can help all your students to be aware of how sentences work together, to recognize the essential elements in any drama, to speak succinctly, and to use complex sentence structures. A paragraph like this might be a major accomplishment for some of your students who don't know how to put one together logically, so don't throw this method aside because it seems simplistic. It is as complicated as the skills of the writer allow.

Help your students understand the connection between grammar and punctuation and style.

Ask your students how to express fear or anxiety in writing. How do you think they will answer?

"I don't know. Why don't you tell me?"

"Use adjectives or those '-ly' words such as quickly."

"Use dialogue and have someone say that they are frightened."

These are not great answers. So what do you do? You need to help your students understand that grammar and punctuation—sentence structure, use of punctuation, the intentional breaking of rules—create style as much or more than the use of adjectives and adverbs. Teaching this may sound intimidating, but it can be great fun. I have developed this exercise:

To Kill a Mockingbird is both my favorite book and movie, and I think it is an excellent choice when teaching style because most of your students will have at least heard of it, it is entertaining, and it is stylistically sophisticated. I use the book and the movie as the basis for a style exercise that involves eight steps:

1. Show your students a clip from the film. I like to show the scene where Scout and Jem are walking home from the school play and are attacked. This scene is quite dramatic and uses cinematic techniques to create a sense of fear, anxiety, and danger. Also, it contains very little dialogue.
2. I place the students in groups and ask them to write a description of what they saw occurring in the film, trying to duplicate the mood and the tone as accurately as possible.
3. I give the students copies of the same passage from the book and ask them to take it home and read it.
4. I ask the students to take turns reading aloud portions of their versions of the passage followed by portions of the original, and we discuss the results.
5. I ask the students to analyze the original portion of the novel in an attempt to understand how the author used grammar and punctuation to create a suspenseful style.
6. Each group is asked to report its findings to the class.
7. As a class we discuss how the students can apply the same techniques to their own writing.
8. I provide the students with another appropriate movie clip and let them try again.

You will find that your students both enjoy and learn from this exercise. It not only teaches them to use style to achieve effect, it also allows you to keep reinforcing the principles and the necessity for grammar and punctuation.

Conclusion

When I started teaching, I was more terrified by the prospect of having to teach grammar and punctuation than almost any other part of writing. I remembered how much I hated it myself, and I remembered how inadequate I always felt when I tried to learn it. If you feel that way, your students feel that way ten times as much. If you remember this, and don't try to become a quiz master or a drill sergeant, you and your students will be fine. Teach them as much as you can as best as you can. Don't expect them to be perfect, and don't expect yourself to be perfect either.

Exercises

Writing Exercises

1. In a brief paper remember a past writing experience that you had that concerned the use of grammar and punctuation. Do you have any bad memories of past teachers? How would you have done things differently if you had been the teacher?
2. Develop a writing exercise that includes the following elements:
   - Asks your students to use grammar and punctuation to create style.
   - Provides an opportunity to discuss how stylistic choices are based on the need to create a rhetorical effect.
   - Includes the opportunity to write and evaluate writing.
   - Includes the opportunity for your students to reach a collaborative consensus regarding the above issues.

Be prepared to share copies of your exercise with the class.

Collaborative Activities

1. Get in your groups and share the exercises that you developed. What worked and what didn't? Share your findings with the class.
2. Choose one section of the handbook that you are using and learn it inside and out. Be prepared to present this material to the class in a format appropriate for a thirty-minute presentation to a class of beginning writers.

   Get in your peer groups and answer the following questions for each presentation:
   - Did the exercise you observed have a specific objective? Did it meet those objectives?
   - Did the exercise provide the students with the opportunity to apply to their own writing the skill being taught?
   - Did you consider the exercise effective?
   - What specific recommendations for change would you suggest?

As a class, present your findings and discuss further techniques for teaching.

Chapter Eight

Using Readings to Teach Writing

I have to admit that I rarely use readings when I teach writing, other than my students' papers or my own. I never feel that I have time for other readings, but I have only recently come to feel this way, and in the act of writing this, I have begun to change my mind (It's nice to know that I can still be taught.). When I first began teaching writing, I did not have a file cabinet full of papers written in past semesters that I could use whenever I needed an example of student writing. Now I do. I also lacked the confidence to share my own papers with my students, not to mention the time to write them. Now I feel comfortable sharing my own writing. I'm not really a better writer, I just care less when my students gleefully spot my errors. I also strongly believe that students can best spend their time in class discussing the ideas they raise in their own papers, as opposed to ideas they find elsewhere. But despite my own prejudices, there are many reasons for having your students read professional writing, yet none of them work if you don't remember some basic principals. Let me share an example with you.

How Using Readings Can Go Wrong

I attended the class of one of my new teaching assistants recently, so I could offer him some much-deserved praise and possibly some helpful advice. He had asked his class to read an essay, "Was Benedict Arnold a Traitor," by Robert Graves. When the class that I attended began, he gave his students a handout that contained the following essay questions:

- How does Graves define (or redefine) the term traitor? What does his definition and use of the term suggest about the role of relative perspective and interpretation in writing history in particular, and writing considered generally?
- How does Graves, an Englishman, seem to feel about the United States? How do his opinions about the United States, as presented in this essay, affect the reader's reaction to Graves's argument?
- Do you believe that what you have learned about the war in history classes was American "propaganda"? How do you react to such possibilities? Do you agree or disagree with Graves's argument? Why? How does it affect your view of American history?

After passing out these questions, he asked his students to get into groups and begin trying to answer the questions. He then told them that after they had talked a few minutes they would have a class discussion of the questions.

As he finished giving his instructions, the students began to apathetically shuffle their chairs into loose semblances of circles. They seemed to feel that by refusing to actually form tight circles they could also avoid discussion, which many of the groups did. As I sat watching, I overheard the following comments: "Did you read this? I didn't." "Naw, I didn't read it either. Should we read it now?" Blank looks were exchanged all around. Books were half-heartedly flipped opened; students began making a pretense of reading. As best I could tell, if any student in the room had actually read the material, he or she wasn't saying. One group even asked the teacher for his book because none of the students in that group had brought theirs. Their teacher very kindly ignored all of this and allowed his students to read the essay before beginning the discussion.

When the discussion began, the students, with the exception of two young men, steadfastly refused to participate. They picked at their fingers, they looked at their desks, they shrugged their shoulders, they doodled on the study questions. The teacher did an admirable job of trying to keep the conversation going, but he was fighting a losing battle. They were still stumbling painfully along when I left thirty-minutes later.

Again we need to return to that question that keeps rearing its ugly head—what went wrong? The instructor provided his students with an interesting essay to read, and he provided thought-provoking questions for them to consider as they discussed the essay. So why didn't it work? The instructor was working under the assumption that providing his students with outside reading would enable him to enrich class discussion and broaden his students' understanding of how different writers address difficult topics. An excellent motive. However, he failed to realize that this assumption was based on the premise that they knew as much about the teaching of writing as he did. For this exercise to work, he needed to begin by telling his students theses things:

The purpose of the exercise: The students did not understand how the act of reading an essay and discussing it would help them improve their writing or write their next paper. Until they understood that, they were not willing to commit to the exercise. The instructor needed to begin by helping them understand that everything we write is based upon our own motives and our perceptions of events and those of our readers. Graves was arguing that Benedict Arnold was not a traitor. The students could make a similar argument on their own behalf or that of someone else.

How the exercise pertained to the purpose of the class: The students also did not understand how the exercise pertained to the goal of the class—to learn how to write persuasively. Again the instructor needed to tell the students and then help them discover how the questions he wanted them to consider would help them learn to write. Specifically, the questions were intended to help the students understand how a writer's perspective and an audience's perspective affect their interpretation of an event. Graves's perspective on the Revolutionary War is affected by the fact that he is British and has a different concept of who was right and who was wrong. The questions themselves are good, but the students could not make such sophisticated connections themselves.

What was lacking was preparation and follow-up. The instructor needed to begin the exercise by discussing his choice of reading material, how it pertained to the students' next essay, and how the discussion that followed pertained to the students' understanding of writers' and readers' perceptions of events. Having prepared the students for the discussion, the instructor needed to reinforce these issues throughout the discussion, rather than abstractly discussing the essay, and then conclude by reinforcing the connections he had established. He should not have depended upon the reading to do all the work. The focus of the discussion should always be students' writing and students writing. The reading merely provides a more sophisticated vehicle for engaging in such discussions.

Reasons for Using Readings in Class

There are many reasons for having your students read professional writing:

- Reading will help your students develop fluency in their own writing.
- Reading will help your students understand how other writers achieve particular rhetorical effects in writing.
- Reading can help students develop ideas when they have none.
- The academic world will demand that they be able to respond to writing in writing.
- A student must learn to read critically if he or she is going to effectively conduct research. Without the ability to research, your students will never move beyond the personal essay.

Reading will help your students develop fluency in their own writing.

How do you explain to a student that even though the following paragraph is not very good, it is correct:

> Enforcing a strict dress code, for example, regulating the colors of students' wardrobes, takes away a student's sense of pride. A student tends to feel like a criminal. When treated like a criminal, one will act like a criminal.

It is difficult to try to explain to a student why this passage fails, but is very easy to demonstrate a better way of saying the same thing by revising the sentences to look like this:

When students lose the right to choose clothing that expresses their personalities, they also lose the sense of pride that accompanies such freedom. Students who have no rights, have no freedom, and people without freedom feel like criminals. It stands to reason that people who feel like criminals, because they have been treated like criminals, will begin to act like criminals.

Obviously you can't spend your time revising all your students' papers. You don't have the time; your students probably wouldn't appreciate your efforts, and most importantly, they wouldn't learn anything. So how can you instill in them a sense of the flow and elegance of well-written prose? Make them read and make them read often. Only by reading effective prose will your students develop an ear for it and begin to both recognize it and imitate it. Someone whose only experience of *Swan Lake* is the local dance school's yearly recital has not really seen *Swan Lake*. Until that same person sees the same ballet performed by a professional dance troupe, such as the American Ballet Company, he or she won't have an effective criteria by which to judge the difference between an amateur performance and a professional performance. On a similar note, until someone reads the works of Shakespeare, he or she may consider the Marvel Classics version of *Hamlet* great stuff—pictures and everything!

Reading will help your students understand how other writers achieve particular rhetorical effects in writing.

Suppose you tell your students to look frightened or angry or pensive. They can probably ham it up and do a good job of physically expressing these emotions by using facial expressions. Suppose you ask them what emotion they should appeal to when asking a friend for a loan. They will quickly be able to tell you depending on who the friend is. Ask them to write a passage of prose that demonstrates any of these emotions, and they may be at a loss. Ask them what rhetorical effect is appropriate in a given writing situation, and they may be more at a loss. How do you tell them to use words, phrases, and sentence structures to create such stylistic effects? This is a case where showing is better than telling. Consider the following examples:

> Shuffle foot had not stopped with us this time. His trousers swished softly and steadily. Then they stopped. He was running, running toward us with no child's steps.
> "Run Scout! Run! Run!" Jem screamed.
> I took one giant step and found myself reeling: my arms useless, in the dark, I could not keep my balance.
> "Jem, Jem, help me, Jem!"
> Something crushed the chicken wire around me. Metal ripped on metal and I fell to the ground and rolled as far as I could, floundering to escape my wire prison. From somewhere near by came scuffling, kicking sounds, sounds of shoes and flesh scraping dirt and roots. Someone rolled against me and I felt Jem. He was up like lightening and pulling

me with him, but though my head and shoulders were free, I was so entangled we didn't get very far.

We were nearly to the road when I felt Jem's hand leave me, felt him jerk backwards to the ground. More scuffling, and there came a dull crunching sound and Jem screamed. (Lee, pp. 264–265)[1]

He wanted to move from the bed, but was afraid he would stumble over something and Mrs. Dalton [who was blind] would hear him, would know that someone besides Mary was in the room. Frenzy dominated him. He held his hand over her mouth and his head was cocked at an angle that enabled him to see Mary and Mrs. Dalton by merely shifting his eyes. Mary mumbled and tried to rise again. Frantically, he caught a corner of the pillow and brought it to her lips. He had to stop her from mumbling, or he would be caught. Mrs. Dalton was moving slowly toward him and he grew tight and full, as though about to explode. (Wright, p. 84)[2]

> Foresake me not thus, Adam, witness Heav'n
> What love sincere, and reverence in my heart
> In bear thee, and unweeting have offended,
> Unhappily deceiv'd; they suppliant
> I beg, and clasp they knees; bereave me not,
> Whereon I live, thy gentle looks, they aid,
> Thy counsel in this uttermost distress,
> My only strength and stay; forlorn of thee,
> Whither shall I betake me, where subsist?
> While yet we live, scarce one short hour perhaps,
> Between us two let there be peace, both joining,
> As join'd in injuries. One enmity
> Against a Foe by express assign'd us,
> That cruel Serpent: On me exercise not
> Thy hatred for this misery befall'n
> On me already lost, mee than myself
> More miserable; both have sinn'd, but thou
> Against God only, I against God and thee,
> And to the place of judgment will return,
> There with my cries importune Heaven, that all
> The sentence from the head remov'd may light'
> On me, sole cause to thee of all this woe,
> Mee only just object of his ire. (Milton, p. 428)[3]

[1]Lee, Harper. *To Kill a Mockingbird.* New York: Warner Books, 1960.
[2]Wright, Richard. *Native Son.* New York: Harper & Row, 1987.
[3]Milton, John. *Paradise Lost. John Milton: Complete Poems and Major Prose.* Ed. Merritt Y. Hughes. Indianapolis: Odyssey Press, 1957.

Your students should be able to very easily identify the ways in which these different writers achieved very specific rhetorical effects. In the first example, Harper Lee creates a sense of fear and anxiety through her use of sentence structure, punctuation, and word choice. For example, in the opening lines, her sentence structure imitates the movements of the stalker: "Shuffle foot had not stopped with us this time. His trousers swished softly and steadily. Then they stopped. He was running, running toward us with no child's steps." When he is moving, the sentence moves. When he stops the sentence stops. The movement of the words perfectly imitates the movement of the action. This is even more apparent later in the passage: "Metal ripped on metal and I fell to the ground and rolled as far as I could, floundering to escape my wire prison. From somewhere near by came scuffling, kicking sounds, sounds of shoes and flesh scraping dirt and roots." The quick, almost frenetic movement of these sentences, caused by the writer's intentional failure to use commas coupled with the piling up of verbs and adjectives, again imitates the frantic movements of the story's participants. The reader is left as breathless as if he or she were participating in the action.

In the second passage, Richard Wright uses words to give the reader access to the protagonist's mental and physical condition: " Frenzy dominated him. . . . He grew tight and full, as though about to explode." The actions of the protagonist after the first sentence demonstrate the extent of his frenzy as he frantically smothers a young woman to prevent her from betraying his presence. The second sentence indicates the extent of his mental anxiety. He is a gun about to go off.

The final passage demonstrates, verbally, the despair that the speaker, Eve, feels in contemplating not only the loss of God's grace, but of Adam's love:

> In bear thee, and unweeting have offended,
> Unhappily deceiv'd; they suppliant
> I beg, and clasp they knees; bereave me not,
> Whereon I live, thy gentle looks, they aid,
> Thy counsel in this uttermost distress,
> My only strength and stay; forlorn of thee,
> Whither shall I betake me, where subsist?

Eve is not merely asking Adam to forgive her, she is begging, clasping his knee. He is not merely her love, he is her strength, her stay. These metaphors contain a power that cannot be denied.

Reading can help students develop ideas when they have none.

The problem your students will most often face is a lack of ideas. Where can they find ideas? In the words of other writers. Send your students to the library with instructions to find material on several different topics. Just perusing the computer for the libraries holdings should inspire interest. Give your students readings that will inspire them to think, such as the one my teaching assistant used: "Was Benedict Arnold a Traitor." Another teaching assistant asked groups of her students to choose a recent event and find five to seven articles from different magazines on that topic. Her students had at least one idea by the time they were finished.

The academic world will demand that students be able to respond to writing in writing.

Many students have the mistaken idea that, if they get through their composition classes in their first year, they won't have to write anymore. But we hope that our students will be expected to write throughout the remainder of their college careers because it will be demanded of them when they enter the work force. Consequently, we are doing our students a disservice if we do not prepare them to respond to writing in writing. When your students study literature, they will be expected to write about literature. When your students study biology or chemistry, they will be expected to write lab reports. When your students study law, they will be expected to write legal briefs. When your students study medicine, they will be expected to fill out medical charts. The world expects us all to read, to understand, and to respond in writing.

By asking your students to read and respond to writing, you are providing an opportunity for your students to improve their abilities to access a text and verbalize their understanding of what they have read. Specifically, you can use the activities below:

- Ask your students questions in response to a reading assignment. Allow them to discuss their answers verbally, but require them to also put them in writing. This exercise gives students practice in understanding a text and sharing that understanding with other readers.
- Ask students to write their own study questions. Such an activity encourages students to find ways of attempting to discover ways of entering a text.
- Expose your students to many types of reading: fiction, nonfiction, drama, poetry, song lyrics, satire, etc. Your students have different backgrounds and areas of interest. Try to consider everyone's preferences.
- Ask your students to write abstracts of the essays and articles that they read. The process of learning to condense a lengthy piece of writing will help your students develop an ability to identify the major points in a piece of writing.
- Ask your students to write critical responses to the readings you assign. Again, this will help them to develop critical reading skills.
- As preparation for all of the above activities, do in-class and group work that allows your students to practice critical thinking skills.

These are only suggestions, but activities such as these will allow your students to become better writers by becoming better readers.

A student must learn to read critically if he or she is going to effectively conduct research.

Gathering research is much easier for our students than it once was. Computers have made information and articles on any subject available with the click of a mouse and the whir of a printer. Our students can gather more articles than they will have time to read without ever leaving the computer to go to the library, but this new availability of information is not without attendant problems. Yes, the Internet is a wonderful source for information. No, not everything your students find will be useful or even credible. Unless our students have the ability to read critically and learn to distinguish between what is a credible source and what is not, they will be lost on the information superhighway.

Lock your students into a room full of jeans and ask them to find the real Levi's 501s, and they'll be home for dinner. Throw them into a store full of a million CDs, and they'll quickly find the one or two they want and be able to tell you why they chose them. Give them three articles and two books on the topic of the Kennedy assassination, and they'll freeze like a deer in headlights. Why does this happen? Your students know Levi's intimately. They know what the real thing looks like, from the side rivets to the stamped buttons on the fly. Show them a pair of jeans without the pocket stitching, and they'll know they're in the presence of a fraud. Put them in a CD store, and they will know how to find what they want because they know how the music is categorized, and they know in which categories their favorite artists will be placed. They even understand the concept of cross-referencing. Jeans and music are important to our students, so they've learned how to categorize them, and they know how to distinguish what they want from what they don't. Unfortunately, they do not always consider articles on topics such as the Kennedy assassination, or information of this sort, important enough to learn in the same way. Your job is to help your students learn to understand how to categorize the information that they need to find, how to find it, and how to evaluate it after they have found it. All of these skills depend upon their ability to read critically. Your students dress critically; they listen to music critically; you can teach them to read critically.

Specifically, you need to help your students learn these skills:

How to evaluate the credibility of a source: You can help your students learn to evaluate the credibility of a source by first pointing out to them that there is such an issue as credibility. Your students may not be familiar enough with the publications in their fields to know which ones have the best reputations. They may never have considered things such as the target audience or the education level of that audience. They may never have considered the necessity of comparing the transcript of an on-line chat session with a published article. An exercise I like to use to teach these skills involves giving my students a list of publications and sources, putting the students in groups, and asking them to rank the material and defend their ranking to the class. I then ask them to create a ranked list of sources appropriate for their topic.

How to identify the major points in an article: You can teach your students this skill in several ways. I suggest that you begin by having your groups identify the major points in essays that you assign. You can progress to having them supply their own articles for analysis. This skill will help them to learn how to quickly identify the material pertinent to their research.

How to evaluate these points for their usefulness and credibility: Once they have learned to identify the major points in an article, your students need to have a way of determining whether they are useful and credible. For example, a student may identify the conspiracy theory as one of the main points in an article about John F. Kennedy's assassination, but that the article appeared in *Soldier of Fortune* magazine should indicate that this source may not be as credible as one that discusses the same issue in *Smithsonian* or *U.S. News and World Report.*

How to compare differing views on the same topic and determine the significance of those differences: Suppose that your student finds three articles on the Kennedy assassination, and they all offer different opinions on what happened. What is the student to do? You need to help your students understand the significance that *Soldier of Fortune* is arguing for conspiracy, while *Reader's Digest* claims that the government should not be blamed for the act of a criminal, and the *Harvard Law Review* is questioning why certain documents pertaining to the assassination have been considered classified. Each journal presents different views based on their readership. An exercise that asks students to compare how several sources discuss a similar event is an excellent way to help your students understand the significance of such differences.

Conclusion

Reading cannot be separated from writing. How can you expect a student who does not have critical reading skills to have success in reading and editing another student's paper? I like to think of the acquiring of reading skills as a progression. First, your students begin to develop critical reading skills as they read each other's papers and peer edit. Next, they sharpen those skills as their writing improves. Then they continue to use these skills as they begin writing persuasively, in this case applying them to the reading of professional writing. Finally, they use their skills to learn how to process, evaluate, and use the research that they collect. By linking your student's writing skills with their reading skills, you have given your students the tools that they need to succeed both academically and in the work world.

Exercises

Writing Exercises

1. You've almost survived a complete semester of teaching writing. What do you think? Are you ready to give up? Have you found your calling? Are you too confused to know? Refer to Chapter Six for specifics on the response paper and then respond to your experience teaching writing.
2. Choose three readings (either whole or partial works) that you would use in class and a handout (questions, an exercise, etc.) that explains how you want your students to read and respond. Prepare copies for everyone in class.

Collaborative Activities

1. Get in your peer groups and compare your experiences. Next, write a letter addressed to "Dear New Teacher," that you can give one of the new teachers next year. After you finish your letter, share it with the class. How would you have felt about getting one of these letters when you first started?
2. Share your exercises with the group and then decide which readings and exercises you found most effective. Then develop a list of criteria for choosing readings and creating exercises. Share your criteria with the class, then create a master list.

Part II

Selected Essays

The essays in the following section are of three types: essays by first-year students, essays by graduate students, and essays with multiple drafts by graduate students. However, all of these essays have two things in common—the students who wrote them were either studying composition or studying how to teach composition, and they were all written in response to one of the writing prompts from the communities of discourse assignment in Chapter Six.

I wanted you to have actual examples of student papers to look at for several reasons:

- You can use these papers to help you develop ideas when you are preparing to write your own papers.
- You can use these papers as the basis for practice in responding to and evaluating student writing.
- You can take comfort from and laugh with some of your colleagues who have been first-time teachers themselves.
- You can compare first drafts with rewrites and get a sense of how students can improve their own writing.
- You can use these papers with your own students as examples of the different types of papers that other students have written in response to the community assignment.

I hope you enjoy these essays and find them helpful.

First-Year Student Essays

Susan Marrufo

Rainbow

New experiences are what make you who you are. Everything that has happened to me each day for the past eighteen years has had an effect on how I handle situations and how I interact with other people. They are the reasons why I am who I am. They are why I am considered to be somewhat of a loudmouth, why I despise the color purple, or why I take one day at a time. All of us have lived different experiences, and been taught many lessons along the way. The way that we choose to handle our problems is a result of the way we have been taught to react or feel about a certain subject. All of this goes hand in hand with critical thinking. Thinking critically is something that happens on a day to day basis. We do it without even realizing it. That certain catastrophe that occurred twenty minutes ago, that you are trying to figure a way out of, is thinking critically. We have all manipulated situations to where we have benefited from something that we probably should not have. It is called dealing with your life the way you know how. The way you solve your problems is directly or indirectly related to things you have been taught. Our society is made up of so many different ideas and lifestyles that there is a need for understanding one another. The fact that we are all different and share different view points is what makes up our attitudes towards different kinds of people. Meeting somebody new is like opening up an undiscovered door. When you walk in, you either find a room with a cliff that drops off, somewhat of a trap, or you find a room containing what you would consider to be your own personal heaven. People are so different, and hold so many different beliefs that each personality complements another who is completely opposite. There is a personality under the t-shirt, or the cowboy hat, or the spiked dog collar worn around the neck (we have seen it). The experiences we've had and what we are taught lead us all to our own unique ways of dealing with and thinking about everyday situations.

I think we, as a society, have an obligation to educate ourselves on variety, not just about different cultures, but about different lifestyles. One of the things that I love to see when I look outside a window is this certain guy walking down the street sporting a blue mohawk, or this random person coming around the corner with the Star of David proudly hanging across his chest. What are this person's experiences? Why do they handle situations the way they do?

Misunderstanding somebody else is probably one of the most common things that happens everyday. We need literacy in the variety of life. Ignorance is something that comes from years of either not being taught anything, or just being taught the wrong thing. The ignorant person has to go through his life blindly, being scared or what they can not understand, which is usually a great deal. Let's relate this to my life and how I've learned some of the most important lessons of my life. Somebody that I love very much is gay. It's a fact that has taught me a lot about people and the way they think. I have stood by and seen this person suffer. I know about their pain first hand because I have witnessed people's reaction to the "big revelation." It's just that I wish that this was something that I could change, but that's impossible, because people already have their opinions about this sort of thing; an opinion based on their upbringing, and their past experiences. The funny thing is that I'm not going to hate them for their opinion. That's what makes them who they are. I am positive that at least one person reading this paper will think that homosexuality is wrong, or sick, or whatever; this being a conclusion that he or she formed a long time ago. Either you will strongly agree with an issue, or you have the right to feel uncomfortable about it, but first try and understand what is different then what you believe in. You don't have to adopt it as your new way of thinking, but just trying to understand is so much better than being afraid of what you can't understand. Sometimes critical thinking means breaking away from the things that you have believed in for as long as you can remember. It's thinking for yourself, forming your own stances about life. The fact remains that how we treat other people has an effect on them. It does.

People hold incredible power by being educated and being able to form intelligent hypotheses, and then, intelligent conclusions. I hate to sound cliché, but knowledge is power. If you don't think for yourself, and just accept what you've always been taught, if you don't ask questions, then what power do you have? You do not know enough to be powerful Maybe that's good, though, because do we want ignorant people in power? It happens, of course, but it ends in hatred. Think. Question. Questions lead to answers. Critical thinking leads to answers. In "Crossing Boundaries", peoples differences, mostly in terms of culture, make the story. Rose explains how the great thing about all of those people that were back in school was what set them apart from everybody else. The mistakes made on their papers were almost like a technique used to enforce their ideas. They added to the stories. The choppy grammar that the students turned in, or the misspelled words gave the work character. It became a necessary part of the essay. It wasn't that the bad grammar was praised, it just defined the paper's character. When you accept somebody's different views and look at them from a different angle, you start THINKING and realize that they make a person who they are. Without those mistakes, the essay would have all resembled each other, much like people. What kind of essay would you be more willing to pick up and read: one with character and variation or one stripped of all feeling and emotion? Think about that.

Nekeya Evans

From Great Generation to My Generation

Once upon a time in 1972, there was a young teenager who just couldn't wait to finish school and begin her life as an adult. She was so in love with this guy, that all she looked forward to was finishing high school, and getting married. She always wanted to go to college and told her parents so. She felt that she could attend college, even though, she was married. Her parents begged her not to get married and to think about her future. She, like most teenagers, thought she knew best. She felt this was her life and she knew what she was doing. She got married after she graduated from high school. Her parents were very upset because they knew she was making a mistake. She did indeed start college, but her husband became jealous, and caused problems. She also got pregnant and after the baby was born she had to quit school to take care of her. Years later, this girl has become a woman and is still trying to finish college. She looks back on her life, and wished she had listened to her parents. She realized now all the mistakes she made. She is my mom.

"Nekeya, what I am trying to tell you is, just like me, you think you know what is best, and although, it is your life, and you still want to make your own mistakes and learn from them. I don't want you to have to go through all the heartaches, trials and tribulations I did," Mom wrote me in her letter.

I realized that I don't have to go through hard times. I know my mom would want life to be better for me than it is for her. I also know that it will hurt her dearly to see me make mistakes that can last a lifetime. Life is only getting tougher for my generation. The government is cutting out all kinds of programs that assist with financial problems. There will not be much help for the future generation. We, my generation, still have time; the help is available right now. Why don't we take advantage of it? We need to think about our future and get an education. We need to start watching the news, read newspapers, and pay attention in class. Hell, we need to do a lot of things. For once, get our butts up and become deeply involve and our college work and stop partying and fooling around. After we graduate from college, we don't have to stress ourselves to hard working. Whenever we want to go on a vacation, we will not have to wait for years until we can afford it. Everything would be readily available at our fingertips.

In Mom's letter, she said, "All you have to do is work for it now, and reach for it later. It will be there at your disposal." I know my mom loves me a lot and that is why she's giving me so much grief. She doesn't want me to suffer a hard life later on and she knows that I'm too intelligent and a very beautiful young lady and that I don't have to settle for less.

I used to have a weakness and it was guys. I thought that I was in love once, instead I was infatuated. I tried to keep my relationship with my sweetheart alive, but I failed. I thought that he was the only one for me, but it takes two to make a relationship work. Since our separation, I have only gained strength and learned that there are other fish in the sea. My mom told me that there is some-one special out there for me and she said not to look for him because he will find me. I've learned that guys come and go and they are definitely not my ticket to success! Now, I listen to what my mother is saying instead of arguing with her. Just like my grandmother told her, she knows best; and she had been where my mom was trying to go. It is a coincidence because of the trends of events that took place from my grandparent's generation down the line to mine. History has a way of repeating itself. Now, it is my turn. I'm going to make it and let not one obsta-cle stand in my pathway.

People wake up! The world is growing rapidly and before you know it, you will be a grandparent. It is time to take the world seriously now and make a change to better the future. Education is the key to gain more knowledge for the world tomorrow.

Works Cited

Evans, Lenora. "Cause I Love You, Baby." *Typed Letter.* Dallas, Texas: Fina Oil Company, 1996. 1, 2.

Shanna Whitley

No Time to Think

The secondary level of education, high school, should prepare individuals for university level courses. College students must be able to apply critical thinking skills in their studies. In "What High School Is," author Theodore R. Sizer explains, "One certainly doesn't learn these things merely from lectures and textbooks" (88). Presently in the United States' high schools, students determine the quality of their education by how much time at home they spend teaching themselves what they cannot learn in the classroom. Many educators believe the fault does not lie within the present school systems. They find the cause of this problem to be a result of the large number of students dedicating their free time to extracurricular activities and after school jobs instead of their homework. Even though these activities take away from the time students can spend on academic studies, they also instill character attributes that the American society values and expects in well rounded individuals. Such attributes include the ability to use teamwork, good time management skills, and the potential to take on a wide range of responsibilities.

Well rounded students get involved in non-academic activities such as sports, theater arts, band, and many others. These dedicated students spend hours of class time training and rehearsing, in addition to hours of their free time. There are many teenagers who find themselves entering the work force during their high school years. Earning minimum wage, these students finance wardrobes, weekly entertainment, vehicles, savings funds for college, and in some cases help finance their families.

This large group of teens do not come straight home after school to relax and tackle their homework assignments; they hit the locker rooms or rush over to the local hamburger joint to begin working. So what happens when their algebra teacher announces at the end of class that if anyone did not understand the concepts of functions, they would learn it while doing their homework? It seems that learning has not only taken a back seat in high school student's lives, but is now being stuffed away into trunks to be dealt with later. Later usually never comes for those students who cannot manage to complete their homework.

Are these dedicated athletes, thespians, waitresses, and other active young adults obliged to quit participating in other activities so they can stay home and learn what their teachers did not have time to explain? Some people believe eliminating extracurricular activities and teenage participation in the labor force is the only answer, because it returns time needed by the students to concentrate on their homework. This extreme answer would raise significant opposition and would block some students' avenues for a higher education. Individuals who value the importance of students being studious as well as capable and experienced in many aspects of life disagree with those who support strictly academic based high school systems. Several scholarships awarded to high school students are received by teenagers who take part in their school's student government, compete in varsity sports, and earn a grade point average of ninety percent or higher. This becomes an unfair disadvantage when there are no more hours left in the students' days to learn the lessons needed to earn high grades.

Our nation's educational system creates a problem for these excelling students by operating under schedules in which teachers have limited time to present new information before a bell rings signaling the pupils to move to their next subject. Taking notes on new facts and figures does not mean the information was learned, or that the students even had to think. It only means that it was recorded. According to Sizer, "The school schedule is a series of units of time: the clock is king." Schools blocked into "time units" leave teachers mainly concerned about how much time they have with their students (86). With such time restraints, the instructors expect the students to retain information during the school hours, then learn and critically think it through while doing assigned homework. "[A] low premium is placed on reflection and repose" when teachers rely on the students to learn the information outside the school environment (Sizer 87).

When involved young adults finally get home, they still must wash their uniforms, inhale a late night meal, and then begin the self teaching process for all the subjects they had during school. If these exceptional students push themselves to finish their homework, how much do they learn while exhausted and in a race with the clock? Some spend valuable sleeping hours analyzing and trying to grasp the full concepts of the subject matter, while others do not even try to do the work. They always have the easier option of borrowing their friend's homework the next morning.

With the problem identified and exposed, how can our educators top this process without diminishing the activities so many American teenagers rely on? One quick answer would be for teachers to split class periods in half. In the first half teachers can utilize their time to present the new information through lectures, while the second half can be used for the purpose of discussion, analyzing, and practicing. Within this time period, students would have the option to ask questions and the opportunity to digest what they received before being hurried to the next subject. Another possibility is dedicating the last quarter of the classroom time to working on problems or reading quietly, and then when that class meets again spending the first quarter of the time reviewing the work and developing a full understanding of the old material before advancing on to new material. As a result, a greater percentage of the students will spend an equal amount of time trying to learn their lessons.

These two methods of change could be put into effect immediately. Homework would not be completely eliminated; there would always be plenty of studying to do for examinations. The major part of the learning process would not be the responsibility of the students at home. Maybe there would be fewer players studying on buses, drama students squinting at notes backstage in the dark, and grocery stockers calculating geometry problems during their fifteen minute breaks.

Even if students did get the opportunity to do more work in the classroom, the question still remains whether the students are learning it. After rotating to their next class, they begin discussing another subject not related to the one on which they were just concentrating. This on and off technique of learning brings the level of education down to a point that merely scratches the surface of each subject. Teachers simply do not have the proper amount of time, "and as a result the opportunity of teachers to challenge students' ideas in a systematic and logical way is limited" (Sizer 88). This especially cheats the students determined to attend a college or university.

Since no one has the power to create more time, this problem may be answered by extending schooling hours for secondary schools, or by terminating the summer break. With this extra time, teachers would be able to expose students to the deeper layers behind the material that they were previously only allowed to scratch. The answers may sound drastic to some high school students, but many students would welcome them before quitting their involvement in non-academic activities. The real pay back would come when they would no longer have to teach themselves what the clock did not allow their teachers to explain. They would have the freedom to stay involved in whatever after school activities they choose, thus creating a larger chance for our nation's young adults to become excelling, well-rounded individuals.

Works Cited

Sizer, Theodore R. "What High School Is." *Reading Culture: Contexts for Critical Reading and Writing.* Eds. Diana George and John Trimbur. New York, New York: Harper Collins College Publishers, 1995. 81-9.

James Swann

Shakespeare vs. Cartoons

Most people consider animated cartoons to be an entertainment medium. Animation is not viewed as art like the Shakespeare's plays and I am not suggesting that cartoons should be considered on the same level as Shakespeare. However, cartoons contain similar ingredients as renown masterpieces of art. Art, as defined by Roger Fry, "is a stimulus and an expression of this imaginative life, which is separated from actual life by the absence of responsive action" (219). Likewise, cartoons simultaneously mimic real life and entertain us, allowing people to experience human conditions in an imaginary form.

As a father of a six year old, I watch my share of cartoons. My son, Justin, loves to watch *Rugrats* and *Looneytoons.* Justin says he does not know why he likes the *Rugrats,* he says he just does. The cartoon is about toddlers in the babbling stage, and they only communicate with each other as opposed to the adults. Tommy, a sweet and good tempered boy, is the main character and Angelica is his foil. I hope the reason Justin likes the Rugrats is because he identifies with Tommy. Angelica is the mean big sister type, so there is a constant conflict between Angelica and Tommy because of their different personalities.

The plot usually evolves from Angelica's selfishness or desire to dominate the other children. The issue of selfish, dominating people verses kinder, gentler persons is common to adults. Shakespeare's Hamlet contained the themes of selfishness and domination. Hamlet was dealing with a selfish, domineering uncle that had murdered his father and married his mother. Shakespeare used the play to show the problems that people experience when the status quo is disturbed. Similarly, the toddlers experience problems when Angelica ruins their normal routine. Children can be entertained and experience social situations in a form they enjoy watching.

When I was a kid, I loved Saturday morning because cartoons were only aired on Saturdays. One of my favorites was *Bill Cosby's Fat Albert.* I can remember Fat Albert singing—"Hey, hey, hey, it's faaaaat Albert, naa, naa naa, were goin to have a good time." The show was about the adventures of Fat Albert and his gang of friends.

Fat Albert and gang always got themselves into some dilemma. The plot usually involved one of the characters getting into trouble and how they arrived at a solution for their predicament. The story line always included some of Bill Cosby's famous humor. Fat Albert's side kick Rudy made cuts at smart alecks like—"You gotta elevator mouth. Yea, it is always going up and down."

The cartoon always ended in a song that summarized the adventure, then Bill Cosby appeared after the cartoon and reiterated the moral of the story. Bill inserted comedy in animation to stimulate children and simultaneously give them an example of how to deal with problems.

Shakespeare used comedy in his play *"As You Like It"* to evoke laughter and stimulate his audience. The play has three brothers; Oliver, Jaques and Orlando.

The three brother's father had recently died and they must learn how to face the world without him. Although the play is not Shakespeare's most famous work, it is my favorite. The play created an imaginary world that parodies humanity and allows the audience a chance to laugh at what otherwise would be a serious situation. Cosby also used humor and dealt with serious situations with comedy.

Shakespeare used the medium of the play to communicate his ideals to an audience. He had a vivid imagination that fueled his pen to create literary masterpieces. Likewise, animators have an unlimited ability to create imaginative ideas that are versatile and can appeal a mass audience. Cartoons are drawn, so they can take whatever shape the artist imagines. Animation's unlimited possibilities allow for exploration of any subject without overpowering the viewer. Animators create imaginary characters to represent their version of real life to the audience. As Fry said, Art is the imaginary life representing the real life (221).

Animation will never be a produce a catharsis equivalent the masterpieces Shakespeare created. Cartoons are not as grand in form. They create a more subdued effect and allow us to relax while experiencing emotions. Animation contains the same attributes as all sublime art; they mimic real life, stimulate and allow for a removed experience of human condition. Cartoons cannot compete with Shakespeare as art, but they are a type of art that many enjoy.

Works Cited

Fry, Roger. "An Essay In Aesthetics." *Communities of Discourse The Rhetoric of Disciplines.* Ed. Gary D. Schmidt et al. Englewood Cliffs, New Jersey: Prentice Hall, 1993. 217-36.

Diane Castro

The Importance of Art In Society

In a restricted and confined society, art serves as a freedom of expression. In every society there are social norms which may repress many strong emotions in people. In the early ages, and still today, certain feelings and actions were viewed as inappropriate by society. Many people turned toward forms of art in which they could, fully and freely, express their thoughts and ideas. Through art, ideas from slavery and the opinion of women to Emerson and Picasso have been conveyed. Today people still use art as a freedom of expression which will continue through the ages. But why? Why is art so important to society? Art is beneficial to society in learning about one's own self, people in the world, and other cultures.

The interpretations of poems or paintings can guide a person into the depths of their souls to bring about new feelings and ideas never before revealed to them. According to Roger Fry, some people may feel an artist "has expressed something which was latent in us all the time, but which we never realized, that [the artist] has revealed us to ourselves in revealing him[or her]self" (Fry 224). Artists and writers, such as Salvador Dali and Plato, encouraged many to search beyond face value and stretch to the farthest reaches of their imagination to find meaning in their form of art. Many people may find a brief escape from reality to imagination in different forms of art. For example, many may feel "really moved at the theatre" and became so engrossed in a play that they may be "both on the stage and in the auditorium" (222). Literature and art can also provide the creator with new revelations. Personally, I find painting and poetry as an escape. I can curl up and be taken away by a certain novel or take a paint brush and express the emotions which I can't put into words. Art can be looked at as a therapeutic measure. It can be something done on your own or instructed by a professional counselor. Art is used in therapy to help people express feelings which they aren't capable of putting into written ideas or speech. Different medium can be used such as clay, paints, crayons or just pencil. It is a very productive form of therapy used on children and adults. It is used for many cases such as rape, abuse or any other traumatic cases.

Learning about other people (the artists in particular) can also be deduced from all forms of art. By learning about the artists themselves, we can view a particular time in history through their eyes. We can learn their thoughts and ideas which may possibly influence and inspire our thinking. From writers such as Frederick Douglass, we can feel empathy towards their experience and gather knowledge from them. Through the presence of art we may have two sides of one story. At times, history books may be biased in mentioning topics such as slavery or Indians due to white authors. Yet art allows people to tell the other side. It has no rules or restrictions so the author writes, paints, and sculpts freely through pure emotion. The thoughts and ideas of people in certain ages, such as the Renaissance and Age of Romanticism, are also reflected in the art created.

For example, during the years of Emerson and Thoreau we know that nature was the major theme of the times. Through sculpting and other art forms, we are able to recreate a vision of tribal people. In some places African, artifacts were found which resembled the people of that time. In other paintings and pictures found we are able to know what Washington and Jefferson looked like and all the other great men of that time. Before the camera, there were oil-painted portraits which were able to survive the ages and teach us about other people and cultures.

Culture is another prevalent characteristic found in many forms of art. There are many poems and stories which have been influenced by the artist's culture and experience. One such novel would be *Uncle Tom's Cabin* by Harriet Beecher Stowe which focused on the life of slaves and slave holders. In other pieces of literature, such as Euripides' *Medea* and Homer's *Odysseus* the influence of Greek culture can be seen in the structure of the stories. For example, male domination can be viewed in both stories which is a characteristic of that society. In African-American and Mexican-American paintings and murals, figures, such as Benito Juarez and Martin Luther King Jr., which shaped their culture and development as a people are depicted and a cultural pride is shown. Through such works of art, history and culture are shared with those who want to gain that knowledge.

The different forms of art help to expand the minds of people, both intellectually and emotionally. Art itself has been and always will be a freedom of expression used for many purposes. In many of those purposes, people can find a useful way to interpret that art as a form of learning about the things around us, individually, culturally, and intellectually.

Works Cited

Fry, Roger. "An Essay In Aesthetics." *Communities of Discourse: The Rhetoric of Disciplines.* Eds. Schmidt, G. D., and J. V. K. William. New Jersey: Prentice Hall, 1993. 217-228.

Diane Castro

Spiritual Discovery

Plato's *The Allegory of the Cave* can be interpreted as a person's experience in acquiring new knowledge. In the story, Plato speaks of prisoners trapped in an underground cave that has only one opening towards the light. They have been chained up by their legs and neck since childhood and can only see before. Behind them is a small wall, a screen, and a fire. Along the wall, men pass by carrying different objects. The prisoners only see the shadows of these men. The story then goes on to describe the ascending of a prisoner towards the light of the upper world. Men move back and forth learning in many ways. I believe *The Allegory of the Cave* can be interpreted as a person's discovery about the knowledge of God. The prisoners in the cave represent two types of people according to where they stand and what they believe in religiously. The chained prisoners portray people who know nothing or very little about God. The reality of life to them is only what they can physically see. The shadows on the wall are what is true and to them nothing else exists. According to this doctrine, some may believe life is only composed of the days we live on earth with no afterlife. They can't see behind them because of the chains around their neck. Stubbornness, lack of information, or any other negative ideas could be expressed by using the chains as a symbol. The chains are restrictions, such as media and other people.

At times, the media produces discouraging articles or programs about religion which can create negative attitudes in people. Certain people, such as t.v evangelists, can make the teaching of God and christians appear hypocritical and undesirable. Yet people can get beyond the restrictions by gaining an understanding of the Word of God and learning not to set their eyes on man.

The freed prisoner represents the people who overcame restrictions and have come to know more about God. The prisoner goes through three levels of enlightenment which lead him to learn more about the Lord. The first level is to receive knowledge which is displayed when the freed prisoner turns around and acknowledges that there is something else besides the shadows. The first step in learning something new is listening to what is being said and having an open mind. Believing is the second level, which is entered into when the prisoner moves toward the light above the cave. When people begin to believe in God, or any other new kind of knowledge, they bravely take larger steps toward learning more. Lastly, the third level is acceptance which is represented when the freed prisoner's vision becomes clearer. The more knowledge that is learned about God, the clearer everything becomes and finally, people can accept the whole concept of God in their hearts.

The prisoner's "journey upwards" (37) represents "the ascent of the soul" (37) towards spiritual wholeness and knowledge. There are three levels which he goes through. The first can be classified as doubt. Pain strikes the freed prisoner as light is first introduced to him. He is unable to see in front of him or the shadows which were once behind him. This inability to see ahead or behind represents doubt. When new ideas come into our lives we may doubt those new beliefs and the old ones in order to reconstruct our way of thinking. The sharp pains and blurred vision describe the difficulty in acquiring entirely new ideas about life, especially when we are set on one way. People approach new ideas and concepts with caution and are slow to accept. The second level is learning. The more people learn about God the more they may understand and accept Him. This can be represented by the vision of the prisoner, which slowly became clearer as time went on. Finally, the third level is the acceptance of God or knowledge which is when the prisoner is able to view the "sun". As Plato says, not in "mere reflections of [H]im in the water, but he will see [H]im in [H]is own proper place, and not in another; and he will contemplate [H]im as [H]e is" (318).

The return of the freed prisoner can be viewed as a person going back to his friends to tell them of what he has learned. Just as the prisoner's vision had changed, so has the attitude of the person who has gained a new understanding of God. Seeing the changes in their friend, they decide this new knowledge is undesirable if it's going to make them different. They want to live life the way they always have and refuse to turn around and see what's behind them as the freed prisoner did. The actual ascent out of the cave is faith.

In my opinion, *The Allegory of the Cave* can be interpreted as someone who finds a new knowledge of God. He or she has lived a certain way for their whole life until a new discovery is made. At first, it is hard to believe and accept all that is being told to him. He or she slowly finds out more, then begins to believe in something until he fully accepts the knowledge of God. With this information, he runs back to share his new knowledge with his friends who live the way he used to. But they don't believe him and don't want anything to do with the new knowledge. All his friends see are the changes in the "freed prisoner." He or she returns to them acting, talking, and perhaps dressing differently and they want nothing to do with him or the cause of his change. They chose to live the way they always have, chained up.

Graduate Student Essays

Angela Drummond

Writing and Composition: What Are We Doing Here, Anyway?

I never had to take composition in college. I placed out. I am teaching a class which I have never taken. This shouldn't be a problem. I am a writer. I know how to write. As a writer, I have my own ideas about what writing is and how writing instructors should teach it. But, coming into contact with the community of teachers of writing has caused me to question whether my ideas are completely sound.

I took classes in creative writing as an undergraduate. In those classes, the party line was that creative writing was one thing and academic, technical, or scientific writing was another. The hope was that one of these so-called disciplines did not ruin your art. To me, it seemed logical. One of my high school English teachers would not allow less than five sentences per paragraph. Every essay had to have at least five paragraphs or sections. Her students were never allowed to use the first or second person pronouns. They had to refer to "the reader" or the mysterious "one." If any of her rules were broken, a mandatory rewrite was in order. This rewrite would be considered late. It was to be handed in no earlier than two days from the date on which it was returned to the student and those two days would constitute a deduction of two letter grades from the final grade. Arbitrary rules and conventions espoused by high school English teachers didn't make students into good writers. It caused them to write highly formalized, stilted prose. These "critical" or "analytical" papers were usually unnecessarily complex and boring. To creative writers, they were examples of bad writing.

When I took "Scholarly Writing" at UNT, I was surprised to find out that the "informal" essay was gaining more acceptance. This was good news to me because I was used to considering myself as existing on the creative side of the writing fence. The critical and technical writers to whom I had been exposed seemed to have little respect for creative writers. They thought that creative writers broke too many rules. They split infinitives. They wrote in run-ons and fragments. They didn't know how to write. Creative writers expected worse grades on critical papers and vice versa. To each side, the other had no idea what writing was.

I still believe there is a distinction between "critical" and "creative" writing. The difference is one of quantitative versus qualitative, or empiricism versus aestheticism. It is analogous to the difference between walking and dance. Walking will get your body from point A to point B. Dance does the same, but with beauty. The two are not opposites, but exist on a continuum with varying levels of creativity throughout. Some people walk beautifully. Some people write very personal, very beautiful analytical essays.

Developing what I will call my craft, though it sometimes seems more like an addiction, I spent a lot of time studying other writer's habits. Some wrote in public; some wrote alone. Some never showed anything to anyone before going through several revisions. Others collaborated with their peers in all stages, from pre-writing to product. Some wrote every day for a certain amount of time, whether or not they had any ideas to write about. One wrote entire novels only to throw them away and write them again from memory so that each draft would not be limited by the one before it. Some had been writing since they were children. Others didn't start until after school, or therapy, or their children had grown up. There seem to be as many different approaches to the process of writing as there are writers. So, what are we attempting to teach when we teach entering freshmen to write?

I assumed that by taking on the position as teaching fellow I would be teaching from the "critical/analytical" side of the writing fence. I prepared myself to learn and follow that party line. In this department, the catch phrase seems to be "writing as process." The descriptions sounded interesting and plausible, but I was confused. I kept looking for the party line. It didn't take me long to discover the source of my confusion. The readings in the teaching methods class revealed that I had been "writing as process" all along. What was going on here? Where were the note cards, the outlines, the footnotes? Of course there should be collaboration in writing, of course rewrites. But wasn't that my line?

In my observation and experience, the desire to write seems to manifest itself as a disease of compulsion. As with any disease, there are certain associated symptoms common in afflicted individuals. One primary and identifying symptom of a writer is the tendency to workshop. Before the young writer even knows what he or she is doing, he or she demands, or at least desires, that friends, enemies, teachers, subordinates read what he or she has written and comment upon it so that it may be rewritten. Before creative writing workshops were available in universities, communities of writers shared their work with one another, solicited opinions from friends and colleagues. I've never heard or read of a writer who did not show his or her work to at least one other person. How did it come about that anyone should teach writing any other way? Perhaps I had read too much Joseph Epstein as an undergraduate, too many articles about how universities and their so-called writing classes (creative and composition) were ruining new writers and subsequently writing as an art. But, I am having a hard time identifying with and understanding the community of teachers of composition. The questions of who they are, who they are said to be, and who I thought they were are all mixed up in my head.

Likely, I have internalized biases from creative writing teachers: "Forget what your high school and freshman composition teachers taught you about writing. They don't know what they're talking about." But, composition is starting to look a lot like the creative or informal essay, in which there is an "I," a flesh and blood individual behind the text instead of the formal, impartial authority. Is this right? Is all writing at the academic level suddenly emancipated? Was it always this way or does this represent a dramatic change? I feel a bit like I have walked in on the twelfth episode of "Twin Peaks," never having seen the first. Clearly, I have missed something. People say, "Surely you have read thus-and-so, on writing theory," and I have to say no. Creative writers have no theory, other than Nike's "Just Do It." For me, and many creative writers, an idea gestates, or alternately, festers, within until it comes to term or to a head, and then is birthed, or erupts onto the page. Someone once described the writing process as staring at a blank sheet of paper until drops of blood bead up on your forehead and drip onto the page. I don't think this is what we want to tell the freshmen.

I don't want to sound like I am privileging creative over academic writing. I love all forms of writing, and have fun writing them all—from scientific to critical to creative. But, I guess I am privileging my own experience over this new information, something I tell the students I tutor never to do. I need to learn more about his community of composition teachers, not just where they are now, but where they were. I need to learn about writing theory, not just what is now, but what it used to be. I see many signs of the transitions between then and now in writing theory and they sometimes seem just as strange and elusive as the characters of Lynch's bizarre series, like the kid with the creamed corn, the letter under the dead girl's fingernail, the red curtain, the dwarf and his strange dance. I am not yet in a position to put it all together.

Taking the teaching methods course will teach me a great deal about what it is we're doing when we teach students to write. In fact, it already has made me think about writing theory in ways I hadn't before. I also want to read more of the books that seem to be staples of writing theory. I have been making a list of the works I hear mentioned in class and outside of class that seem appropriate and to the point. Lastly, I want to observe other teachers of writing and talk to them about their ideas. I hope that, by doing these things, I will gain a better understanding of the community of teachers of composition and, more importantly, begin to feel like I am a part of it.

Postmodernism and Composition:

A Proposal

Tom Connelly

Tom Connelly

Postmodernism and Composition: A Proposal

"Deconstruction is not a method or a theory; it's something that happens—it happens."

—Jacques Derrida[1]

As I drove home from the university recently, a peculiar thing happened to me. It was the beginning of the semester and I was a little anxious about how I was going to handle my duties both as a graduate student and a new teaching fellow. At the moment, however, my attention was on the radio. I was searching for some fragment of noise that could carry me the rest of the way home. Often in situations like these, the dial will gravitate towards one of the many Christian radio shows that airs around town. This does not disturb me. I enjoy listening to these programs for their "entertainment" value. For some reason, I am comforted by the knowledge that there is a community of people whose personal ideologies conflict with my own—that I would, if I were to ever confront them, piss them off.

This day's Christian offerings promised to be interesting. An author of some great new book was explaining how people like him could deal with people like me. Certain phrases jumped out, "Charles Darwin released his *Origin of Species*... most Christians had no idea anything was happening ... the church wasn't ready ... the result has been devastating."[2] I was hooked. The topic, however, was to be about something that threatened the fabric of society even more than evolution. The voice continued:

> Now, in the late twentieth century, we face a new revolution that likely will dwarf Darwinism in its impact on every aspect of thought and culture. The new onslaught against truth is coming under the general heading of "postmodernism."[3]

I am not a stranger to the term "postmodernism." As a student of literature, I utilize several postmodern/deconstructive strategies of reading that enables me to understand a text. I might, for example, pay close attention to the way characters in a novel interact with one another, focusing on the language they use as it conforms or challenges the realities around them. Shifting my focus, I could also examine the metaphors authors use to create narratives not explicit in a text. I could study how, for example, aspects of a fictional work comments on the historical period in which it was written. The general rule for applying such reading strategies is that if it helps elucidate the text, then its worth using. There are no real consequences to this methodology and there is no risk, since the only thing at stake is my relationship with the text (something I can always put down, or pick up, at my leisure).

The voice that was coming out of my radio, however, was not interested in any literature that I had read. He was not interested in my belief that such reading strategies invigorate and empower the reader. I believe the readers generate their own meanings, claim their own truths. He believes that there is only one real truth, and that people like me should stop and consider the consequences.

I am hesitant to dismiss this author's complaints out of hand.

If these postmodern theories liberate the reader from any definite, concrete truth associated with a text, as I believe, what happens when these same readers then "read" the law, the government, medicine, society, or even themselves? Critics of postmodernism, like my author, argue that such a road leads to despair. They would point to a growing population of young adults who feel inadequate in a society where following the rules is no guarantee of success or security. The author, Dennis McCallum, would contend that postmodernism deconstructs and renders meaningless, those narratives necessary for society to function; it is for him nothing less than a death of the truth.

As a reader of texts I am comfortable with postmodern strategies. As a teacher of composition I am suddenly less so. Postmodern theory applied to teaching would necessitate that teachers no longer function as the guardians of "privileged information."[4] They would instead serve as guides for students. They would fill the role, as Paul Northam suggests, of "competent judges of the expectations of society"[5] (without, I might add, ever knowing what exactly those expectations are). What is at issue for me, is the sudden change of the playing field. If I am at odds with a text, I can always put it down and pick it up later, the same is not true with my relationship with a student. There are now risks; there are now consequences.

In order to incorporate postmodernism into classroom, without compromising our duty as teachers, it seems imperative that we seriously examine not only the ways in which postmodernism enriches our classes (the movement from product to process, teacher as guide instead of authority), but also the effect it has on student's attitudes and beliefs. For example, troubling notions of the teacher-student relationship may help students to become better writers, but what if a student were to deconstruct all relationships which involve authority?

Perhaps I am overreacting, placing too much weight on my ability to make an impact with my students. After all, they are adults capable of making their own choices, learning from their own mistakes. This, I believe, is just a rationalization to avoid culpability. Underestimating the extent of my influence would be just as disastrous as pretending that postmodernism does not exist. I can not shrug off my responsibility, just as I can not turn back the clock. My students will come from a culture of sound bites and mixed mediae, hyper-reality and fractured families. I may not be able to offer them in good faith, the same solace that McCallum does, but I can attempt to help them bring focus to their lives.

In order to contend with the issue of postmodernism in the composition classroom, I propose three actions. The first involves observing the ways in which postmodernism is present or absent in the classroom. This would also include reviewing scholarly criticism which deals with this issue. Second, I would contact the author of *The Death of Truth,* Dennis McCallum (via e-mail). McCallum's commentary offers a sense of practicality that is absent in most theoretical discussions. I would like to know what recourse he would take in light of postmodernism's presence. How would he set things "right"? Third, I would teach composition that tries to recognize the limitations of all theories of reading/writing. Such a class, would be critical not only of strategies not-postmodern, but postmodern as well.

What I hope to achieve by this experience is a sense of balance, a sense of trust in what I am doing. By seriously treating McCallum's complaint that Postmodernism equals the death of truth, I hope to be able to offer a way of dealing with postmodernism in good faith (i.e., without ignoring it) while instilling in my students an understanding that central to narratives are not only the tools for deconstruction but also their construction.

Notes

[1]Gary Olsen, "Jacques Derrida on Rhetoric and Composition: A Conversation," *The Journal of Advanced Composition* 10:2 (1990) 12.

[2]An excerpt of McCallum's reading appears in Dennis McCallum's *"From The Death of Truth Are We Ready?"* (Bethany Publishing, 1996).

[3]Ibid.

[4]Paul Northam, "Heuristics and Beyond: Deconstruction/Inspiration and the Teaching of Writing Invention," *Writing and Reading Differently,* Eds. G. Douglas Atkins and Michael L. Johnson (University Press of Kansas, 1985) 123.

[5]Ibid.

Kevin M. Clay

Proposal: Can Writing Be Taught?

Cormac McCarthy, an author of some current note, and one who I personally admire, once expressed the opinion, in an interview with the *New York Times Magazine,* that teaching writing was fundamentally "a scam." He might have been a little nicer about it. It horrified me when I read it. Such a statement, from such a source (at least for one who wishes to enter upon a career doing that precisely) is disturbing. In that situation, the question—is it possible to teach writing at all?—takes on a certain urgency. Then, too, as a worst case scenario—what if he is right?

I do not think that many composition teachers would purposely scam anyone—least of all their students—but the possibility that it *might* be so nags irritatingly. What if he is right? Do other teachers worry about this at all? I do know that it was a topic in other graduate-level Rhetoric classes that I have taken. On that basis, the question seems to have at least some standing in the community of composition instructors. Regardless, the question is an important one to me, for several reasons. First, because at this juncture of my nascent career, I have no choice about what I am going to teach. I *must* teach writing, whatever I ultimately think about it, and teach it to Freshmen at that, if I am to begin—much less complete—the Ph.D. program in English at this university. If the teaching of writing *is* a scam, then the sad fact is that, in my case, a beginner has been charged with teaching beginners how to do something that possibly cannot be taught all. If scam it is, in other words, it is also a scam that I am obliged, willynilly, to participate in.

And for a second reason, I admire McCarthy. What he thinks is important to me. Perhaps he is merely unkind, and curmudgeonly to boot, but he is also indisputably a notable practitioner of the art that I am trying—that I am obliged to try—to teach. The fact is, that irrespective of how ill-tempered and uncharitable McCarthy may be, here I am; a teaching fellow and a Teaching Fellow, thrown figuratively (perhaps literally also) to a pack of Freshman wolves, who snap at me hungrily with large, wet teeth. The teaching *must* begin. From my vantage point, the immediate future holds not less writing instruction (as McCarthy might wish) but more—*lots* more. I see no reason why I should be at ease about the possibility of effort that might well be much worse than merely wasted. What should I do; go back where I came from? Run screaming back to a sewage plant somewhere? It was at least a living wage. Resign myself to a lifetime of gravity thickeners, clarifiers, cyclone degritters, process control, *sludge?* I think I will not do that.

For myself alone, then, the entire question is badly in need of inspection. Can writing be taught at all? If it can be taught, what aspects can be taught best? Of all possible aspects, which are most pertinent to the question? If some narrowing can be accomplished, how then do I proceed? To address it in the most realistic and personal terms conceivable, put it like this: *Have I wasted all of the last three years? It was a struggle just getting to this level. What do I do now?*

McCarthy makes no distinction between creative and academic writing. If he meant only the creative writing programs that have proliferated so widely since the mid-century, then doesn't his complaint—thank God—have nothing whatever to do with the composition teacher? But his condemnation reads both as sweeping, and as absolute—"Teaching writing is fundamentally a scam." Can *any* sort of writing be taught? Exclusive of McCarthy, exactly what sort of writing is it that I am talking about?

Academic writing in my opinion, has grown increasingly amorphous. The number of different approaches, at any given point in time, is literally staggering. I took two courses in Rhetoric at Tarleton State University: *Classical Rhetoric* and *Practicum of Teaching Composition.* They exposed me to an incredible range of opinion on the teaching of writing. Based on that experience, it is in my opinion arguable that the teaching of composition in colleges and universities is so many things now, that it is almost nothing at all. Or to qualify that in terms more becoming to the novice, it is certain that the methods said to be useful for the teaching of writing are nothing short of bewildering in their abundance.

Freshman Composition, once upon a time, concerned itself exclusively and unmistakably with what most of us have been taught to regard as academic writing: mechanically perfect, objective, third-person exposition. Dewey-eyed Freshman, fresh off the turnip wagon, were expected, not so long ago, to mimic the dry agonals of desiccated scholars. Yet the days of the current-traditional—as I was taught to name these traditional, Hugh Blair flavored rhetorics—are supposedly long since over, and since at least the 1960s, students in these courses have been encouraged to do any number of things. Actually, as we shall see, the proliferation of rhetorics had begun much earlier than that, though it did, in that chaotic decade, gather quite a head of steam. Some of these competing approaches seem exactly opposite of that stereotypical academic writing—and so they have often been. But what sort of instruction is it that is being taught instead?

Berlin's history of American Rhetoric paints a picture something like what follows: in the late 19th century, American colleges were attempting to supply industry with the scientifically trained professionals it needed, and in that period, the modern university curriculum was shaped. Along with it, the current-traditional, structuralistic and/or mechanistic rhetoric that most Americans are still, to the exclusion of much else, exposed to in High School, were also developed, based to some extent on the work of 18th century rhetoricians such as Blair, but moreso influenced by the empirical thinking of the scientifically literate. By about 1900, some schools had begun to practice what came to be known as *Liberal Culture*—the beginning of the modern Liberal Arts education. In the 1930s, Liberal Culture began to give way in the composition classroom to various *social rhetorics,* first in response to the shallowness of the Roaring Twenties, and later to the distress occasioned by the Great Depression. The CCCC was born after World War II, and at about that same time the fashion shifted to *semantic rhetorics* informed by the work of Freud, Piaget, and B.F. Skinner, alongside the florescence of linguistics initiated by Noam Chomsky. Also, beside and within all this, *expressionistic rhetorics* had begun to appear as early as 1915, and with these the notion of writing "process" as opposed to "product," which has been the subject of much discussion in the present class. The 1960s and 1970s saw a proliferation of expressionism, which had begun to take on its modern form in the work of Bilsky, Hazlett, Street, and others as early as 1952. Linda Flower and her partisans then appeared, in the late 50s and early 60s, and the *cognitive rhetorics* began to develop. By about 1967, both cognitive and expressionist rhetorics reached a sort of culmination in Robert L. Scott's *epistemic rhetoric*—an entire rhetoric of discovery, where the written expression of knowledge embodies the pursuit of it, and indeed, the definition of "knowledge" itself. Into all this hothouse exuberance of competing rhetorical models, Foucault and others of his deconstructing ilk appeared in the early 1980s. Complicating the picture still further, American universities already had a heritage from the classical, and one more immediate than ancient Greece or Rome. Throughout this time, there were periodic upheavals in favor of it—in favor of that take on *classical rhetoric* that was actually older than the nation itself, going all the way back to pre-revolutionary Harvard, where it amounted to a sort of *transactional* or *democratic rhetoric* in itself. Yet another of the competing models proposed at or near the mid-century was this rebirth of the transactional model, and another movement all the way back to antiquity. It is all of this that presents the novice with a clamor that is deafening: my God, what *does* it all mean?

One thing it means is that the transactional is currently triumphany—after Foucault and Derrida, it is simple inadmissible that writing be divorced from its social context—as indeed, was one major tenet of ancient rhetorics. But that is a side issue here. What is important to note is that the thrust of development, for about a century, has arguably been toward a fuller expression of the student's own identity, and *that* means somehow tapping the student's creativity. I do not assert this in a vacuum; I believe this trend is clear, beginning at Harvard before the Revolutionary War, and running through all of the above, to remain distinct in our own day. Many approaches to composition did and do attempt to partake in some way of the student's creativity, as opposed to his or her ability to mimic "scholarly" models—which is not to say that "modeling" *per se* is out of place, nor for that matter any other method that will work. I submit, though, that recent permutations—back to classical, forward to deconstruction, sideways to cognitive—continue in some degree to be attempts to tap the creative root of the individual personality—just as all the preceding were (and all the current are) responses to prevailing cultural conditions in specific places and times. With all this in mind, it is reasonable to assert that the intent of the modern composition classroom can productively be regarded, whatever the flavor of rhetoric, as seeking most fundamentally to improve or promote, in some systematic way, the creativity of the student. I seems quite clear to me, then, that the one truly global intent of the modern composition classroom is to systematically improve creativity. If it seems reasonable to take for granted that mechanics—spelling, punctuation, grammar—can be taught (and it does seem reasonable) is it also reasonable to believe that creativity can be taught as well? Heretofore, the assumption seems to have been that it can. Intentionally or not, that seems to be exactly what teachers have been trying to do, and at that for quite some time. Well and good, then: the questions with which we had begun focus on that single question. *Can creativity be taught?* And if it can, how? how can *I* do that?

The thrust appears to devolve, in one way or another, to the desire to promote the creativity of the student writer. When we say that, though, aren't we are really saying that the composition classroom has in many ways evolved into a sort of creative writing program in composition clothing? We are indeed, in my opinion, saying exactly that, because the focus of instruction is then the same for creative as for expositional writing—to enhance the student's access to his or her own creative roots. That said, returning momentarily to McCarthy, it follows that if he did mean strictly creative writing programs, his complaint is *still* legitimate in the composition classroom, and so my question—among other reasons, out of concern for McCarthy's utterance—stands with it. Or put it another way: given all this as preface, if one type of writing instruction is a scam, then so is the other. The best option seems to be to find out for one's self, and the best place to do that would seem to be in the writing classroom, in the midst, as it were, of the attempt. But that assertion does not occur in a vacuum, either—as we shall see.

Of course, as seems to be the case with any attempt to investigate writing—as perhaps any other enterprise that smacks of the creative—a degree of subjectivity inevitably arises. The simpler terms of the question minimize this to some extent, but the criteria ought also be in some measure quantifiable. The simplest equation possible, then, would be some comparative of what the student's work was like at the beginning of the course, with what it is like at the end. It is possible to count grammatical errors, or misspellings, or awkward constructions, or some other list of like measures, and compare totals, but that does not get to the heart of it, and getting down to cases is precisely what is desired—can it be done, or can it not? If so, what aspects, and to what degree? What *is* the heart of it? Any assessment of *how best to do it* woukd have to await the verdict—it seems pretty futile to spin out a pedagogy to a purpose that might be unfulfillable.

But I do not begin without opinions—who could, whose life and livelihood depend on it? That is, I am no different from those who have created all of these theories, nor ought I pretend to be. I do have my own axe to grind, that is. And I do have an opinion. I believe that it is possible to *nuture* creativity, if not exactly teach it. I do not think I at present have sufficient background, knowledge or experience to propose anything that claimed it could actually do that. But if I look at the work of my students in just the way proposed, I *will* find out something about what I have done and not done in class this semester. What I want above all else to do is nurture creativity.

This is something that is at once very similar to and totally distinct from teaching it. I also think that the best way to do it has a great deal more to do with the teacher him or herself than it does with the rhetoric he or she is pushing. The anxiety, then, over *what I have to do* turns out to be rather grossly misplaced. If I must be anxious, I ought really be more anxious about the sort of atmosphere I will create in my classrooms. That, in my opinion, is more important than how I will address either the fundamental problems of basic writers, or the real possibility of creativity among the more advanced. Overweening questions about the profession itself are well and good, but not as practical matters, it would seem. I ought to be most concerned with the students themselves, and I cannot be that while emoting from the horns of a self-imposed dilemma. So it *does* all come down finally to a matter of the classroom itself. The exercise itself—this inquiry—does not seem to me to be specious, or a waste, so long as I might learn something from it. And it is not, because I have done so already. You hold the evidence in your hand.

Writing is above all communication. But to be effective, it must also be in some degree *creative*—the flower-flinging 60s were quite correct in this—and correct also in the placement of the act irretrievably in a social context, vis-a-vis both the transactional approach, and the deconstructive. Of course, judgments of creativity will themselves, inevitably, be subjective—yet creativity *can* be recognized, and some unanimity in that recognition is likewise inevitable—otherwise, there would be no canon of any literature, no measure or consensus of any aesthetic. It is proposed, therefore, that a comparison be made between beginning and ending student production in one or more of my own sections of Freshman Composition, with assessment on the basis of creativity. Does the student show an improvement in getting his or her point across clearly? Does the student show imagination in achieving that clarity? With what frequency does the student show this? Is there more of it at the end of the course than there was at the beginning? To answer these question is to assess the student's creativity, and whether or not an increase in it is detectable.

Kathryn Hickerson

Another Person's Moccasins

"What gives you the right to teach like this?" asked the cow-eyed girl in the front row, her lips snarled as if she had just caught a whiff of spoiled milk, her arms tightly crossing her chest with her fists clenched. And for a second I couldn't answer. "Do I have a right to be teaching at all?" crossed my mind, and then I thought, "Of course this is happening to me today," as I rubbed my bloody left heel against the back of my comfortable black loafer. I was glad I had gone home between classes to get some shoes after throwing away, out of sheer frustration and discomfort, the pair I had originally chosen to wear that day. Defending your position of authority is much easier when you are sensibly shod.

After a moment's consideration, I realized that the student was not questioning my right to teach per se, but my right to teach "writing as process," my right to teach in this nihilistic manner which had absolutely no regard for the eminent importance of the introductory paragraph, with its general to specific structure and clearly stated thesis. Following quickly upon the heels of my initial insecurity was a bit of self-righteous outrage. I glanced back over my left shoulder at the blackboard, at the lofty terms which I had been scribbling in my enthusiastic, pre-challenge euphoria. The words 'Honesty,' 'Insight,' and 'Exploration' floated against the dusty background of the board in a pristine, idyllic state.

"What does she mean by asking such an asinine question?" I thought to myself, "Can't she see the obvious inherent value of these things?" Once again wrapped in my cloak of invincible abstract ideals, which need no justification, I glanced back toward the class, my mouth slightly open, eyes blinking, while I searched for a response, attempting to walk the fine line between confidence and cockiness.

I walked around to the front of the desk, which was in the front and center of the room, leaned back against it, and crossed my arms in front of my chest. I glanced around at the rest of the students, who were not sharing in her anger or my defensiveness, but who sat with their mouths slightly agape and a sparkle in their eyes, waiting for the ball to drop. I then launched into my defense.

"Writing as process is not some way-out, maverick concept that I have concocted on my own. This theory of writing is widely accepted by scholars in the field, and this is the method which has worked for me personally and has always worked in my previous classes. In addition, this is the method which is supported by the department. Instructors at the college level have the freedom to teach in whatever manner they deem appropriate . . . ," and then I halted mid-sentence.

I looked to my right, at the girl who had thrown the pebble into the peaceful pool of my lecture, and saw that her expression had changed. Now that her knee jerk response had passed, she no longer looked as if she were smelling something rotten, but rather as if she were cutting onions. Her eyes were shiny with the tears she was blinking back. Her clenched fists were no longer a manifestation of her barely repressed desire to pummel me, but rather an expression of fear. As I stumbled in my own soliloquy of self-defense, I followed her line of vision. She was looking over my left shoulder, and I saw that she was transfixed by my newfound mantras that I had scrawled on the board with the flourish of certainty. I then realized that she was not angry at me; she was afraid of the words on the board.

I looked down at my crossed arms, at the shoes I was so glad to be wearing, and I looked back at the pebble tosser. "I know that you are uncomfortable with this," I said to her. "Writing is frightening if taken seriously, and I appreciate that." She was not consoled, as the defiant tilt of her head informed me. And neither was I.

I remembered my mother telling me, "When you go on a long trip, the most important thing to remember is to bring really comfortable shoes." I wanted to share this with the pebble tosser; I wanted her to know that I really understood where she was coming from, that I really understood the need and desire for comfortable shoes.

But I couldn't give her the advice my mother gave me. I was asking her to exchange her comfortable shoes for a new pair, which were actually a few sizes too big, promising her that she would grow into them. I was then making matters worse by asking her to climb a mountain in these shoes, and expecting her to do so willingly and gratefully. Because I had been struck by awe rather than fear at the sight of the mountain, and therefore had been driven to climb it, I expected everyone else to feel the same. I was wrong.

I wanted to share my realization with the pebble tosser. I wanted to tell her my version of my mother's adage, that comfortable shoes aren't necessarily the best footwear for an expedition. I wanted her to know that I appreciated her reservations, but that sometimes the first step in a journey is outfitting of one's self in something new. I wanted to share, but I couldn't explain. I didn't understand the advice myself.

Angela Drummond

Ethics and the First Year of College

I remember my first year of college when I look in the faces of my students. I remember the excitement. I remember trying to look on-top-of-it while others tried to look cool—though all of us failed. I see these kids doing the same thing. They go far out of the way to prove to their friends, to themselves, that they can handle this huge change in their lives. Yet, they are still confused at every turn, and afraid.

When I assigned journal-writing to my students, I explained that I would be reading them, so they shouldn't write anything that they would feel uncomfortable with me reading. Still, they used the opportunity for mild catharsis in many cases, and I found myself in a strange position. In medicine there is doctor/patient confidentiality. In law there is attorney/client privilege. Where is that line in teaching?

I took up the first set of journals on Friday. My friends and I had planned to go out that night, but we all had work to do, so we agreed to take it along. Brad and his girlfriend Kim met Donald and me at "That Special Blend" in Oak Lawn for coffee, conversation, and company while we worked. Brad was making up assignments for high-school English; Kim was clipping articles for a project she had in a social services class; Donald was writing music, and I was grading journals.

We sat on the patio of the coffeehouse at a plastic table. The patio was full; there were people all around us. We each had our coffee, and started working. As I read each journal I put a check-mark on it and recorded it in my grade-book. Reading these journals in public was, I now know, throwing all professional ethics to the wind. I couldn't help laughing at some of them. And when I did, I had to explain my outburst to the rest of the group.

"This person wrote, 'I should have known I was doomed from the very beginning'!"

Everyone looked up from their work. "She's *doomed?*" Brad said, incredulous.

"Oh, my God! She wrote that?" Kim put her scissors down. She works in a psychiatric ward for troubled teens and has seen a lot more doom, real and perceived, than we imagined this student could ever have experienced. We assumed this student to be the typical small-town college freshman—sheltered, naive, very much unlike the violent, suicidal, drug addicted sociopaths with whom Kim works.

I was laughing. "It's not really funny. It's that kind of sad/funny. It's just so bad that it sounds like a sitcom version of a bad first day of college." Here is where the ethics went out the window. I told them what was in the student's journal. "First, when she left to come down to Denton from Amarillo, her parents were out of town, so she had to go alone. Then, she had a flat tire on the way and had to change it in the rain. When she finally got to the dorm, she was too tired and miserable to unpack. She just made up her bed, got in, and tried to call her parents for some consolation. They weren't home. Then she gets a roommate from hell. The girl has a boyfriend with her and he stays in the room until morning. The whole time, they are talking and watching TV. So, this girl can't even get any sleep. It turns out that the roommate expects to bring the boyfriend in the room all the time. Also, she has to sleep with the lights on and the TV on loudly. So the girl never gets a moment of peace. They aren't writing sitcoms this funny."

Brad, Kim and I were laughing. Brad said, "Let me read one of those." I handed him one at random. Really, I didn't think about the ethics until later. It crossed my mind, but I let the idea go. I have been around a lot of teachers and they always let me read their students' work. Was it okay, then, because I didn't know those students? Were my actions in this case out of line? My friends will probably never meet my students. I looked at Donald. He was smiling with his mouth, but not with his eyes. I wondered whether he was just preoccupied with his music or if he, too, sensed that there might be something wrong with what I was doing.

"What's wrong?" I said. He shook his head. "I shouldn't let other people read their journals, should I?"

"No, It's not that," he said, "I'm thinking! Lyrics! Lyrics!" He pursed his lips seriously and pointed to the notebook he was writing in. I smiled.

Kim said, "This is like these kids I get in all the time. Only they're worse. I had to remove this genital piercing from this one girl—"

"Genital piercing?" Donald's attention shifted abruptly. Momentarily, he put down his pencil.

"Yeah, they're not allowed to keep them in in the hospital."

"Why? What difference would it make?" I asked.

Brad looked up from the journal in front of him and wickedly raised one eyebrow. "They might get torn out in a fight."

I started, wondering if, perhaps, he was kidding, "What kind of a fight could you get in that someone could—"

"You'd be surprised. You can't put anything past these kids." Kim said. She took a sip of coffee.

Donald shuddered. "I still can't get past the idea of a genital piercing. Ouch!" He winced.

Kim continued her story about her patient. "Anyway, this girl was crying, I mean, she was really bawling." She imitated the girl's voice. "'You just don't understand! This is the only thing about myself that I really love! I'm not even supposed to be here!' I said, 'Honey, if that's the only thing you love about yourself, that's why you're here.' Her mother said she was like that all the time."

Brad was reading one of the student journals. "This guy says he just realized he doesn't have any real friends."

"Geez, that's sad." I said, sobered. "I went through that same thing."

"What does he mean 'real friends'? Like what?" Kim said, cutting out an article from the newspaper.

Brad said, "He says like in the movies or on TV, a real friend that will be there for you. He doesn't have that."

"And now that he's at school, he really doesn't have that. He'll have to make all new friends," I said.

Donald looked up from his lyrics. "I ought to read those. There are two or three songs in every one."

Many teachers, myself included, often take our liberties with students' work. We let other people read, without the student's permission, almost anything we see fit to discuss. I have had teachers share student work with me and, as I have just described, I have done the same. One thing that made it easier to share the student's work, was that with the exception of Donald, everyone at the table was or had been an English teacher. But, I still feel strange about it. Perhaps, I feel that way because the journals were so personal. I remember when I was working in a doctor's office and had access to people's medical and psychiatric records. Secretaries and nurses regularly discussed patients' psychoses, foibles and personality flaws, even between offices and with their friends. The rule was that with non-medical personnel, you simply left off the name of the patient. I saw that rule broken many times, but, I don't know that anyone was ultimately hurt. How does that apply here? I don't know. But, I feel I should be more careful and give more respect to my students' journals.

Lisa Hartsell Jackson

Peer Editing: The Event

Four weeks have passed since school started, and I no longer get that queasy "Oh my God, I have to teach" feeling in the pit of my stomach, or the clammy hands that accompany it. For a while, I was living on peppermints, hoping the soothing taste would calm my frazzled nerves as well. At least I could be assured of facing my class with minty fresh breath. As I begin to eat my tenth peppermint of the morning, I realize I have begun to look forward to my classes. Each day, as I make the long drive to Denton, I listen to classical music and think about what I will say to my class. If I have time, I stop somewhere to grab a quick cup of coffee. Not only do I crave the caffeine, but the steam rising from the Styrofoam cup seems to help open my head.

Finally, I arrive at the university, park my car, and make the five minute walk to the Auditorium building. I climb the stairs to the third floor, and try to catch my breath. As I walk down the dimly lit corridor to room 301, I usually see a couple of my students waiting for me. Amy, a particularly ambitious student, is often the first one there. "Hi, Lisa! How was your weekend? What are we doing today in class?" Amy almost moves a little too quickly for me. I find myself silently wondering how much Valium it would take to tone her down. In truth, I love having my students talk to me this way. We both sit down on a faded, burnt-orange bench which is in the hall. Amy is relaxed right now, and she looks me in the eye as she leans back against the wall. We both talk about little nothings. I think to myself about how pleased I am that I seem so approachable to her. I would have never spoken to an instructor like this when I was a freshman.

The class before us finally leaves, and Amy and I head into the tiny, cramped room. I step behind the podium, get out my digital travel clock, and shuffle through my papers to get my notes for today's class. Amy is still chattering away, but now she is talking to Tami and Robyn. I start to greet each student as he or she comes through the door. I'm glad they no longer act surprised that I know all their names. I wait for a few moments for them to get to their desks and rummage through their backpacks for a notebook and pen. Some of them, especially Parrish, look like they just woke up. "Today is your first peer-editing day," I announce in my official "I am the teacher" voice. "I want you to use this opportunity to make your paper better. Take your time and do a good job. Now, go ahead and get into your groups."

Now the kids begin talking and scraping their desks along the floor. A couple of the groups, Amy's included, ask "Can we go in the hall?" I answer, "Yes, as long as you keep the noise down. Don't disturb other classes." Saying this makes me think that teaching is often a lot like parenting. As they begin to work, I can sense the awkwardness my students feel. They are totally silent. This is an uncommon occurrence for this class, who are usually very talkative. I am still behind the podium, not just for the protection it provides me, but also to give the kids some distance from me. I really want them to do this on their own, without my instruction.

Slowly, they start to read aloud. Amy is out in the hall, giving direction to her group. "Okay, y'all. Let LaMecia read first. Everybody needs to get out a piece of paper and make the positive negative column thing they made in the film." I love Amy's bossiness. Actually, this is exactly what I wanted to have happen. I continue to just listen for a long time, keeping a careful eye on the students I suspect will try to goof off. Brian gets up to throw away a gum wrapper. I smile sweetly at him while I secretly tell myself how much he drives me crazy. I look at the face of the clock. Only five minutes have passed. I stare even harder at it, hoping my concentration will make the time pass more quickly.

Finally, enough time has elapsed for the kids to have gotten started by themselves. I slowly, quietly make my way to each group. I choose Paul's group first because they seem to be being too quiet. I ask Paul, "How are you guys doing?" He looks at me and says, "We're already done." "Oh," I answer. "Why don't you go ahead and start on your revisions?" "We already have," Paul replies, almost a little defensively. "We were hoping you would let us do this again on Wednesday so we can revise some more." For a minute, I am dumbfounded. These are the same students who, only a week ago, looked at me like I was Sigourney Weaver with an alien coming out of my chest. What has happened? Suddenly, they are directing themselves without my help. "I think that's a great idea. When we get close to the end of the period, I'll ask everybody else."

The rest of the groups seem to be getting on just fine. I walk back to the front of the room and think about what has just happened. I knew before I started this job that a lot of the kids I taught wouldn't care about what we were doing. I've told my husband that teaching feels a lot like a roller coaster ride, with all its highs and lows. Right now I feel like I am at the top of the highest part of the ride, full of enthusiasm and waiting for the next rush. My little black clock tells me we have only two minutes left. I quickly call the class back to order and ask, "Would you like some more time on Wednesday to re-edit the revisions you are going to make?" Amy and Paul respond "Yes!" The other class members mutter their approval or disinterest. "Well, that looks like a yes to me," I say, since I have not gotten a conclusive response. The kids begin to stuff their papers and books back into their backpacks. Some of them actually seem to sprint out of the room. Amy and Paul both stop and say "Thanks, Lisa," before they leave. It's time to get off the roller coaster again. I stay behind and erase the board, rearrange the chairs and turn off the lights. Another class session is past, and I feel good and excited that at least two people understood me today.

Kate Hickerson

Learning to Fly

I want to make a confession to you. I was once madly in love with the three-point theme, a.k.a. the five-paragraph essay. I spent my entire undergraduate career writing three-point themes. I could write a three-point theme that was three to five pages long, or I could write a fifteen page paper that was a series of three three-point themes. At that time, I attributed all of my academic success to my ability to write a three-point theme, and I was very certain that my mastery of the three-point theme would lie at the heart of any future scholastic achievement which I might enjoy.

I was dreadfully wrong. I turned in my first graduate school paper to my professor, a man whom I considered a paragon of scholarly ability, only to have it returned with my entire conclusion crossed out, and a grade scrawled on it which I would rather not repeat. When I discussed this with my professor later, I was told that the whole point of graduate school was to unlearn everything I had learned as an undergrad. I was furious. If he took my three-point theme away from me, with its lovely conclusion, which is a restatement of the introduction in different terms, then what did I have left?

I now realize that I was a horrible writer. Very correct and structured of course, but dreadfully dull and formulaic. And worst of all, I was incredibly complacent. I felt that I had figured it all out, and that there was nothing more to writing. Or perhaps I had a sneaking suspicion that there might be something more to it, but what I had worked very well, so I was not in the market for anything else, thank you very much.

So what I am saying is, I was saved by "writing as process." I was blind, but now I see. "Writing as process" has enabled me to be the author of texts such as the amazingly witty and exploratory personal essay you see before you. I am a convert, lock, stock and barrel. And this frightens the hell out of me. I now hear myself defending "writing as process" with the same zeal with which the recovered addict defends sobriety. I now attribute my current academic success to my triumph over the three-point theme and to my acceptance of "writing as process" as my personal savior.

Am I too hasty in my condemnation of the three-point theme? Perhaps only someone who has such a long and rich tradition of three-point theme production could benefit from "writing as process" to the extent which I do. Am I wrong to renounce the virtue of the three-point theme to my students, mere freshmen in college, denying them an additional four to five years of undergraduate three-point theme production? Perhaps the three-point theme has a place and a purpose. Perhaps the structure of the three-point theme operates as the experienced co-pilot, which the novice needs before she can fly solo.

Or maybe I am doing my students a favor. Maybe the production of three-point themes is the fog that lowers visibility and grounds the pilot. Maybe this essay which you are reading right now would be vastly more informative and entertaining if I had renounced the three-point theme during my freshman year of college. If I had been encouraged to fly solo at a younger and more inexperienced age, risking occasional failure certainly, would my writing soar higher now?

Maybe my emphasis is off. Perhaps instead of discussing weather conditions and piloting assistance I should be scanning the horizon in search of a new perspective. Maybe the answer lies in the willingness of the future pilot. Weather conditions could be fabulous, and a person could have had a few practice runs with a co-pilot, and the fear of flying solo could still freeze her in the hangar.

I was going to submit my first abstract for a conference last week. My very first abstract ever. I had no mental model of an abstract, and I was scared stiff. I inquired as to the proper form of an abstract from several sources, and though the format did not sound difficult, and though I supposedly possess the writing skills necessary to accomplish such a basic and unimaginative task, I had a very difficult time getting my abstract off the ground.

So I guess what I am saying is this: the three-point theme does not ground writers because of its rigid structure and formulaic nature. These aspects of the three-point theme could actually be beneficial in that they supply the writer with a mental model which she can use at her discretion. The more mental models a writer has at her disposal to assist her in the writing process the better.

However, there will always be new situations which will require a writer to push herself. It is in these situations that the three-point theme can be a hindrance. The safety of the three-point theme's structure allows frightened solo pilots to stay in the hangar. When the conditions are optimal and the flight lessons are completed, it all comes down to the writer and her willingness to take risks. Welcome to the great, wide open.

Angela Drummond

Marilyn Manson and Garfield
A Diametric Opposition in the Classroom

I was substitute teaching for an algebra teacher at W. T. White High School. I had subbed there before. I had a hall duty at that time, and I ran across a student who was wearing a Nine Inch Nails T-shirt. He was the typical "alternative"-looking teen, long hair, baggy clothes. He was still too young to successfully pull off the unshaven look, but he was appropriately unkempt. The shirt was black with the band's name on the front in blue letters and the lyric "God damn this noise inside my head" upside-down on the back. It was the same shirt I had at home which I had gotten from Nails' recent concert with David Bowie. I mentioned this to the student as I checked his hall pass.

"You like Nine Inch Nails?" he said, incredulous. I had forgotten that as an adult I was supposed to have given up fun in the form of pop culture. I assured him that I did like the group and had in fact gone to the concert. He was amazed, and we had a brief chat before we went to wherever he was supposed to be.

On this particular day, to my surprise, the same student turned up in my class. I found out that his name was Gene. This time he was wearing a Marilyn Manson T-shirt. He remembered me and we chatted again. He was a bit disruptive, but no more than some of the more clean cut students I had taught earlier in the day. After I passed out the assignments, he came up to me and stated that he had to go to "Concept Mastery" to get help with his work. I gave a hard time, because as a sub, I am always worried that the students will lie to me in order to get out of class. But, I finally found documentation in the teacher's desk that he indeed had to go for this special help, and I let him go. Shortly thereafter, he returned saying there was no one there to help him. I asked him why the teacher didn't help him herself. He replied with a shrug. But then another student, who was quietly working a problem at the board said, "The teacher doesn't like him."

Usually, when a student says that the teacher doesn't like him or her, I assume that the reason is because the student is disruptive. Children often equate discipline with dislike. However, I have never had another student say that a teacher didn't like a particular student. The student who made this comment was not a friend of Gene's. It didn't appear that she made the statement out of solidarity. When I suggested that Gene's behavior might have had something to do with the teacher's reaction, she shook her head to indicate "no." It made me think that maybe there was something to it. I said, "Well, I'll help you with it."

We started working on the problems, and it turned out that he didn't have any trouble with the work. I began to wonder why the teacher regularly sent this student out of the room. He made good and rational conversation, albeit on Trent Resnor and whether or not Marilyn Manson was his puppet or not. He was pleasant and personable and relatively eager to please, at least he behaved that way with me. We continued to talk and I tried to tell him that he should take his algebra more seriously because he would see it later in college. I related that I had made that mistake and lived to regret it. He laughed.

"Oh, I'm not going to college."

"Why not? You should," I said.

"College is for people who are really smart and stuff. I'm not all that smart. That's why I go to Concept Mastery. I'm going to drop out, anyway."

It really struck me that this student had been given the impression that he was not capable as a student when there was nothing wrong with his ability to master the problems I explained to him. I could imagine that he probably had not listened well in class and that could have been the source of his problems. But few of the other students were able to do the problems without assistance. "What are you going to do to make money?" I asked.

"Oh, I don't know," he said, "There's all kinds of things I could do. Like, I could work at a gas station or something. Maybe learn to fix cars . . ." I tried to redirect him in this regard. I told him that he was smart enough to go to college. I pointed out how easy the math problems were for him. "But, I go to concept mastery and everybody says college is real hard." he said.

"That doesn't mean you can't do college work," I said, "Besides, people will get you psyched out that something is really hard. Then when it's time to do it, you get freaked out and you can't do it. But, it might have been easy all along. It's like when I had to take organic chemistry in college. Everybody said, 'It's so hard, it's so hard.' So when I got there, I was like, 'Aaaaaaugh!' But when I calmed down, it turned out that it wasn't that bad."

He considered. "Yeah," he said, "But you're smart. You probably never had to take concept mastery."

"They didn't have concept mastery," I said.

The bell rang. He jumped up with the other students. But before he left he said, "I liked talking with you."

I got up to straighten out the desks and pick up some of the paper that had been left on the floor. As I did, I looked around the room. It was decorated with posters of Garfield and kittens or puppies with happy and benign captions. I looked at the teacher's desk. Everything was immaculately neat. The accent items, pencil holders, in/out baskets were decorated with lace, curlicues, or teacher apples. I realized why this teacher didn't like this student. I surmised from her choice of decor that this woman was the type of person I used to be. I used to like the frills and lace, cheerful affirmations attributed to fuzzy animals, cuteness, sweetness and light. I had no clue about people who dressed as if they had been hit by a bomb (my description at that time for "alternative"). If she was anything like I had been when those were my favorite things, there was no way she could relate to this boy, nor be interested in finding out where he was coming from. I know that I am making a gratuitous assumption about this teacher and her motives. There's no way I could really know why she made the decisions she did. She could be quite open to counterculture among her students. And, I guess it is easier to handle a problem student when you are not faced with that student every day. But that day, I was appalled that, rather than help the student, she seemed to have labeled him as stupid and sent him out of her room every day. It was less than six weeks into the semester and she seemed to have already made up her mind about him.

Some people I know would argue that this doesn't happen on the college level. They say that the professors are used to this being the time that young people go to great lengths to express themselves. But I couldn't begin to count how many times I have heard teachers and professors express things like, "I just don't understand these kids," or "Look at that one. He's going to be the one I'll have to spend the most time on," or "I'm dreading reading that one's papers."

How can you teach if you are not willing to meet the student where he or she is and lead him or her to where you want him or her to be? I think that as a teacher, knowing what your students are "about" (as in who they are, not as in "about" to fail) is as important as any teaching method or course structure. It is actually more important because it precedes them. Without that information, a teacher is building his or her tower of knowledge on sandy soil. The student's current knowledge, presuppositions, tenuous world views may not make for the firmest foundation, but we should relate what we want them to know to what they already know. Even if we have to modify that foundation in order to build upon it (as, undoubtedly, we shall), we will be better served as educators than if we expect the students to meet us on our level.

Shane Shukis

A Brief History of Laughter in the Classroom

I have opined to my fellow TFs frequently this semester about my strange importation of Mikhail Bakthin's theory of laughter into the classroom environment. In *Rabelais and His World,* Bakthin has outlined how laughter, beginning in Medieval folklore and migrating to Renaissance literature and beyond, pervades as official genre and undercuts any serious rules, destroying a hierarchy of 'official' values. This paper is not about Bakthin at all, but it is about me. And I have been fascinated by Bakthin's ideas for years. Hence, I felt the need to introduce some of the need to introduce some of the background material from where I get my ideas.

When I started teaching freshman composition this semester, I was nervous as hell about alienating the students. I was afraid of using words that, although they seemed common to me, made students feel like there was a distance between us. An example is 'erudite.' One day, my class had to ask me to define that word before I continued with my lecture. Not one student had a clue what it meant, and I was mortified because I felt as if I had tried to go over their heads and appear, well, erudite. I have also feared acting like some concept I am discussing is simple when, in fact, it's not. I've certainly been guilty of perpetuating this ruse in the past to avoid calling attention to my own uncertainties about a subject. Frequently, I have rattled off about Bakthin as if he were my brother and not this obscure Russian theorist who had a few helpful but esoteric ideas.

My anxiety is based upon my own personal experiences in which a teacher seemed like this distant figure who was above us, the students, on a higher level of understanding. I've never liked these classes because the teacher talked "down" to us, and we were there only to take notes because we had nothing to contribute to the class.

I can remember classes and teachers I've been in all the way back until high school that were based upon the idea that the teacher was an "authority" there to preach the word, so to speak. The attitude was that there was a right, unquestionable way to approach a subject, and the teacher, like a preacher, would show the students the way to the promised land. Many of the classes I've taken were run similarly, and I can even remember a special incident from high school.

In an English class during my sophomore year, we were reading John Knowles' *A Separate Peace.* When our teacher gave us our essay assignment for the book, she put an introductory paragraph on the overhead projector, complete with a three-part thesis statement about the book, and told us to copy everything down. Our assignment was to finish the paper she started.

I had been completely enthralled with the book, and when I read the thesis statement she provided, I felt that it didn't address the parts of the book I liked. Being inquisitive, I approached the teacher and asked her if I could do a different thesis statement. She said *no,* that everyone had to do the same assignment. I tried to explain to her that I wanted to do the same assignment, just a different thesis. *Shane,* she said with that disinterested yet condescending tone of hers, *I'm sorry that you cannot understand the directions. But I will not waste my time allowing you to disrupt the teaching process.* I remember vividly to this day how mad I became at her. The rest of the class was mindlessly churning-out assembly-line crap about Knowles' touching story, vacantly repeating what she had said the day before (the topic sentence mirrored her stunning one-day lecture about the book), and I was impeding her *Teaching!* To shorten the story, I ended up in the principle's office shortly thereafter. In my hand was a pink discipline-slip, and on the line that asked for the reason I was sent to the office was scrawled "being smart." Of course, she was too demure a proper-lady to write that I was being a smart-ass or smart-alec, but serendipity contrives with irony in such sublime ways at times.

I have developed a preoccupation about the classroom environment from this distinction. My instructor from that fateful class rightfully claimed that she was concerned with the *teaching* process. And that is exactly what she and others of her pedagogical orientation are concerned with. They believe that their purpose in the classroom is to disseminate certain established rules and formulas of successful writing, and that they are only successful if they get each student to absorb these important paradigms. Therefore, they must be perceived as an authority, an elevated presence, within the classroom. This is the teaching process.

Now that I have begun to teach writing, I realize that, conversely, I am overly concerned with the learning process. If writing is to be considered as a "process," an activity of evolution and growth, or even change, then the teaching of writing must be considered in a similar light. Instead of looking at the teaching of composition as the dispensation of particular grammar rules and styles to the masses, I attempt to help my students learn how to shape experience through writing and, more importantly, to interpret and learn from the process. One of the ways I do this is to "challenge" my students to explore themselves through writing. I encourage them to take a chance when they write, and not to just "fulfill the assignment." The idea is that, instead of resorting to a particular formula, each student may try new strategies to explore how they feel and think about a subject. Hopefully, because they wrote to suit themselves rather than a pre-existing structure, they will have discovered something personal through the experience. Hence, to me, the teaching of composition is very much the process of helping others to discover their own ability to learn. In a weird way, teaching is a type of learning, a type of learning that relies on the teacher's ability to listen to and understand each student's own experiences expressed in the papers and to respond individually, personally. Consequently, teaching composition is learning about one's students and their own ability to learn.

The majority of this process happens in the classroom and is accomplished through teacher-student interaction in an open and honest environment. It absolutely amazes me how little attention has been paid in the past to the classroom environment. For the learning process to really happen, students must trust their teacher's motivations enough to sincerely explore their writing abilities in relation to themselves and their experiences instead of just fulfilling an assignment's requirements. If they write with trust and sincerity in that the teacher truly cares about what the students have to say for themselves, then they should learn as much about themselves as they do about the act of writing. This trust cannot happen if a teacher only expects a student to "fulfill the assignment." The teaching of composition at the college level is much more than a matter of literacy. For me, it is a matter of the aided evolution of a critical ability to read events in life and formulate them in a coherent manner. To do this, I must convince my students that I am not concerned whether or not they consider what I say as the correct answer, I would much rather that they discover their own truth for themselves. This is the way I try to run my classes.

Very early this semester, I discovered how laughter in the classroom loosened up my students and facilitated the learning process. At first, they would begin class by focusing on taking notes instead of participating in class discussion. I attribute this to their training in the teaching process in which they were taught to "learn" simply what the teacher told them to. I discovered that when I told jokes, lots of jokes and plenty about myself, they progressively lightened up and participated more because I seemed less distant, less elevated. I believe that I used their own laughter to convince them that I really, truly wanted to hear what they thought instead of having them repeat what I told them back to me. Preachers and prophets don't tell jokes, but Mr. Shukis does.

Very quickly, I began to make a peculiar connection between my experiences in the classroom and my personal studies. Bakthin posits that, in a text, the existence of laughter and humor is used to tear down a serious, monologic/logocentric control of the text by a single voice/ideology (they were synonymous to Bakthin), such as an Anthony Trollope novel. It opens up the text to a discourse of many voices or ideologies, such as a Dostoyevsky novel. When this happens, it is impossible to tell who is in control, and all voices seem of equal value.

As the semester wore on and I told more and more jokes, my students really began to take the initiative in class discussions and their writings. At times, all they would let me do was sit back and enjoy the ride. I believe that they could do this because I convinced them that their voices were equal to mine. I have even had two students come tell me that they had always been incredibly shy and bad in English because they could never "fulfill the assignment" to the teacher's liking. Now, thanks to my class, they have become vocal, confident, and pretty effective writers in my opinion.

I started bragging about all of my success to other TFs, lauding my use of laughter as a device. I imagine that I sounded pretty smug, and many TFs were interested in my methods. But after awhile, they all asked me a certain question: "Just how far would you take it?" That question has stuck with me. "How much humor is good in the classroom?" I realize that this is a legitimate concern. Certainly, there has to be a point where too much laughter can impede the learning process because nobody can take anything seriously, like in a Three Stooges routine.

There was one moment recently this semester when I felt I might have crossed that imperceivable line and invited chaos. I was priming my class for an in-class writing assignment. We were going to defend an aesthetic position, something not grounded in empirical standards. I could easily tell that they did not like the assignment as I began to set it up: "It's very difficult to argue for something that is not defined universally. Your opinions are the ultimate arbiters of your perceptions and tastes, but they are not adequate arguments and defenses by themselves." The students were leaning their heads back a little and rolling their eyes as if begging for deliverance from above. They did not want to read their half-hearted responses.

Thinking as quickly as I could, I remembered an event from earlier in the semester. One night, I went partying on Fry street with two other TFs, Chad and Keith. We had bought a six-pack of beer and were standing on the street-corner talking to some friends. I had released my hair from the ponytail I usually keep it in and was looking very casual. While standing there with beer in hand, I heard a car screech to a halt. To my left, I then heard "Hey Mr. Shukis! Don't come to class drunk on Monday!" I looked over and saw a car-full of my students. They were all laughing and saying "Look how long his hair is! What a long-haired hippie!"

Remembering this event and the look of joy and derision on the students' faces, I unbound my hair and quickly made up a story that my sister-in-law told me to get a hair cut because I looked like a hippie. I told my class that I needed to make a decision on what to do and that I wanted their help. I then began a class discussion by giving them my "Teflon-guarantee, meaning that anything you say about me or my hair won't stick." Immediately, the class began a lively discussion about whether or not my hair was very aesthetic. The response was absolutely amazing. The students felt completely uninhibited and compared my hair to 'hard spaghetti" and such bad celebrity hairdos as Michael Bolton and Billy Ray Cyrus. Other students rushed to my hair's defense, citing personal aesthetics and a rebellious motivation. In almost an instant, the class had begun to raucously laugh every time a humorous comparison was made about my hair, which was followed by a fervent defense of it. All I had to do was encourage each student to speak freely and then show them certain ways they could shape those opinions into arguments using any number of the literary devices we had learned. At times, the laughter was so tear-inducing loud that the class could hardly breath much less elucidate the subject clearly. And I did have one student become very upset at me for being so flippant an authority figure. After class, he claimed that I should have respect for my position and myself and should not let students laugh at me so; I wouldn't if I had any self-respect. He has a point, and he certainly would have approved of my sophomore English teacher from high school. But, when the students turned in their response assignments on my hair, the care and effort put into their positions were evident and everybody scored well, even the guy who ripped me apart for being a charlatan—his support for his argument was strong and eloquently stated.

I have pondered over the query of *how far?* for a while now and do not have an answer. I do not script the jokes I tell. That would probably be transparent and backfire on me. Instead, I trust in *Kairos* and rely on inspiration to fuel my antics before the class. There is a time for inviting levity and a time for the business at hand. Hopefully, when I sense a lull in my students' attention or a wavering of their sincerity, I can come up with whatever chuckle-gag or knee-slapper I can, many times at my own expense. So far, all has gone well.

Graduate Student Essays
with Multiple Drafts

Reading to Write

First Draft

Jim Burrows

Jim Burrows   **First Draft**

Reading to Write

I remember precisely the professor's comments on my first college essay. "You are very talented and very intelligent," he had written. The comments had been scribbled in green felt-tip pen in the kind of frantic and weary hand I sometimes notice myself using now on my students' papers. The "o" in "you," for example, was an incomplete circle; one of the "t's" in "intelligent" had been left uncrossed, and each successive line of neon green dwindled further and further toward illegibility. I don't remember reading his other comments, though they must have existed—suggestions on how I could improve my writing, corrections in the text. I don't recall the topic of my paper, its thesis, or if it had one. I don't remember the writer whose work I was writing about. I do remember my grade: D.

Probably I should have spoken to my professor about the apparent conflict in his comments and my grade, but I didn't. I was so flattered by his comments that I didn't care about the grade. I didn't care because I knew then that I could write, that it wasn't unattainable. My essay, I'm sure, had lacked structure, a thesis, focus. But in whatever had poured unedited onto the page from the nebula of my subconscious mind, my professor had recognized something, some spark, even if he hadn't felt justified in rewarding me for it.

Years later, as a new graduate student, I was visiting my family when I ran into my seventh grade English teacher. When I told her what I was doing, she asked, "Do you want to teach or write?" "Both," I said. She nodded, and a knowing smile of contentment crept onto her face. "You always just understood the language," she said. "You always had it."

What is this "it" she was talking about, and is "it" really so intangible, so unnamable? Is "it" creativity? Facility with language? Talent, we usually call it. Only I don't want to call it talent because to do so elevates effective writing to an unreachable level. Talent, whatever it is, isn't something students feel they can acquire. Either they're born with "it," or they're not. It's a dangerous word. We may as well go back to invoking muses, a practice generally frowned upon as a method of teaching composition. It's an archaic idea, this invocation of the muse, and yet many of our students, in the quiet morning hours of the day their first essay is due, will be appealing to a higher power for assistance.

I'd rather think of writing as an acquired talent, a learned ability so closely aligned with reading that the two are inseparable. This last statement, that reading and writing "go together," seems obvious, and yet I believe that many students—probably most of them—forget this when they write. They forget that muses do actually exist—they're called writers. Reading is writing's nourishment. Great writers are great readers, without exception, but there is a specific kind of reading during which this nourishment occurs, a kind of reading not required in other disciplines. When students are asked to read their Chemistry books, for instance, they are reading for information—they scan, they highlight, they scan some more, skipping happily over the words like a flat rock across water. They never learn to sink, to slow down and drift down deep into the language. I believe this kind of reading is indispensable to writers. When it happens, the mechanics, the technology of the language is ruthlessly and automatically absorbed.

How do I teach this? How do I make my students understand that they don't need to reinvent the wheel, that they can carry what they've learned from other writers in their sensibilities? How do I get them to shift their reading emphasis from content to style?

Since I'm advocating learning writing from other writers, I would be remiss in not consulting professional writers in this matter. I have already begun this consultation. Donald Hall's essay, "Four Kinds of Reading" was very helpful. So were Donald Murray's "Reading as a Reader," Eudora Welty's "A Sweet Devouring," and "Of Speed Readers and Lip-Movers," by William Gass. These are all essays that discuss the especially intense kind of reading I want to promote as a method of teaching writing.

My second point of attack is the journal section of the library. Certainly I plan to consult journals published by and for teachers of composition, but it occurs to me that journals directed toward the study of linguistics might be especially helpful in this area. The kind of reading I'm advocating is physical—the words come in through the eye, are decoded into sound in the throat (even if the reader is reading silently), and filter into the understanding. Exactly how this happens isn't nearly as important as that it does happen.

Obviously, I'll make sure my students do plenty of reading. The first essay I'm asking them to write is an autobiographical essay. I've made copies of essays by Langston Hughes, Alice Walker, and James Thurber, and I plan to give them more and more examples as the due date for the first essay nears. This isn't enough, of course. The point is to get them to read a certain way. I plan to make copies of handouts which ask them to identify sentences, phrases and even single words from the essays they've read. Handouts which ask them, in other words, to identify the author by his or her style.

Essentially, I want to help my students improve their writing by helping them to improve their reading. I know this is a tall order, and the objection might even be raised that since my students are college freshman, it's already too late. Nonsense. I believe the capacity to read in this way, to swallow and digest not mere facts but language, is innate. My students have it, they just haven't been made to use it. In fact, much of their education in other disciplines has probably discouraged this kind of reading by rewarding the regurgitation of facts picked from their reading. This kind of reading, of course, is necessary. We read papers and news magazines in this way. We read road signs this way. But one cannot reach his or her full potential as a writer without learning another kind of reading. I believe that when my students learn this, when they learn to stop skimming the surface of language and drift downward into its depths, they will reemerge as better writers.

Jim Burrows   **Rewrite**

Reading to Write

I remember two things about the first essay I wrote in college: one sentence of my professor's response, and my grade. "You are very talented and very intelligent," Dr. Hemenway had written. The comments had been scribbled in green felt-tip pen in the kind of frantic and weary had I sometimes notice myself using now on my students' papers. The *o* in you, for example, was an incomplete circle; the final *t* in intelligent had been left uncrossed, and each successive line of neon green dwindled further and further towards illegibility. I don't remember reading his other comments, but they must have existed: suggestions on improving my writing, corrections in the text, questions about my ideas. I don't recall the topic of my paper, its thesis, or if it had one. I don't remember the writer whose work I was writing about. I do remember my grade: D.

I didn't feel compelled to ask Dr. Hemenway about the apparent conflict between his comment and my grade. I was so flattered by that one comment that I didn't care about the grade. I didn't care because I had his stamp of approval—I sensed approval, somehow, in that word *talent*—and I knew then that I could write, that it wasn't unattainable. My essay, I'm sure, lacked structure, a thesis, focus. But in whatever had poured unedited onto the page from the nebula of my subconscious mind, my professor had recognized something, some spark, and his recognition of that meant more to me than any grade.

Years later, as a new graduate student, I was visiting my family when I ran into my seventh grade English teacher. When I told her what I was doing, she asked, "Do you want to write or teach?"

"Both," I said.

She nodded, and a knowing smile of contentment crept onto her face. "You always just understood the language," she said. "You always had it."

What is this *it* she was talking about, and is it really so intangible, so unnamable? Is it creativity? Facility with language? Talent, we usually call it. Only I don't want to call it talent. As a teacher, I'm almost afraid to use that word in my classroom for fear of perpetuating that old image of the automatic writer, the one who goes into a trance-like state during the process of writing and becomes the mere instrument of his muse or God or the Buddha or whoever. Of course the perpetuation of this image, though flattering to talented writers, is detrimental in the classroom, where the focus should be on revision. I'm reminded of lines from Yeats's poem, "Adam's Curse," in which the speaker discusses the toil involved in producing great writing, and the misconceptions that exist concerning writing:

> I said, "A line will take us hours maybe,
> Yet if it does not seem a moment's thought,
> Our stitching and unstitching has been naught.
> Better go down upon your marrow-bones
> And scrub a kitchen pavement, or break stones

Like an old pauper, in all kinds of weather;
For to articulate sweet sounds together
Is to work harder than all these, and yet
Be thought an idler by the noisy set
Of bankers, schoolmasters and clergymen
The martyrs call the world."

Each work of writing is first of all work; still, there is such a thing as talent in regard to writing—no writer can be great without it. According to Hemingway, "Real seriousness in regard to writing is one of the two absolute necessities. The other, unfortunately, is talent." Most of my students are not what I would call talented writers. Most of them also don't take themselves seriously as writers, and these two problems are not unrelated. I think most of my students feel that if they're not born with this nebulous thing called talent, they'll never be good writers. They don't feel it's something they can acquire, so why try? They forget that talent isn't really required for good writing; it's only required for great writing, the kind we find in Shakespeare, Hemingway, and Morrison. I believe that most of my students—there are few exceptions—are capable of lucid, intellgible, insightful prose, but their concept of what it is to write short circuits their ambition. Many of them come to me with confused ideas about the process of writing; they seem to think of it as mostly inspiration, a dream-like state in which the muse is invoked. That's an archaic idea, the invocation of the muse, and yet many of my students, in the quiet morning hours of the day their first essay is due, will be appealing to a higher power for assistance. That *talent,* it's a dangerous word.

As a creative writer, I'm attracted to the image of the writer as an individual with heightened powers of perception and seemingly magical abilities of communication, but as a teacher of writing, I'd rather think of writing as an acquirable talent, a learned ability so closely aligned with reading that the two are inseparable. This last statement, that reading and writing go together, seems obvious, and yet I believe that many students—probably most of them—forget this when they write. They forget that muses do actually exist; they're called writers. Reading is writing's nourishment. Great writers are great readers without exception, but there is a particular kind of reading during which this nourishment occurs, a kind of reading not required in other disciplines. When students are asked to read their Chemistry books, for example, they are reading for information. They scan, they highlight, they scan some more, skimming over the words like a flat rock across water. They never learn to sink, to slow down and drift down deep into the language. I believe this kind of reading is indispensable to writers. When it happens, the mechanics, the technology of the language is ruthlessly and automatically absorbed. Our students are in the infancy of their writing lives, and they must learn to write in the same way that they learned to speak: by sheer mimicry. We know, of course, that in writing, as in speaking, there is no such thing as true mimicry. Each writer's individual perception, experience, and ability tinge his or her attempts to mimic. Students don't need to reinvent the wheel as they seem to think they do. They can carry what they've learned from other writers in their sensibilities. Their mimicry will seem like babble at first, but eventually a voice unmistakably their own will emerge. I believe that advocating this mimicry in my class is the closest I can come to teaching talent.

Since I'm advocating learning writing from other writers, I would be remiss in not consulting professional writers in this matter. I have already begun this consultation. Donald Hall's essay "Four Kinds of Reading" was very helpful. So were Donald Murray's "Reading as a Writer," Eudora Welty's "A Sweet Devouring," and "Of Speed Readers and Lip Movers," by William Gass. These are all essays that discuss the especially intense kind of reading I want to promote as a method of teaching writing.

My second point of attack is the journal section of the library. Certainly I plan to consult journals by and for teachers of composition, but journals from other disciplines—Psychology, even the hard sciences—might be helpful. The kind of reading I'm advocating is physical. The words come in though the eye, are decoded into sound in the throat (even if the reader is reading silently), and filter into the understanding. Exactly how this happens isn't nearly as important as that it does happen.

Obviously, I'll make sure my students do plenty of reading. The first essay I'm asking them to write is an autobiographical essay. I've made copies of essays by Langston Hughes, Alice Walker, and James Thurber, and I plan to give them more and more examples as the due date for the first essay nears. This isn't enough, of course. The point is to get them to read a certain way. I plan to make copies of handouts which ask them to identify sentences, phrases, and even single words from the essays they've read. Handouts which ask them, in other words, to identify the author by his or her style. That is, after all, what we should focus on as teachers of writing, even though we must assign grades based on complexity of thought and quality of ideas. Ultimately, I want my students to view writing as a mode of thinking, as the highest linguistic expression of an emotion or idea, as a process that not only expresses their particular way of viewing the world, but informs and affects it as well. I believe, however, that if they are made to focus intensely on how they write, what they write will be subjected to this intense scrutinization as well.

Essentially, I want to help my students improve their writing by helping them to improve their reading. I know this is a tall order, and the objection might even be raised that since my students are college freshmen, it's already too late. Nonsense. I believe the capacity to read in this way, to swallow and digest not mere facts, but language, is innate. My students have it, they just haven't been asked to use it often enough. In fact, much of their education in other disciplines has probably discouraged this kind of reading by rewarding the regurgitation of facts picked from their reading. This kind of reading, of course, is necessary. We read papers and news magazines in this way. We read road signs in this way. But one cannot reach his or her full potential as a writer without learning another kind of reading. I believe that when my students learn this, when they learn to stop skimming the surface of language and drift downward into its depths, they will reemerge as better writers.

Project Proposal: Crash Course in ESL

First Draft

Michelle Niemczyk

Michelle Niemczyk   **First Draft**

Project Proposal: Crash Course in ESL

The questionnaire seemed harmless enough. "Circle the sections that you would like to teach," it urged. So, in my enthusiasm I circled all the sections of freshman English I thought I could possibly teach: developmental writing, freshman composition, computer composition, technical writing, and English as a second language (ESL). Since the university had a department dedicated to language acquisition and aspects of teaching and learning ESL, I thought they would only use me, a plain old literature grad student, in an emergency. Well, faster than you can say 911, I was standing in front of about thirty international and non-native speaking students, who were looking at me with big trusting eyes, and attempting to teach ESL.

The problem with this situation is that the pedagogy course for new teaching fellows did not address ESL specifically. Having taught both regular freshman composition and ESL composition for a couple weeks now, I am convinced that there must be a difference in approach for the ESL class to be effective. Although I have received some useful advice on teaching ESL students, there is still much I don't know. I fear my lack of knowledge of their particular needs will effect the quality of the education that I am trying (in my amateurish way) to give them. How much English are they required to know before taking my class? What sort of English have they been taught (i.e., British versus American English)? What discourse has been used to teach them that English? How can I make *my* English more comprehensible to them?

The answers to these questions can be found by joining the community of teachers of ESL. Veterans of the field can fill me in on the probable educational background of my students. They can help me with approaches to meeting the specific needs of students suffering from a language deficiency. They can introduce me to the discourse used in teaching these students. Once I have this information, I can better judge their educational gaps and work to bring them up to speed. I can also speak to them in the same way in which they are used to speaking about English, for as a native speaker, I have not spoken *about* my language since I was in grammar school, and even then, not in the terms that they are used to hearing. Specially trained and experienced teachers of ESL can help me comprehend the academic world of my ESL students, and help me to give those students the education I feel they deserve.

I plan to familiarize myself with those who teach non-native speakers and also academic world of the international student in three specific ways. First, I will go to Office of International Affairs at Kendall Hall and discover what the international student's "port of entry" at the University of North Texas is like. There, I can get an idea of what sort of leveling education the international students receive when they arrive, if any. Second, I will interview the head of the ESL department, Dr. Cukor-Avila, on the various schools of thought concerning the teaching of ESL. Her comments should help me decide what approach or approaches to use in teaching ESL students. Last, I will attend a lecture class on the teaching of ESL. From the lecture I hope to gain practical knowledge that will be of use in my classroom. I also plan to talk to members of UNT faculty that teach ESL, in order to answer in questions the above-mentioned activities do not address.

I anticipate that my foray into the ESL department and my research into the academic lives of international students will result in knowledge that will ultimately help me to become a better teacher. I know that all the faculty and staff associated with the international office and the ESL department are concerned with the quality of education that we give international and non-native speaking students, therefore, it is my hope that my own concern will foster in them a willingness to help me succeed with this project.

Project Proposal: Crash Course in ESL

Rewrite

Michelle Niemczyk

Michelle Niemczyk   **Rewrite**

Project Proposal: Crash Course in ESL

One day early in the semester, I asked everyone in my ESL class to sign a copy of the university attendance policy, so that I could keep it on file as proof that each student was aware of attendance rules. When I tried to file the copies in the students' files, I found that I couldn't read most of their signatures. So, the next day, I asked the students to come up as I called their names and print their names underneath their signatures. All but a handful of the class looked at me with uncomprehending cheerfulness. I called the first name. "Here."

I explained the situation again, but slower, making sure that I enunciated. I called the name again and motioned for the student to come up to my desk. I showed him the sheet and asked him to print his name beneath his signature. "This *is* my signature." O.K., deep breath. I wrote instructions on the board, read them, and tried again. The concept caught on; the ball was rolling. Then, I called Florence Meresse. Florence was beleaguered, with two of her classmates signing and explaining, she flipped hurriedly through her French/English dictionary to decipher "Print Your Name." What had I gotten myself into?

Looking back, the teaching preference sheet had seemed harmless enough. "Circle the sections that you would like to teach," it urged. So, in my enthusiasm I circled all the sections of freshman English I thought I could possibly teach: developmental writing, freshman composition, computer composition, technical writing, and English as a second language (ESL). Since the university had a department dedicated to language acquisition and aspects of teaching and learning ESL, I thought they would only use me, a plain old literature grad student, in an emergency. Well, faster than you can say 911, I was standing in front of about thirty international and non-native speaking students, who were looking at me with big trusting eyes, and attempting to teach ESL.

The problem with this situation is that I know nothing about the educational background of the international students I am trying to teach. NOTHING. I need to know what level of learning my students are responsible for before entering my class, so that I know what gaps to fill and which to assume have been filled by previous education. I fear that the lack of knowledge of my international students' particular needs will affect the quality of the education that I am trying (in my amateurish way) to give them. My confusing first weeks of teaching ESL kids prompted several questions: How much English are they required to know before taking my class? What sort of English have they been taught (i.e., British versus American English)? What discourse has been used to teach them that English? How can I make *my* English more comprehensible to them?

The community of teachers of ESL should be able to provide the answers to my questions. These veterans of the field can fill me in on the English language requirements of my students. They can help me with approaches to meeting the specific needs of students suffering from a language deficiency. Teachers of ESL can introduce me to the vocabulary used in teaching non-native speakers, so that

I can discuss English grammar in the same way in which they are used to discussing it—I have not spoken *about* my language since I was in grammar school, and even then, not in the terms that they are used to hearing. Once I have this information, I can better judge my students' educational foundation, as well as their gaps, and work to bring them up to speed. Specially trained and experienced teachers of ESL can help me comprehend the academic world of my ESL students, and help me to give those students the education I feel they deserve.

I plan to familiarize myself with those who teach non-native speakers and also academic world of the international student in three specific ways. First, I will go to Office of International Affairs at Candle Hall and discover what the international student's "port of entry" at the University of North Texas is like. There, I can get an idea of what sort of leveling education the international students receive when they arrive, if any. Second, I will interview the head of the ESL department, Dr. Cukor-Avila, on the various schools of thought concerning the teaching of ESL. Her comments should help me decide what approach or approaches to use in teaching ESL students. Last, I will attend one of Dr. Cukor-Avila's lectures on the teaching of ESL during her Thursday night class in the Language Building, room 322. From the lecture I hope to gain practical knowledge that will be of use in my classroom. I also plan to talk to members of UNT faculty that teach ESL in order to ascertain their opinions on the teaching of ESL students compared to native-speaking students.

I anticipate that my foray into the ESL department and my research into the academic lives of international students will result in knowledge that will ultimately help me to become a better teacher. I know that all the faculty and staff associated with the international office and the ESL department are concerned with the quality of education that we give international and non-native speaking students: therefore, it is my hope that my own concern will foster in them a willingness to help me succeed with this project.

Lisa Jackson   **First Draft**

Investigating Teaching Fellow Training: A Proposal

I have never taught a class before. I have tutored individual students, and I have trained new people at my former place of employment. However, I have never been solely responsible for fifty-eight college freshman. As I eagerly anticipated the beginning of the fall semester, I found myself asking a multitude of questions: What would my students be like? What is their attitude toward writing? How prepared are they to write at the college level? Will we like each other? Most of these questions answered themselves on the first few days of class. My students are young, and they are both excited and scared about college. Most of them are writers of average capability, while a few already write very well. I have been pleased with their timid attempts to talk to me, and we are working daily on getting to know each other. Now I am faced with the big question I have been considering daily: What can I, as a first time teacher, do to prepare myself that will enable me to reach my students, to inspire them, and to help them overcome their fears about writing?

I have spent the greater part of my life as a student. While this makes me prepared as a scholar, I also realize it does not make me prepared for the practical aspects of teaching. Much of my preparation must, and will, occur in the classroom as I teach. One of the first steps I have used to ready myself is to take a personal inventory of myself as a person and as a student. I know that I have maturity and experience, both in life and as a student, on my side. For years I have watched what my teachers have done that has been effective, and what has been ineffective. I have already begun to incorporate those good ideas, while simultaneously trying to avoid the bad ones. After each class, I have reviewed what has and has not worked. My journal has served as a terrific sounding board. Writing down the events of each class has enabled me to review the day more objectively.

As I have begun my career as a teacher, I have become interested in researching what type of training other departments within the University of North Texas offer their teaching fellows. I would be interested to know if they conduct a course as the English department does, of if they hold a series of workshops before school starts. If the method of training does differ in this way or in others, I would like to know which is more effective and which makes the teaching fellows feel more prepared. I am also curious to know if the other departments provide any preparatory materials other than textbooks, and what they are.

In the next few days, I plan to talk to at least three teaching fellows outside of the English department to obtain this information. In addition, I will try to get feedback from them on what they would have liked to have to prepare themselves. I hope this information will not only illuminate me as a teacher, but will also help me determine if the way we as a department, and the university as a whole, is effective in its training of teaching fellows. I think this information is important to me as an individual, but it is also of vital importance to this university. What is paramount to me in this issue is not my needs as a person, but our students' needs as they begin the lifelong journey toward learning. The training of teaching fellows touches on our most important obligation—ensuring that our students get the best education possible.

Lisa Jackson   **Rewrite**

Investigating Teaching Fellow Training: A Proposal

I have never taught a class before. I have tutored individual students, and I have trained new people at my former place of employment. However, I have never been solely responsible for fifty-eight college freshman. As I eagerly anticipated the beginning of the fall semester, I found myself asking a multitude of questions: What would my students be like? What is their attitude toward writing? How prepared are they to write at the college level? Will we like each other? Most of these questions answered themselves on the first few days of class. My students are young, and they are both excited and scared about college. Most of them are writers of average capability, while a few already write very well. I have been pleased with their timid attempts to talk to me, and we are working on getting to know each other. Now I am faced with the big question I have been considering daily: What can I, as a first time teacher, do to prepare myself that will enable me to reach my students, to inspire them, and to help them overcome their fears about writing?

I have spent the greater part of my life as a student. While this makes me prepared as a scholar, I also realize it does not make me prepared for the practical aspects of teaching. I am uncertain about how much time I will need to allot myself to prepare for class each day, and I am also unsure of how to teach a subject that I have always considered to be an intuitive skill. The fact that I have never taken a formal writing course, which I never previously considered a problem, has now become one. If I had had this experience, it would have given me some idea of what was going to happen in my classroom. It would also have prepared me for some of the things that my students will find difficult, since I might have experienced the same dilemmas. Since I am faced with these deficiencies, I have decided that much of my preparation must, and will, occur in the classroom.

One of the first steps I have used to ready myself is to take a personal inventory of myself as a person and as a student. I know that I have maturity and experience, both in life and as a student, on my side. For years I have watched what my teachers have done that has been effective, and what has been ineffective. I have considered how these things have effected me as a student, and how they can effect my students as I teach them. I have already begun to incorporate those good ideas, while simultaneously trying to avoid the bad ones. After each class, I have reviewed what I have perceived to have worked, and what has not worked. I have used the reaction of my students as a measure. I have tried to attentively notice what type of questions they have asked, while noticing if they were questions that indicated they understood my line of reasoning, or were confused by it.

As I have begun my career as a teacher, I have become interested in talking to other teaching fellows in the English department to see what type of methods they use in their classes. I would like to know how many use the community assignment in teaching 1310, and what they see as the benefits and drawbacks of the format. I want to know if they use the textbook we are provided with and if they like it. If they choose not to use the available text, I wonder what text they use, if any. I also want to determine how to handle more problematic issues, such as what to do with combative students, attendance problems, and disruptive students. In the next few weeks, I plan to talk to as many teaching fellows as possible so I can try to answer my questions. After all, my peers are my most valuable and accessible resource. What is paramount to me in this issue is not my needs as a person, but our students' needs as they begin the lifelong journey toward learning. Preparing myself as a teaching fellow touches on my most important obligation—ensuring that my students get the best education possible.

Peter England   **First Draft**

Literary Theory, Freshman Composition, and Me

At the graduate level, we discuss rhetorical strategy, intertextuality, and whether the reader brings meaning to a text or the text brings its own meaning to the reader. The act of reading is inextricably linked with that of writing, yet these two ideas have been stressed to the students in different ways. The students need to be inspired to go beyond the beginnings of reading and writing, which they have learned in high school, and to start considering themselves as readers/writers.

My first impulse is to emphasize personal style and strategy instead of standardized forms. What I should actually do, however, is introduce the students to different ways of reading, and from there, to different ways of writing. I hope to let them practice enough so that they begin to get the feel of their own personal style. My most inspirational classes have involved a teacher who brought new insight into how things worked, whether the topic was physics, or philosophy, or writing. However, the semester is only so long, and the students already have several papers to write before the end of the term. Would the introduction of post-structuralism inspire the students or intimidate them? My solution is to introduce the various topics by means of essays designed to convey the necessary information while using a style easily understood by college freshman.

A specific plan of action must necessarily fall by the wayside, as any course should change itself during the semester. Any course that deals with post-structuralist modes of thought could easily be designed to flow with the learning ability of the students involved. One of the most important facets of the writing process is the reading process. Short reading assignments, to be read before or during class, would help to bring about a greater awareness of multiple possible interpretations. For instance, if we were discussing a work that had the term "gangster" in the context of 1920s Chicago, the class would simply work off the ideas gleaned from black and white movies, or stories handed down to them from relatives. If, however, we were discussing a work that used the word "gangsta," obviously in a more contemporary context, we would then leap into the realm of direct and personal experience. The majority of my students have encountered "gangsta" in music, television, pop culture, and even in their neighborhoods in the form of people who label themselves using the word "gangsta." Most of my students will have had a different level of experience with "gangsta" and will be able to share with the class their interpretation of this word. From this point, the class could then discuss a few other ideas which they share commonly, but which they use in various fashions.

The class discussions brought about by playing with the possibilities of interpretation are fun, but not all that is required to teach the students to care about their writing. Peer editing assignments, in which groups of students read and interpret each other's writing can also serve to reinforce the idea that a writer is always communicating something, and needs to be careful about how he/she communicates it. One of the final, and more difficult concepts to teach, is stressing to the student that a document is not a static entity, and its effect changes each time it is read, and each time it is read by a different person. I am not sure how to convey this idea. My desire is to create a greater awareness and sense of care about the writing process, therefore encouraging each student to work harder and write better. This approach allows students to feel as though their writing is more important than as a mere grade. However, I am sure that many of them will simply think that the teacher who talks about "living documents" and "ever-changing texts" is just carrying on in a different language.

One problem shared by the community in which I teach is that it is still in the early stages of writing development. Therefore, I need to hold back the tides of post-structuralism just enough to ensure that the students are not lost in the multitude of possibilities presented by post-structuralism. At this moment in time, they still need strict delineation of paper format, length, and style. I hope that by the end of the semester, they will need less deliberate instruction as to style. One of the most important aspects of writing is to develop your own style and yet still be able to communicate accurately, but without requiring too much effort on behalf of the reader. One way to avoid this problem is to give them topics to write on, whether for short, in-class assignments, or more lengthy compositions. These assignments would be presented in addition to the papers they are writing concerning topics of their choosing, and would theoretically serve to allow the student to focus more on writing than on worrying whether or not their topic is important enough to grace my desk.

Freshman composition students in school during this portion of the century are already post-structuralists. They have been taught that multiculturalism is "good," plurality is "good," and that different people see things different ways, and that all this is "good." But these are also students who, during high school, have been given a reading assignment and then had the teacher spend the next class period telling them what they have read, revealing the "true meaning" of the text. Encouraging these same students to have confidence in their ability to read and interpret will inspire the same confidence in writing and communicating.

Peter England   **Rewrite**

Literary Theory, Freshman Composition, and Me

At the graduate level, we discuss rhetorical strategy, intertextuality, and whether the reader brings meaning to a text or the text brings its own meaning to the reader. The act of reading is inextricably linked with that of writing, as both actions are different end of the same stick. However, reading and writing have been stressed to high school students as different topics. Freshman composition students need to be inspired to go beyond the beginnings of reading and writing, which they have learned in high school, and to start considering themselves as readers/writers. As a teacher of freshman composition, I feel it is my duty to find a way of emphasizing the interconnectedness of the reading/writing process.

Because of my agonizing memories of high school English classes, my first impulse is to emphasize personal style and strategy instead of standardized forms. But maybe I should introduce the students to different ways of reading, and from there, to different ways of writing. Instead of teaching a writing class just by having students write, wouldn't it be possible for them to incorporate different reading skills into the process? As a matter of fact, since proofreading is a part of the process-oriented approach to writing, any sort of reading practice could be beneficial to the class. I hope to let them practice enough so that they begin to get the feel of their own personal style of reading *and* writing. My most inspirational classes have involved a teacher who brought new insight into how things worked, whether the topic was physics, or philosophy, or writing. However, the semester is only so long, and the students already have several papers to write before the end of the term, not to mention years' worth of built-up dread towards the writing process. Would the introduction of post-modernism inspire the students or intimidate them? My solution is to introduce various topics by means of essays designed to convey the necessary information while using a style easily understood by college freshman. The whole idea of post-modernism, as I see it, is to allow everyone a voice. What better place to introduce that idea than in the first year of college instruction?

A specific plan of action must necessarily fall by the wayside, as any course should change itself during the semester. Any course that deals with post-modernist modes of thought could easily be designed to flow with the learning ability of the students involved. One of the most important facets of the writing process is the reading process. Short reading assignments, to be read before or during class, would help to bring about a greater awareness of multiple possible interpretations. For instance, when I was discussing a work that had the term "gangster" in the context of 1920s Chicago, the class worked off of ideas gleaned from black and white movies, or stories handed down to them from relatives. If, I suggested, we were discussing a work that used the word "gangsta," obviously in a more contemporary context, what would the effect be? The students immediately understood the difference. The majority of my students have encountered "gangsta" in music, television, pop culture, and even in their neighborhoods, in the form of people who label themselves using the word "gangsta", and were able to share with the class their interpretation of this word.

The class discussions brought about by playing with the possibilities of interpretation are fun, but are not all that is required to teach the students to care about their writing. Peer editing assignments, in which groups of students read and interpret each other's writing can also serve to reinforce the idea that a writer is always communicating something, and needs to be careful about to communicate it. One of the final, and more difficult concepts to teach, is stressing to the students that a document is not a static entity, and its effect changes each time it is read, and each time it is read by a different person. I am not sure how to convey this idea. My desire is to create a greater awareness and sense of care about the writing process, therefore encouraging each student to work harder and write better. I want the students to feel as though their writing is more important than as a mere grade. However, I am sure that many of them will simply think that the teacher who talks about "living documents" and "ever-changing texts" is just carrying on in a different language. But it's a language they need to recognize and relate to their own writing in such a way as to sharpen their communication skills.

One problem shared by the community in which I teach is that the students are still in the early stages of writing development. For the most part, my students would improve a great deal simply from rememdial grammar instruction. Therefore, I need to hold back the tides of post-modernism just enough to ensure that the students are not lost in the multitude of possibilities presented by post-modernism. At this moment in time, they still need strict delineation of paper format, length, and style. I hope that by the end of the semester, they will need less deliberate instruction as to style. One of the most important aspects of writing is to develop your own style and yet still be able to communicate effectively without requiring too much effort on behalf of the reader. One way to give my students practice is to give them topics to write on which were unrelated to their semester-long projects. If I emphasize that these shorter assignments are not graded so much for mechanics, but for the writer's ability to express an opinion, or interpretation, then maybe the students would learn more about the process of reading as related to writing. These assignments would be presented in addition to the papers they are writing concerning topics of their choosing, and would theoretically serve to allow the student to focus more on interpreting their own writing than on worrying whether or not their topic is important enough to grace my desk.

Freshman composition students in school during this portion of the century are already post-structuralists. They have been taught that multiculturalism is "good," plurality is "good," and that different people see things different ways, and that all this is "good." But these are also students who, during high school, have been given a reading assignment and then had the teacher spend the next class period telling them what they have read, revealing the "true meaning" of the text. Encouraging these same students to have confidence in writing and communicating.

Epiphany

First Draft

Laurie R. Renegar

Laurie R. Renegar   **First Draft**

Epiphany

The hard wooden bench made me fidget. I yawned, not bothering to cover my mouth. It was early, too early even for a morning person. I sat waiting for Dr. Angelotti, my English professor at the University of Oklahoma. He was late, or perhaps I was too early, I couldn't be sure; the hands on my Mickey watch were often out of synch with the "official" school time. A janitor opened the heavy doors at the end of the bright hallway. His weathered hands clutched the long broom handle as he began to methodically sweep the floor. The push broom made long hissing sounds like a cat warning an enemy to stay away. I was mesmerized by the movement.

"Hi Laurie! Glad to see you made it! I know it's early." Dr. Angelotti said as he jangled his keys in an effort to find his office key among the countless others.

"Here, let me get that," I offered as he juggled his briefcase and coffee while pushing the door open.

I felt like I was walking into a library. Books lined the walls, and sat stacked three feet high in the corners opposite his desk. It seemed to make sense that the office was in disarray; Dr. Angelotti gives me the sense of always being immersed books and writing. Dr. Angelotti is one of the best professors I have ever had. He strives to bring out the "writer" within his students, which is no easy task. There is no doubt we were a tough audience: seniors, eager to graduate, and busy with student teaching. No one had the time or the inclination to write creative essays. Even with the deck stacked against him at times, Dr. Angelotti managed to make everyone see their natural talent and recognize how they can build upon it. I was here to discuss my final portfolio before I turned it in. It would be the last significant writing assignment I would complete before graduation.

Dr. Angelotti flipped through the pages of the portfolio. He had seen many of the works go from chicken scratch in a spiral notebook to full-blown essays. Finally, he raised his head and spoke. "Why do *you* write, Laurie?" I scrunched up my face in confusion. Why do I write?

"... Because ... it's ... for the class?" I guessed. I couldn't really understand why he was asking. Why did I write?

"Do you really think so?" he probed. "I bet that you have better reasons. Think about it." The question was dropped and he went on to discuss my portfolio, but the question still nagged at me as I left his office.

Two weeks after that, I graduated. I didn't have time to think about the question. I was out of school, and frankly, I didn't care about creative writing anymore. I moved to Texas and began teaching. I taught students to write the traditional five paragraph essay, but did very little writing myself. Then I became a corporate trainer for a telecommunications company, which involved more traveling than anything else. Even if I had wanted to, there was no time to write. Then, when I decided to return to graduate school, I realized that writing would again become a big part of my life. I was scared that I would not be up to par as a typical graduate student. To reassure myself, I got out my portfolio from Dr. Angelotti's class. As I read through the portfolio, I saw a small penciled in comment in the margin of the cover page, "Why do you write?" All the details of that morning with Dr. Angelotti came flooding back. Why did I write? Why was I interested in returning to a writing field?

I wasn't sure of my answer until I actually became a graduate student. Even then, the answer didn't come to me immediately, but after a few weeks, I felt like was getting closer. One day I was sitting at my computer writing an essay for my Post Colonial Literature class, and as my thoughts formed sentences, I realized what motivated me to write. It was more than the class requirement, and more than the grade. I have to admit that my love for writing is out of pure selfishness. I write because it is my own version of immortality. The words will exist long after I am gone. They will represent who I was, and what interested me. My words will reflect my passion for living and learning. My writing will serve as proof that I was here, that I experienced things, and that I had an impact, not matter how small, on the world around me. I remembered back to the "read-arounds" we did in Dr. Angelotti's class. Everyone was required to bring at least one page of text to class each day. We would sit in a circle and read our works one by one. No one was allowed to comment; they just had to listen. At first, it was excruciatingly painful for me to read my papers. I wanted to be as funny, as profound, as some of my classmates. Eventually, though, I got the hang of it, and became more at ease. I learned so much in those read-arounds. Not just about writing, but about the lives of my classmates. As we began to take risks in our writing, we became a support group for each other. When a classmate read a piece of their writing, we were able to take a short glimpse into their world and their reality, no matter how different it was from our own. Those read-arounds taught me that writing joins people together by linking their experiences. I hope that years from now, someone will be able to read something of mine and feel—for even just a second—that they can somehow connect to my experiences and become a part of the world as I know it.

I don't think that I really knew the answer to the question when Dr. Angelotti asked me, "why do you write?" that day in his crowded office. It took being removed from the academic world, then being mercilessly plunged back in, for me to realize why I write. I have to admit that I missed it. I don't miss the spending Saturday at the computer or the due dates, but I do miss seeing my thoughts and feeling take shape within the text. I feel confident now about why I write, and I can't help but wonder if Dr. Angelotti realizes what he started. Even though he is miles away, I think he does.

Epiphany

Rewrite

Laurie R. Renegar

Laurie R. Renegar   **Rewrite**

Epiphany

The hard wooden bench made me fidget. I yawned, not bothering to cover my mouth. It was 6 am, too early even for a morning person. I sat waiting for Dr. Angelotti, my English professor at the University of Oklahoma. He was late, or perhaps I was too early, I couldn't be sure; the hands on my Mickey watch were often out of synch with the "official" school time. A janitor opened the heavy doors at the end of the bright hallway. His weathered hands clutched the long broom handle as he began to methodically sweep the floor. The push broom made long hissing sounds like a cat warning an enemy to stay away. I was mesmerized by the movement.

"Hi Laurie! Glad to see you made it! I know it's early." Dr. Angelotti said as he jangled his keys in an effort to find his office key among the countless others.

"Here, let me get that," I offered as he juggled his briefcase and coffee while pushing the door open.

I felt like I was walking into a library. Books lined the walls, and sat stacked three feet high in the corners opposite his desk. It seemed to make sense that the office was in disarray; Dr. Angelotti gives me the sense of always being immersed in books and writing. Dr. Angelotti is one of the best professors I have ever had. He strives to bring out the "writer" within his students, which is no easy task. There is no doubt we were a tough audience: seniors, eager to graduate, and busy with student teaching. No one had the time or the inclination to write creative essays. Even with the deck stacked against him at times, Dr. Angelotti managed to make everyone see their natural talent and recognize how they could build upon it. I was here to discuss my final portfolio before I turned it in. It would be the last significant writing assignment I would complete before graduation.

Dr. Angelotti flipped through the pages of the portfolio. He had seen many of the works go from chicken scratch in a spiral notebook to full-blown essays. Finally, he raised his head and spoke. "Why do *you* write, Laurie?" I scrunched up my face in confusion. Why do I write?

". . . Because . . . it's . . . for the class?" I guessed. I couldn't really understand why he was asking. Why did I write?

"Do you really think so?" he probed. "I bet that you have better reasons. Think about it." The question was dropped and he went on to discuss my portfolio, but the question still nagged at me as I left his office.

Two weeks after that, I graduated. I didn't have time to think about the question. I was out of school, and frankly, I didn't care about creative writing anymore. I moved to Texas and began teaching. I taught students to write the traditional five paragraph essay but did very little writing myself. Then I became a corporate trainer for a telecommunications company, which involved more traveling than anything else. Even if I had wanted to, there was no time to write. Then, when I decided to return to graduate school, I realized that writing would again become a big part of my life. I was scared that I would not be up to par as a typical graduate student. To reassure myself, I got out my portfolio from Dr. Angelotti's class. As I read through the portfolio, I saw a small penciled in comment in the margin of the cover page, "Why do you write?" All the details of that morning with Dr. Angelotti came flooding back. Why did I write? Why was I interested in returning to a writing field?

I wasn't sure of my answer until I actually became a graduate student. Even then, the answer didn't come to me immediately, but after a few weeks, I felt like was getting closer. One day I was sitting at my computer writing an essay for my Post Colonial Literature class, and as my thoughts formed sentences, I realized what motivated me to write. It was more than the class requirement, and more than the grade. I have to admit that my love for writing is out of pure selfishness. I write because it is my own version of immortality. The words will exist long after I am gone. They will represent who I was, and what interested me. My words will reflect my passion for living and learning. My writing will serve as proof that I was here, that I experienced things, and that I had an impact, not matter how small, on the world around me. I remembered back to the "read-arounds" we did in Dr. Angelotti's class. Everyone was required to bring at least one page of text to class each day. We would sit in a circle and read our works one by one. No one was allowed to comment; they just had to listen. At first, it was excruciatingly painful for me to read my papers. I wanted to be as funny, as profound, as some of my classmates. Eventually, though, I got the hang of it, and became more at ease. I learned so much in those read-arounds. Not just about writing, but about the lives of my classmates. As we began to take risks in our writing, we became a support group for each other. When a classmate read a piece of his or her writing, we were able to take a short glimpse into their world and their reality, no matter how different it was from our own. Those read-arounds taught me that writing joins people together by linking their experiences. I hope that years from now, someone will be able to read something of mine and feel—for even just a second—that they can somehow connect to my experiences and become a part of the world as I know it.

I don't think that I really knew the answer to the question when Dr. Angelotti asked me, "why do you write?" that day in his crowded office. It took being removed from the academic world, then being mercilessly plunged back in, for me to realize why I write. I have to admit that I missed it. I don't miss spending Saturdays at the computer, or the due dates, but I do miss seeing my thoughts and feeling take shape within the text. I feel confident now about why I write, and I can't help but wonder if Dr. Angelotti realizes what he started. Even though he is miles away, I think he does.

Keith Irwin   **First Draft**

Grades Suck

Exordium

I asked my students to write a paper about an event in their lives, asking them to present that event in detail, then practice interpretation by writing what it meant to them in a personal way, and what it might mean to the general reader, or at least in a greater context than the author's personal life and development.

Kristina wrote about the day she went to Charter's, a hospital for substance abusers, after having slashed her wrists on a night of unendurable depression, and Laura wrote about how her family changed after her father was kicked out for abusing her sexually. What amazed me about these papers was the amount of trust Laura and Kristina had in me, as their teacher, to share these things, and in their fellow students, who had to peer edit them.

But these papers have problems, not in the subject matter, so much, but in the way they chose to focus them. Laura wrote about what her family was like before her father's abuse, and what her family was like afterwards, but jumped right over the really painful, and most important part of the story—what her family was like *during* her abuse. Kristina's paper suffers from similar problems in that it would be much more effective if she focused on that one night when everything came apart for her, and used that night to relate the kinds of things that brought her there. Both of the papers opt for vague details and generalized statements about the horrific events they contain, probably because the events are still painful to them, but perhaps also because the writers are inexperienced.

Giving advice about the writing of papers when those papers are about such personal things is difficult, and will take careful phrasing on my part. But giving these papers grades, although not impossible, puts an intense and to my mind unnecessary strain on both me, as the teacher, and on Kristina and Laura, the students. By giving Laura's paper a B-, say, the message isn't a sympathetic desire to help Laura better bring home the tension of the situation, and the kinds of effects trauma can have on the rest of a person's life, but rather something like, "well, sorry about what happened to you, but I couldn't care less because the writing sucks. B-."

How can either of these students think of their stories and thoughts as in the process of development, as getting closer and closer to being both vivid and thought provoking, when grades render them finished, essentially botched products? How can these students continue to trust me as looking out for them, when I smack them while uttering sympathetic advice? Yes, they can revise for a high grade, but it is finally the grade they are thinking about, and about how to please me in order to get it, rather than on the what their chosen event really means, and how they can best evoke that meaning through writing.

Narratio

Most of us who teach Freshman composition find ourselves in institutions in which the final assessment of a student's abilities and development in a course of study is a single letter, a grade, which in fact measures a student's abilities to conform to a teacher's expectations rather than his or her capacity to integrate the subject matter into a larger scheme of knowledge, or to practice a skill in any given context.

Grades also imply a product oriented system of evaluation. It doesn't matter if a student has learned how to learn. What matters is that the student has produced a product suitable to an authority or expert on the matter.

Current composition theory, as well as the testimonies of countless practicing, professional writers, holds that expository writing is largely a process of developing ideas, and that the teaching of expository writing is not the teaching of correct form, but the teaching of this process of development. Students should thus be encouraged to reflect on how they develop ideas through writing, and should be given ample opportunity to practice such developments.

But the idea of "grading" a draft of a paper, which we tell the students is not the end product, but a step in the development of ideas, is contradictory, because by putting a grade on the paper, we are judging not the process, which we are supposedly teaching, but the product. But a number of my students have written, before their first paper was graded, that the process I took them through—multiple drafts, peer editing—seemed to have produced good writing in it—but they'd withhold judgement until their papers were graded. Thus, the quality of ideas, or their own developing interest in writing depends not on how *they* feel about it, but on a letter I'll affix.

Thus teaching process but evaluating on product seems to me an underlying contradiction not only in the composition classroom, but in the university as a whole.

Confirmatio

Although we all find ways to reconcile ourselves to giving grades, and students are used to it as well—expecting it, in fact, I think we would all rather do without them. But, given that we're teaching within an institution, and that a lot of things are going to have a change before grades will be phased out of the educational system, what can we do?

One alternative is to pressure the administration into making Freshman composition a "pass/fail" class, rather than a GPA graded class, and for coming up with a set of guidelines to ensure that "passing" the class requires a much more rigorous program than is extant in most programs. This places the burden on the teacher not to slack, to allow the students to rewrite until both they and the students feel satisfied with any given piece.

Or, a Nancy Atwell approach might be adapted, in which students set their own goals in consultation with an instructor, and are then evaluated on whether they achieved them or not. But, ultimately, we teach here at the University of North Texas and the problem of grades isn't going to go away. I'll have to put some letter on Kristina's paper, on Laura's, perhaps lose their trust, their energy. So what do we do? Given it'll be a cold day in hell before grades go away—well, we do nothing. We pretend grading is objective. We pretend that a revision policy acknowledges and encourages the point of view that writing is a process, and we'll go on attaching letters.

Reprehensio

But maybe the grading system isn't all that bad. People can glance at a student's transcript, for instance, and see that he or she has been consistent, has stuck with a four or five year commitment and is thus, perhaps, a good bet as an employee or a graduate student. Certainly a slim, two page transcript is a lot easier to look at then a thick sheaf of written evaluations such as make up the "transcript" of students from colleges such as Evergreen, in Washington State, where there are no grades. Employers, or Graduate Committees can thus rely on the letter grades—the thumbnail evaluations of unknown professors. Condensing a series of letter grades to a single GPA makes the process even more efficient. Kristina is not a woman who has worked her way back from despair through determination, self honesty, and a willingness to communicate, a woman who has learned not only how to deal with these things, but to communicate some of it through writing—she's a 3.25. We can be objective, keeping personal matters personal.

But—as this obviously biased portrayal points out—numbers and grades dehumanize, not only the people who are graded and numbered, but the people who do the grading, and eventually, the people who rely on that grading to make decisions. What they do is enable people to judge without engaging in the process of interpretation, without having to do the very same thing we're trying to teach them—to take a look at facts, evaluations, and interpretations, and then to examine and test them, to come up with judgements not as a snappy end, an instant assessment, but as an intermediate stage in a learning process.

Perhaps we can even say that the problem with grades is the problem with education in general these days. What matters, as far as the student's bottom line is concerned, is that they do what professors demand in order to get an A. What they've *actually* learned, or what the course is attempting to teach them, doesn't matter. I'm a good case in point. I learned how to pass French tests without learning French. I can get an A, I can't speak the language. What have I learned? How to take tests? Same with math. Same with just about any course which calls for the recitation of facts rather than an interpretation, or evaluation of the facts—for classes which dump the time consuming process of writing, and of evaluating ideas in favor of easily computable numbers.

Peroratio

So—by "grading" students, we judge writing out of context, and at odds to teaching the writing process. What makes it difficult for writing instructors is that we can't *not* see the humanity of our students. They *write* about it, even if ineffectively, in every piece. In fact, it is their very ineptness, in many cases, which makes them most human because they aren't good enough writers to hide themselves. Faced with their emotions, thoughts, growth—and even our own love for them (for how can you not love them?), we cannot dehumanize them with a letter—yet do.

An essay is not a student, of course, but is writing—and as such it can be talked about as a craft, as a means of both conveying and developing ideas, with forms for doing it better given certain contexts. Professionals are not graded by critics. If their craftsmanship is bad—this is pointed out. If their *ideas* are bad, they are challenged, not with a C-, but with more ideas, with questions, or even advice—or worst of all, silence.

Until we end this need to attach quantities to qualitative matters, we are going to have problems developing those qualities which enable our students to produce good writing, to use writing as a means of thought and expression, to function in our complex, post-capitalist, industrial society, and to find the means to live a more connected life, a life in which simplistic numbered quantities are overthrown in favor of the rich complexity of qualities and changes life seems to be when you open it up to interpretation.

Grades Suck

Rewrite

Keith Irwin

Keith Irwin   **Rewrite**

Grades Suck

There's a stack of papers on my desk—all of varying quality or seriousness. Each represents a stage in the development of a writer, and a stage in the writing process. That's how I'll respond to them, anyway, at least as far as margin and ending comments are concerned. But I'll also be assigning a grade, and to me, assigning a grade is like judging meat. The farmer, the feed, the cow's quality of life—none of that matters. Just fat content, taste, quality.

When I passed these papers back the students will flip to the back page, not to see what I think about their subject matter, or style, but to see what the grade is. If they get an "A," they'll be relieved. If not, they'll be upset, perhaps, or resigned, but they'll be interested in "figuring me out," figuring out what I want, how to grow a cow to get that grade "A" rating. Will they be thinking about how to adjust their writing process? Probably not. If they're like me, they'll wonder why I didn't tell them what I wanted in the first place. The last thing they'll think about is the process they went through to develop the paper, especially since, apparently, it didn't work. They didn't get an A, the real purpose for writing the paper in the first place.

According to current composition theory, writing is a process, and in order to get our students to produce good writing and to use writing as a means of learning material in later classes and careers, we must teach this process. But this is not what we "grade" when we grade. A student who re-drafts, peer-edits, collaborates and develops, but whose paper is largely unsuccessful, less aesthetically pleasing, or less effective at its purpose (pick your own criteria), gets a "C." A student who "off the cuff" writes an excellent paper and goes through the motions of the process activities, such as peer editing, revision, invention exercises and the like, gets an "A". The hidden message is that teachers don't reward students for mastering the writing process, but for producing end products, regardless, or in spite of, the process.

But isn't a successful paper the result of a successful process? Aren't those students who get less than an "A" in need of some "process" adjustment? Of course. The process oriented approach to teaching composition emphasizes that the process is different for everyone, and that students must find their own way. A grade on a paper, then, is a signal to students that they must adjust their writing process in order to get a better grade. That's what we would like to think, anyway, and that's certainly the aspect of grading I'll be emphasizing to my students.

And, I must admit, grading works for the more motivated students, the students who already have confidence in their abilities to do college level work. In fact, just about anything works for this type of student. But the message a grade implies, even for such students, is that the process doesn't matter: it's the product. Because a writing process is not "objective" in the sense that you can follow rules and have them always work, it becomes something that doesn't really matter, since just about any process is valid. It's the paper that matters. And, ultimately, why *not* think this way. Isn't a book judged by whether or not people read it? Aren't other pieces of writing judged by whether or not they work or produce the intended effect in a certain context?

Yes. Undoubtedly. But this is not what composition classes are for, comp theory tells us. They're supposed to show students how to learn, how to use writing as a way to learn, and how to see, make adjustments to, and develop the process by which they convert experience into writing, into the language which is the medium of knowledge.

Grades, by carrying the underlying message that papers, and by extension, learning, is to be graded as a "product" subverts the learning process. One solution might be that we can include the "process" in the grade—so many points for rough drafts, freewrites, brainstorms, and peer editing comments. But doesn't this just turn the whole process, and all its techniques into a giant, elaborate product?

For me, the whole problem is the concept of grading in the first place. What would work better is that students set their own goals in consultation with the instructor, and then revise their papers until those goals are reached, in both the instructor's and the students' estimation. In a sense, the teacher and the student collaborate, the teacher offering feedback and experience, the student offering subject material, goals, and style. At the end of this process, the student "passes,' and goes on to his or her education with, hopefully, a sense that he or she and the professors and the university are all in it together, as explorers rather than as master/servant pairs.

But this kind of learning, this kind of acknowledgement of individuality, mutuality and collaboration has its own problems in the classroom setting. For instance, if students work on their own individual pieces of writing, and their own set of goals, what would be the purpose of meeting in a classroom? What would the students work on together if, for instance, papers were not due on any particular day? How could students help each other, and thus learn how to help themselves, if they are all working on separate, perhaps totally different projects?

One solution is Nancy Atwell's, in which class time is where students can write, and where they can get help from the teacher, or from other students. Another might be to jump right in and have students learn about and learn from the other students' projects, perhaps helping each other decide when a project is finished enough.

But aside from all this consideration of practical matters, what seems clear to me is that with current composition theory's avocation of the idea that process is what we teach, and that products are never really finished, the grading process, which emphasizes product, is counter "product"ive, so to speak.

What it ultimately comes down to, for me, as a teacher, as a human being interacting with other human beings, is that I don't want to put grades on my students' papers. I feel like I am evaluating their papers as products, and ultimately, I feel as if I am evaluating *them* as products because their papers are about personal things, events that matter to them, and with which they are still emotionally involved, even if only as a result of writing the paper. I'll grade them, but in order to do it I have to abstract myself a little, and them, too—and in the end, I feel, at grading time, like an inspector at a meat packing plant, treating papers, the people they came from, like dead meat.

Postmodernism and Composition:
The Event

First Draft

Tom Connelly

Tom Connelly   **First Draft**

Postmodernism and Composition: The Event

I am a composition teacher. I instruct twenty-nine students, three days a week, in a room roughly the size of a large studio apartment. Initially, the construction of the room was a little alien to me. As a student I was more familiar with the traditional "English" classroom. Such rooms are usually laid out so that a student can stare at either a teacher, who sits in front of a chalkboard (s)he will use once or twice a semester, or the doorway. Throughout a semester my gaze would move from the figure at the head of the classroom to the doorway, the doorway to the figure, thousands of times. It was like some kind of phantom tennis match: teacher to exit, responsibility or freedom. These two focal points were a constant reminder that I always had a choice, that I always had a way out.

As a composition teacher, in a room I imagine to be almost the size of the "Romper Room" set, I find that the comfortable dynamics of my former classrooms are perversely reversed. The doorway is now on the other side of the room, and there are twenty-nine students barring my way. It is a little unnerving, as well as confining. I have actually been trying, for the past month, to physically position myself in relation to my classroom, trying to find where in the equation of student, teacher, exit, I belong.

One of strategies I have tried is to be as equivocal, and self-effacing as possible. I stand in front of my students as a teacher while at the same time reminding them that I am also a student, that I am of the same generation they are, listening to the same music, watching the same movies, etc. Basically I suck up, but it is only a stalling tactic until I become comfortable with the position of the door.

In order to keep this strange relationship with my students alive, I fashioned lessons around a postmodern notice that "truth" is a social construct. My students and I, for example, collectively establish the criteria by which we will judge each others work. We discuss theoretical issues concerning the process of writing, asking such questions as What is a text? What does it mean to write? During these exercises I do not posit myself as a teacher in the traditional sense; rather, I act as a secretary, organizing and writing down everyone's ideas.

When it comes to issues of management and classroom structure, however, I revert to an oppositional relationship with my students. I make it clear that this is no longer a democracy, that I have the authority to conduct the class as I see fit. So far this heuristic juggling act has worked. But it has created an atmosphere that I believe has led to an impasse.

The trouble began on the first day of peer editing. Each student had come to class with a rough draft and was prepared to present their paper to a group. For the next forty minutes I literally became obsolete. The students were on their own, hopefully discussing what a good paper sounded like, what phrases worked or did not work for them. I, on the other hand, was left in the uncomfortable position of finding a place to simply "be." It was as if I were in a dance hall, when the music suddenly starts and everyone pairs off, leaving me the odd man out. I didn't know where to go. Did I try to blend into a group of students? Or did I retreat to the head of the classroom?

Mistakenly, I chose the former.

At this point, we were about twenty minutes into class. The group of which I was observing had just finished listening to the first paper. They were in a small circle blocking the doorway, trying to get as far away as possible from the background noise. I looked past their shoulders out into a hallway to see a somewhat familiar looking student slowly approach. It had been about a week since I had seen this student last. And even then, I remember, he was twenty minutes late. He quietly came in, trying to make as little noise as possible, and looked around to get his bearings. Then, realizing that his group was the one I was in, he sat down, opened a spiral and began the bewildering task of absorbing the assignment. The confusion in his downcast eyes (a cheap ploy for sympathy, I mentally noted) made it clear to me that he had no idea what was going on. I was certain that if I told him some nonsense like we were each going over our Christmas wish lists today, or our special letters to the President or Brad Pitt, he wouldn't have even blinked.

This student makes me nervous. I know that sooner or later I am going to have to play the bad teacher and ask him why he even bothers to come to class. Part of me is hoping that he will just fade away. He could become a silent face that I will never have to confront, only assign the befitting "F" to and get on with my life. So far, he has made it easy for me. He has never come up after class with the audacity to ask "Sorry I was late, you are not going to count me absent are you?" Nor has he approached me with a cavalier, "Hey, you may not know me since I never come to class, but have I missed any assignments?" I was beginning to feel the urge to say something to this student, something I wasn't ready or prepared to deal with. So instead, I pretended that a group on the other side of the room desperately needed my attention.

In this group I have a student who is afraid to write. She has asked repeatedly why she must work on her writing skills when she is just as capable, and more comfortable, with speaking. At first I thought this was just a ruse to soften me up, to make it easier for her to submit second-rate work. I no longer believe that. I tried to counter her arguments about writing, but she always had a flippant response. "How about when you need to write a letter?" I might ask. She prefers to use the phone. "What about leaving a simple note to a friend?" She reminds me that there is always voice-mail. "Well, I find that when I am trying to remember something, writing notes usually helps." She claims to have a photographic memory. I have stopped trying to win such circular arguments with her, consoling myself that the rest of the world will prove her wrong.

Today she was not in good spirits, and I was pretty sure I knew why. I began the difficult task of convincing her that writing is not something to be afraid of. Big mistake. Sometimes you can feel the air around someone becoming heavier, more constricted, as if that person were choking on their own emotion. I felt that air of anxiety around this student. She was unsure of herself, unsure of her paper, unsure of her ability to continue in this class. I could tell that if I were to press the issue with her, ask what traumatic event occurred that could create such a panic, she would be in tears. Rather than witness my class crumble under this emotional flood, I realized then that it was probably best if I, the teacher, wasn't around. I got up and carefully hid myself at the head of the class.

My initial reaction to the day's events was minimal; I didn't think anything that had occurred was of any real importance—just something as a teacher I had to confront. After later consideration, however, I realized that the spectacle touched on the theoretical issues that I had been grappling with, I was unsure about all this postmodern stuff that I had been reading about. I was unsure about how I should use theory in my teaching. It became clear to me that the trouble I had in the classroom was symptomatic of this confusion.

The two students, I believe, represent opposite extremes of what is required of me as a teacher. The first student is a complete enigma. I don't know why he comes to class; I just know he doesn't have a chance of getting a passing grade. The loose style that I have adopted in order to teach only alienates him. His failure to attend the preliminary classes which explained my process, has made it impossible for him to comprehend what is going on. Since the syllabus offers only a general framework of what is required each day, he has no reference to find out what assignments he has missed or what was covered. What goes on in the classroom, the social interaction, etc., is the class—something that cannot be duplicated outside that particular time and place. Any corrective action would, therefore, necessitate the student being able to recreate the classroom experience outside of its social context. He would, in effect, have to play the roles of teacher and student. Since this is not possible, he remains anonymous.

The other student is a postmodernist's dream. She operates in a purely oral medium, focusing on her abilities as a listener and speaker at the expense of her writing. She wishes to abandon the semester's six paper structure, hoping instead for a dialogue between each member of the class. She too, will become marginalized. She will become weighed down by that unnameable restraint, ultimately failing to impart her ideas to the other students and me. Anonymity, for her, is also imminent.

The preceding experience offers me no solutions; rather, it only highlights the extent of my problem. My inability to come to terms with my role as a teacher: that is, how I should position myself in the classroom, also affects the way students position themselves with regards to me. In an attempt to be both things—the traditional teacher as well as one of the students—I have succeeded, in at least to examples, of being neither.

Postmodernism and Composition:
The Event

Rewrite

Tom Connelly

Tom Connelly   **Rewrite**

Postmodernism and Composition: The Event

"But you're always joking"—*one of my students on why he and others failed to do homework I previously assigned in class*

The preceding quote makes me a little uncomfortable. It reminds me of what Alec Guinness's character must have felt like at the end of "The Bridge Over the River Kwai." In the last moments of the movie, he realizes that building a bridge in the "English" manner probably wasn't such a great idea. The bridge, after all, was for the Japanese war effort, which was against England (WWII was in full swing at the time). Guinness's character then gets to utter the terrific line—"My God what have I done?"—and die, blowing up his bridge in the process. As a teacher of Writing Composition, I am not so lucky.

Okay, maybe I am exaggerating a bit. After my student complained that he couldn't differentiate between my sarcasm any my lecture (or in this case, when I am assigning homework or just joking about it), I didn't feel that I had just committed treason. What I did feel, however, was a sense of disappointment, a sense that maybe the ways I present myself to my class should be more defined.

Throughout the semester I have adopted a posture in front of my students that is both equivocal and self-effacing. I stand in front of them as a teacher while reminding them that I am also a student, that I am of the same generation as they, listening to the same music, watching the same movies, etc. Basically I suck up, but I remind myself that it is only a stalling tactic until I can become more comfortable with my teaching.

To keep this strange relationship with my students alive, I fashion lessons around the postmodern notion that "truth" is a social construct. My students and I, for example, collectively establish the criteria by which we will judge each other's work. We discuss theoretical issues concerning the process of writing, asking such questions as What are texts? and What should we as readers, expect from them? During these exercises I do not posit myself as a teacher in the traditional sense: rather, I act as a secretary, organizing and writing down everyone's ideas.

When it comes to issues of management and classroom structure, however, I revert to an oppositional relationship with my students. I make it clear that this is no longer a democracy, that I have the authority to conduct the class as I see fit. So far this heuristic juggling act has worked. Yet as the introductory quote suggests, it may not have worked very well.

On the first day of peer editing, for example, each student came to class with a rough draft and was prepared to present his/her paper to a group. For the next forty minutes I became obsolete. The students were on their own, hopefully discussing what at good paper sounded like, what phrases worked or did not work for them. I, on the other hand, was left in the uncomfortable position of finding a place to simply "be." It was as if I were in a dance hall and everyone had a partner except me. I didn't know if I should try to blend into a group of students, or retreat to the head of the classroom.

Mistakenly, I chose the former.

At this point, we were about twenty minutes into class. The group that I was observing had just finished listening to the first paper. They were in a small circle near the doorway, trying to get away from the background noise. I looked past their shoulders out into a hallway to see a familiar looking student slowly approach. It had been about a week since I had seen this student last. Even then, I remembered, he was twenty minutes late. He quietly came in, trying to make as little noise as possible, and looked around to get his bearings. Then, realizing that his group was the one I was in, he sat down, opened a spiral and began the bewildering task of absorbing the assignment. The confusion in his downcast eyes made it clear to me that he had no idea what was going on.

This student made me nervous. I knew that sooner or later I was going to have to play the "bad" teacher and ask him why he even bothered to come to class. Part of me hoped that he would just fade away, that he would become a silent face that I would never have to confront. I only wanted to assign him an "F" for the course and forget him. Up to that point, it appeared that I was going to get my wish. He never came up after class to ask "Sorry I was late, you are not going to count me absent are you?" Nor did he ever approach me with a cavalier, "Hey, you may not know me since I never come to class, but have I missed any assignments?" Looking at him at the moment, I felt the urge to say something. I felt like I should somehow make an example out of him, so that other students would understand why this class was so important. The problem, however, was that I didn't feel that I could accomplish this without coming across as a mere distraction. I was confident that I could draw attention to his mistakes, but was unsure how shaming him was more relevant than actual peer-editing. Rather than deal with this issue, I pretended that a group on the other side of the room desperately needed my attention.

My initial reaction to peer-editing day was minimal; I didn't think anything that had occurred was very important—just something I as a teacher had to confront. After later consideration, however, I realized that the spectacle highlighted several problems with my relationship to my students. I was unsure about all this postmodern stuff that I had been reading about, yet was determined somehow to introduce it into the classroom. It became clear to me that the trouble I had was symptomatic of this contradiction.

Both my students, the one alluded to in the introduction and the one in peer-editing, illustrate the problematic nature of my heuristic balancing act. The peer editor was a complete enigma. I didn't know why he came to class; I just know he didn't have a chance of getting a passing grade. The loose style that I had adopted in order to teach, the constant switching of gears between my role as teacher and student, would only alienate him. It was as if we were all staging a play and he walked in not knowing who was acting and who was watching. I had designed the course so that the "knowledge" would be a social construct. His failure to attend, therefore, made it impossible for him to comprehend what was going on. The classroom, the social interaction, etc., was the class—something that could not be duplicated outside that particular time and place. Since any corrective measure was impossible, he remained anonymous.

The other student's situation was/is much more difficult to deal with. My role as a teacher became vague and subject to misinterpretation. I thought that a flippant, sarcastic tone in my lectures would engage my students more; I thought they would be more attentive if I tried to entertain as well as teach. The problem was that my teaching style was ambiguous (sarcasm seems to only work if it can be misread). My students were unsure when I was shifting gears, when I was the joking student, or the serious teacher.

The preceding experiences offer me no solutions; they only highlight the extent of my problem. My inability to come to terms with my role as a teacher— even I was unsure what mode I should be in during peer-editing—also affects the way students position themselves with regards to me. In an attempt to be both things: the traditional teacher as well as one of the students, I have succeeded, in being neither.

Peter England   **First Draft**

Losing and Winning

I decided to read aloud Jim Corder's wonderful essay, "Losing Out," to my two freshman composition classes. I had wanted to teach them something about writing, and somehow include the basic concepts of linguistic philosophy. My best classes have included some sort of subtle insight into how we communicate, and I wanted to pass that on to my students. The essay by Corder was, I thought, a good choice. Easy to read, and yet full of the sort of problems I wanted to present, this essay would really grab their attention. I could change lives.

My first class, an eight o'clock, slogged into the classroom weighted down by sleepy eyes and bad cafeteria food. I was bouncy and energetic, my voice ringing as I called the roll. Some of my energy was bound to rub off, so I spread it liberally about the room. Announcing the lesson plan for the day, I tried to hint to them the excitement in store, the revelations they would uncover, the inspiration they could gain, if only they would listen. As I prepared them, in my oh-so-professional way, I realized I was saying so many of the things I have heard from the most mediocre of teachers:

"I know this may not sound like fun, but I want you to listen."

"Now, don't focus on how hard this is, just relax and enjoy it." Immediately I ended with the lame, "OK, here we go," and began to read.

I read the first page, adding emphasis and emotion, dramatic pauses and light-heartedness. The humor was all there, if they would just listen. If they would just listen, the lesson would be learned. The second page seemed longer than the first, and I remembered to make eye contact. Each student in the room got an eyeful as I glared, meaningfully, at just the right phrases. I was a preacher, a priest, a heuristic holy man delivering a liturgy of literature. They would be inspired, damn it.

I realized suddenly that I could have complete thoughts on an entirely different subject, while still reading out loud. I began to plan the rest of the class, which questions I would ask and to whom, and what would be due on Friday. How could they not appreciate a teacher like me? What awards would I receive, which accolades would I garner?

The thirst came with the third page. I was glad to recall that only one more page remained. My throat was dry, but the message was so important I did not want to stop, I did not want to break the cycle of education that I had thoughtfully and carefully begun. I stumbled over a word, and realized that I had intonated an entire phrase incorrectly, losing its emphasis. I was lost. Which paragraph were we in? I found it, but not before the silence burned into me. I wondered if I had been monotoning while thinking my scholarly thoughts. I chanced a look out over my audience. Two pairs of eyes transfixed me, twenty-seven others studied the floor.

The last page whizzed by, the rhetoric catching them once again. That Corder sure is a great writer, I thought. He saved me from the fires of a freshman mutiny. I wound up reading.

Putting down the book, I waited for the questions. The air in the classroom was as motionless as though I had shot an albatross from the air. Now I had all the eyes focused on me, but now I didn't want them. Where were all the questions? Where were the looks of comprehension? The two students who had been paying attention looked oddly satisfied, but the others looked like they were caught in the headlights of a truck. What to do? I barked out some stuff about Friday, then relieved us all of embarrassment by letting them go about two minutes early.

I collected assorted late papers and re-writes as they exited, then shuffled off the next class. Gathering strength from remembered images of the two faithful watchers, I charged up the stairs to the third flood and my other classroom. This class, the nine o'clock, would surely be more influenced. They would be more awake, more attentive. I let them type away on their journals for a few minutes at the beginning of class. Walking around like a benevolent patriarch, I answered questions, nodding sagely, exuding wisdom and knowledge. Today you will learn something extraordinary, my persona said.

I called roll, then gave a brief introduction to the piece. Once again, I began to read Mr. Corder's excellent essay on writing and construction.

The thirst hit me immediately, before the end of the first page. In my will to create a meaningful experience, I had forgotten my water bottle in the last classroom. The nearest water fountain was halfway down the hall, too far to reach before their little attention spans had collapsed. I bullied my throat through to the middle of the second page, nodding, making eye contact, doing those real teacher things.

On the third page I squeaked. My voice kept ramming itself into the dry wall of my throat. The parched message drifted, lonely, across the background noise of computer fans and electric hums. I began to panic, and wondered what to do. Then the lesson hit home to me: remember your own teachers, what would they have done? With confidence I finished the last paragraph on the third page and said, "Well, ya'll are smart. You don't have to hear the end. What did you think of that stuff?" That was all it took. The classroom discussion took up the rest of the class period, and I did not have to contribute more than a few words. The students took over.

What I had learned was that the students needed a message of hope, but it could not come from something read aloud, something canned and handed over to them. It had to be something directly from me to them. As it turned out, what they needed to hear was that they were adults, and did not have to have an essay read aloud to them in order to learn something. Only a few days before I had ridiculed the high school technique of assigning a reading, then standing in front of the class to tell them what they had read. These students could do that for themselves, they could meet their own meanings without the go-between of a teacher. All I had to do was tell them they could.

Since then I have realized that the meaningful classes in my past, which I wanted to recreate for my students, always demanded a great deal of attention from me. The instructors never lectured non-stop while light bulbs appeared mysteriously over pupils' heads. The best teachers spent much of their time watching, sometimes quieting the class so that a statement may be heard, but most often just setting ideas before the students and letting their minds feast upon the newness of the knowledge. Of course, the hardest part is letting go the first time. It is difficult to trust that your students can make it on their own. After all, they are your students, and they need you, right?

Peter England   **Rewrite**

Losing and Winning

I decided to read aloud Jim Corder's wonderful essay, "Losing Out," to my two freshman composition classes. I had wanted to teach them something about writing and somehow include insight into some basic concepts of linguistic philosophy. The best classes I have taken included some sort of subtle insight into how we communicate, and I wanted to pass that on to my students. The essay by Corder was, I thought, a good choice. Easy to read, and yet full of the sort of problems I wanted to present. This essay would really grab their attention. I could change lives.

My first class, an eight o'clock, slogged into the classroom weighted down by sleepy eyes and bad cafeteria food. I was bouncy and energetic, my voice ringing as I called the roll. Some of my energy was bound to rub off, so I spread it liberally about the room. Announcing the lesson plan for the day, I tried to hint to them the excitement in store, the revelations they would uncover, the inspiration they could gain, if only they would listen. If only they would listen, I prayed, with a glitter in my eye. I would show them how much they needed a teacher, especially one as erudite and knowledgeable as me. As I prepared them in my oh-so-professional way, I realized I was saying many of the things I have heard from my teachers, many of whom were uninspiring:

"I know this may not sound like fun, but I want you to listen."

"Now, don't focus on how hard this is, just relax and enjoy it." Immediately I ended with the lame, "OK, here we go," and began to read.

I read the first page, adding emphasis and emotion, dramatic pauses and light-heartedness. The humor was all there, if they would just listen. If they would just listen, the lesson would be learned. The second page seemed longer than the first, and I remembered to make eye contact. Each student in the room got an eyeful as I glared, meaningfully, at just the right phrases. I was a preacher, a priest, a heuristic holy man delivering a liturgy of literature. They would be inspired, damn it.

I realized suddenly that I could have complete thoughts on an entirely different subject, while still reading out loud. I began to plan the rest of the class, which questions I would ask and to whom, and what would be due on Friday. How could they not appreciate a teacher like me? What awards would I receive, which accolades would I garner?

The thirst came with the third page. I was glad to recall that only one more page remained. My throat was dry, but the message was so important I did not want to stop, I did not want to break the cycle of education that I had thoughtfully and carefully begun. I stumbled over the word "intertexuality", and realized that I had intonated an entire phrase as if it were a question, therefore losing its emphasis. I was lost. Which paragraph were we in? I found it, but not before the silence burned into me. I wondered if I had been monotoning while thinking my scholarly thoughts. I chanced a look out over my audience. Two pairs of eyes transfixed me, twenty-seven others studied the floor.

The last page whizzed by, the rhetoric catching them once again. I could see the focus in their eyes and knew that they were no longer thinking about the early hour. That Corder sure is a great writer, I thought. I wish I could write so personally and in such an insightful way. He saved me from the fires of a freshman mutiny by describing his own creation through written language. I wound up reading.

Putting down the book, I waited for the questions. The air in the classroom was as motionless as though I had shot an albatross from the air. Now I had all the eyes focused on me, but now I didn't want them. Where were all the questions? Where were the looks of comprehension? The two students who had been paying attention looked oddly satisfied, but the others looked like the ghostly crew of a phantom ship. What to do? I barked out some stuff about Friday, then relieved us all of embarrassment by letting them go about two minutes early.

I collected assorted late papers and re-writes as they exited, then shuffled off to the next class. Gathering strength from remembered images of the two faithful watchers, I charged up the stairs to the third flood and my other classroom. This class, the nine o'clock, would surely be more influenced. They would be more awake, more attentive. I let them type away on their journals for a few minutes at the beginning of class. Walking around like a benevolent patriarch, I answered questions, nodding sagely, exuding wisdom and knowledge. Today you will learn something extraordinary, my persona said.

I called roll, then gave a brief introduction to the piece. Once again, I began to read Mr. Corder's excellent essay on writing and construction.

The thirst hit me immediately, before the end of the first page. In my will to create a meaningful experience, I had forgotten my water bottle in the last classroom. The nearest water fountain was halfway down the hall, too far to reach before their little attention spans had collapsed. I bullied my throat through to the middle of the second page, nodding, making eye contact, doing those real teacher things.

On the third page I squeaked. My voice kept ramming itself into the dry wall of my throat. The parched message drifted, lonely, across the background noise of computer fans and electric hums. I began to panic, and wondered what to do. Then the lesson hit home to me: think of your own best teachers, and what they would have done. With confidence restored I finished the last paragraph on the third page and said, "Well, ya'll are smart. You don't have to hear the end. What did you think of that stuff?" That was all it took. The classroom discussion took up the rest of the class period, and I did not have to contribute more than a few words. The students took over. They wanted to explore how it is a person could be created through the medium of the written word. Is language really the glass through which we view the world, they asked, and can we ever escape the discourse and see, really see, with unblurred eyes? Maybe they were not quite so flowery, but those were the questions they asked. I had to kick them out of the classroom so the next group of students could come in. They left reluctantly, in true student form, wanting some more answers and willing to think in order to get them.

What I had learned was that the students needed a message of hope, but it could not come from something read aloud, something canned and handed over to them. It had to be something directly from me to them. As it turned out, what they needed to hear was that they were adults, and did not have to have an essay read aloud to them in order to learn something. Only a few days before I had ridiculed the high school technique of assigning a reading, then standing in front of the class to tell them what they had read. These students could do that for themselves, they could meet their own meanings without the go-between of a teacher. All I had to do was tell them they could.

Since then I have realized that the meaningful classes in my past, which I wanted to recreate for my students, always demanded a great deal of attention from me. The instructors never lectured non-stop while light bulbs appeared mysteriously over pupils' heads. The best teachers spent much of their time watching, sometimes quieting the class so that a statement may be heard, but most often just setting ideas before the students and letting their minds feast upon the newness of the knowledge. Of course, the hardest part is letting go the first time. It is difficult to trust that your students can make it on their own. After all, they are your students, and they need you, right?

The Disappearing Teacher

First Draft

Jim Burrows

Jim Burrows   **First Draft**

The Disappearing Teacher

I am seven years old. My grandfather, recovering from open-heart surgery, lies in bed beside me with his hands folded over his chest, over the long dividing scar. I am reading aloud to him from a book called *Foxfire*. It is evening, early fall, and an uncertain breeze comes in through the open window. Between sentences, I can hear trucks droning by on the distant highway. When I pronounce the word "millenium," my grandfather's chest begins heaving, and he squeezes out a wheezing, painful laugh as I watch the scar jump. The scar is horrific to me, a long ridge of raised, tender skin. I am thinking it is the color of a sunset, of drying blood, and that if I touched it, the skin would split open and I would see his heart. My grandfather never finished grammar school; I know he is laughing in astonishment, and with pride, at my ability to read such words as "millenium," words that he cannot read. My little boy's fierce sense of duty is all that keeps me beside him, for although I am afraid of my grandfather's chest, with its long, sore furrow of violation and the damaged muscle underneath, I want more than anything to please him. I read until his breathing deepens and he seems to sink, warm and sleeping, into the bed beside me.

I am twelve years old. Mrs. Bonham, my sixth grade teacher, has asked us to write a story. My story is about Luke Johnson, a famous basketball player. For the last two days, instead of playing basketball after school with my playground buddies, I have walked excitedly home alone to work on my story. I am in love with Mrs. Bonham because she is beautiful, and because when she read aloud to us from Where the Red Fern Grows, she was unable to finish and left the room crying. Now she reads aloud from my story. Her chestnut hair is pulled back into a pony tail, but a few reddish brown ribbons hang down. These she brushes back, tucking them behind her ears with one hand as she reads, holding my story with the other. She looks up and winks at me as she finishes. My writing career has officially begun.

I am twenty years old. Keith Long, the instructor in my first creative writing class, has called me into his office. Now, as I wait, he sits behind his desk, rereading my poem, sipping occasionally from a can of Dr. Pepper. Mr. Long has a grotesque case of psoriasis, and his knuckles and forearms are covered with scaly red flaking patches. The skin of his hands is leathery and mottled, and their unexplained, constant tremble is communicated to the sheet of paper he holds in them. I have read the poem already in class, and my fellow students have complimented me on it. They have suggested few changes, though I do not remember even these. His eyebrows raise as he hands the poem back to me, and he shakes his head slightly and smiles. "This is a hell of a poem," he says. Then he begins talking to me about publication, about where I should send my poem, how I should prepare it. He is serious. Behind him, through the window of his third story office, I see the plush green campus lawn and the few residential streets and houses beyond; beyond these, miles of wheatfields blaze toward the horizon, where towering gray walls of cumulonimbus cloud are built. I try to focus on Mr. Long's words to stop the sensation of falling, and to detract my attention from the overwhelming clarity of the tableau outside that window, where something seems to have fallen away and my future opens before me.

I am twenty-seven years old. I teach composition. My students are gathered into groups of three and four, editing each other's papers as I sit at my desk, half pretending to read. They have devised constitutions for this purpose. They seem at ease. Doan and Blakely, obviously sidetracked, are laughing. Andrea, who strikes me as a born leader, holds a pen in her right hand as she speaks to her group members, punching her most salient points with it, conducting the symphony of her thought. Angelique nods. Steve seems disinterested, slumped down in his chair, his legs crossed at the ankles. In group four, Jason, the only member of the class who calls me by my first name, is hunched over his desk, peering around the class. Krystyl is talking loudly, and although I can hear her voice above the other snippets of discussion that leap out at me, I have no idea what she is talking about, except that it seems to have nothing to do with writing. Sandra, who graduated high school twenty years ago, is the only member of the class who seems to be uncomfortable. Her pale blue eyes seem to have become fiercer, faceted with desperation. Her forehead is shiny, and her cheeks are blotched with tones of peach and scarlet. Although she is older than me, she comes closer to being a member of my generation than any of my other students. When she looks up, sighing, and catches me watching her, I raise my eyebrows and look away. Sorry. I have suddenly closed my mouth to prevent the word from escaping.

I am thinking I know why Sandra is uncomfortable with peer editing. She is a woman approaching middle age, and she feels foolish among these children. Furthermore, the subject of her essay is delicate. She is writing about a murder which was committed by one of her best friends many years ago. The friend had confessed to Sandra—only to her. Sandra had gone to the police, turned in her best friend, and had sat there at the trial almost a year later as her friend was sentenced to life in prison without the possibility of parole. Sandra told me she felt she had taken a life just as her friend had. "For years, I've tried to forget about this," she told me, "I don't know why I want to dredge it up again now, after all the therapy and after putting it behind me, but I do. It just seems necessary."

"Then it is," I said. We had this discussion in the privacy of my office. Now when she looks at me in class, I feel I have somehow let her down.

After class, Ashli waits for me at the door. Ashli strikes me as diametrically opposed to Sandra in many ways. She is young and attractive, a tall willowy blonde, an animated Barbie Doll, whereas Sandra is overweight, with epicene features further androgenized by a careless, mop-like haircut. The only thing they seem to have in common is that they are both good writers, though for different reasons. Ashli has real talent—language aptitude, literary instinct, and a poet's sense of the aesthetic moment, a penchant for producing the shimmering turn of phrase or terse, resonant statement at just the right moment. Sandra, though, possesses the other necessary quality all good writers share—real sincerity in regard to writing. She is a good writer because her subject—her life—demands that she be good; because she feels it is incumbent upon her, "necessary," she had said, to do it justice.

Ashli is asking about her proposed topic for the next essay. I tell her it's fine. Then I ask her about peer editing.

"It's okay," she says. "I just don't think my other group members are helping me much."

"Are you helping them?" I ask.

"Well," she says, "I think I am. We usually spend a lot of time working on their papers, and not much on mine."

"Why?" I ask, knowing the answer.

"I think," she begins, "It's because they don't want to talk about my writing." I finish for her. "They don't feel their criticism is justified?"

"Maybe," she says.

I tell her that peer editing should be seen as a chance to help each other, not hurt each other. Then I say something that will badger me for the rest of the night. "Peer editing is just that way," I admit to her. "The people who are really talented and who come to class with a polished essay aren't going to get as much out of it, but the people who need the most help are going to benefit from your insight and ability."

At this, Ashli gives me a weary look. I can tell she appreciates the compliment, but I also think I see confusion creeping into her face, or maybe I'm just searching her features for a hint, some expression that will tell me how I'm supposed to feel about what I just said.

It is two weeks later. Ashli and Sandra have spoken to me in conference, and their papers have improved, and they know how impressed I am with their writing. They no longer seem lost.

Last night, there was a lunar eclipse. The moon glowed an eerie blood-red behind a dark gauze of clouds. I took it as a sign of providence when, rummaging through the wreckage of my bedroom, I found a computer disk filled with old poems and essays I had written as an undergraduate years ago. I slid the disk into my computer, and read myself as my teachers must have read me then, equally impressed and frustrated. I was also embarrassed, literally. The words glowing on that computer screen, the person who had written them, tugged at some old forgotten blood deep inside of me, pulling it warm and pulsing into my face, the way the earth's gravitational field, on rare occasions, pulls blood into the moon. Reading my juvenalia, I realized that everything I have ever written that I care about—every poem, essay or story—was written with the explicit goal of pleasing someone I perceived at that time to be my literary superior or equal.

As a creative writing student, I have been told repeatedly that the most important relationship is between the writer and his writing, that the writer must write for himself. I don't believe this. I've never written anything well that wasn't a thinly veiled plea for affirmation as a writer from someone whose opinion I respected, and I'm not generous with that kind of respect. I've always written primarily for my teachers, not my colleagues.

Peer editing, I think, is a very useful classroom exercise. It emphasizes revision. It can help students validate their own critical voices. It fosters essay writing as the communication of meaningful thought and emotion, not just sentences strung together in support of a thesis. In spite of these positive aspects, I am wary of peer editing, just as I am wary of other exercises that have been introduced into writing courses during the shift from product-oriented methods of teaching composition to process-oriented instruction.

I am discomforted by such strategies as collaborative learning, freewriting, and peer editing, and not just because I sometimes feel useless as an instructor while they're going on. I don't know how the fragmentation of literary theory over the past thirty years—the advent of gender theory and reader response in particular—has affected methods of teaching composition. Nor is it possible to measure the effects of the great proliferation of creative writing programs in American universities over the last few decades. But I do know that composition classes are becoming more and more like writing workshops, in which the teacher is not a teacher at all, but more of a moderator who helps the students help themselves. In writing workshops, the channels of energy do not go from student to professor and back to student; the class is seen as a community of writers working with each other under the leadership of a senior writer.

In conferences, I hear myself telling students to be more creative. "Show, don't tell," I say. "Use more dialogue. Begin with narration." I tell them to write from personal experience, to be honest and sincere. I find myself, in my comments, referring to essays as "poetic," "good stories," or to essay writers as "good storytellers." I tell them they can make things up. I especially like to tell them that they don't have to try to plug their own thoughts and ideas, which are precise and unique, into a formulated five paragraph paradigm. I hear my colleagues saying similar things to their students. I am happy for all of this, and I think my students are too.

And yet I fear, when I recognize this trend, that the teaching of composition is in danger of going down the long, sad slide to "workshopping." As a creative writing student, I have been privy to many workshops. I've taken fiction and poetry workshops as both an undergraduate and graduate student. I've written short stories, "creative" essays, formal poetry, free verse, "flash fiction," "prose poetry," and one lamentable screenplay. If ever there was a product of the workshop system, I'm it, and yet I know that the quality of my output in every workshop I've ever taken was directly proportional to my perception of the instructor's critical or literary abilities. In some workshops, the instructors let so much of the burden of criticism fall on the students, and fostered such a relativistic, "anything goes" attitude, that my work suffered despite my best efforts.

Teachers of composition, I think, are becoming more and more activity-oriented. They are becoming less authoritative in the classroom. Composition classrooms are becoming more and more like workshops, where the burdens of criticism are dispersed throughout the class, where students' possibilities for becoming successful writers are more interrelated than ever before. This is a hopeful trend, but I also see an inherent danger in it. It probably raises the general level of writing among composition students. The worst students get better, the average students probably get better; the best students, the ones with real talent and conviction as writers, are the ones who suffer. These students, in effect, are taking on some of the burden of the instructor by becoming the most avid editors and critics in peer editing groups, and by dominating their collaborative learning groups. Many of these students view writing as a personal, laborious activity, which it is, and so they probably don't benefit nearly as much from free writing exercises either.

As I teach process, I sometimes feel envious of those instructors of my past who expected a polished product from me and who judged that product based on what it was, not what I might become. I also wonder, remembering those teachers, why writing, the actual business of it, the process, seems always to have been so secret. I'm not sure I know why, but I think I have an idea. When I write, I shut myself up in my room, and turn the lights down, and sometimes unplug the telephone, and what I do during that time is secret, and I am ashamed of it. I am ashamed of it because the words, as they come, are not good enough for Mrs. Bonham, or Mr. Long, or any other teacher whose affirmation I need, because I am still writing for those teachers; they're not good enough even for my nearly illiterate grandfather, dead now ten years. I still feel sometimes, even with all I know about the process of writing, that the actual act of writing is a secret, lonely act; that first drafts are dreadful secrets, things to keep hidden, and that these feelings, which strike me as a curious mixture of shame and price, are necessary to great writing.

The Disappearing Teacher

Rewrite

Jim Burrows

Jim Burrows   **Rewrite**

The Disappearing Teacher

I am seven years old. My grandfather, recovering from open-heart surgery, lies in bed beside me with his hands folded over his chest, over the long dividing scar that stretches above the collar of his undershirt. I am reading aloud to him from a book called *Foxfire*. It is evening, early fall, and an uncertain breeze comes in through the open window. Between sentences, I can hear trucks droning by on the distant highway. When I pronounce the word "millenium," my grandfather's chest begins to heave, and he squeezes out a wheezing, painful laugh as I watch the scar jump. The scar is horrific to me, a long ridge of raised, tender skin. I am thinking it is the color of certain sunsets, of drying blood, and that if I touched it, the skin would split open, and I would see his heart. My grandfather is functionally illiterate, having never finished grammar school; I know he is laughing in astonishment, and with pride, at my ability to easily read such words as "millenium," words that he would have to sound out phonetically. My little boy's fierce sense of duty is all that keeps me beside him, for although I am afraid of my grandfather's chest, with its long, sore furrow of violation and the damaged muscle underneath, I want more than anything to please him; not just because he is my grandfather, but because he is an authority figure in my life who has recognized an ability of mine, someone whose opinion I respect. I read until his breathing deepens and he seems to sink, warm and sleeping, into the bed beside me.

I am twelve years old. Mrs. Bonham, my sixth grade teacher, has asked us to write a story. My story is about Luke Johnson, a famous basketball player. For the last two days, instead of playing basketball after school with my playground buddies, I have walked excitedly home alone to work on my story. I am in love with Mrs. Bonham because she is beautiful, and because when she read aloud to us from *Where the Red Fern Grows*, she was unable to finish and left the room crying. Now she reads aloud from my story. Her chestnut hair is pulled back into a pony tail, but a few reddish brown ribbons hang down. These she brushes back, tucking them behind her ears with one hand as she reads, holding my story with the other. She looks up and winks at me as she finishes. My writing career has officially begun.

I am twenty years old. Keith Long, the instructor in my first creative writing class, has called me into his office. Now, as I wait, he sits behind his desk, rereading my poem, sipping occasionally from a can of Dr. Pepper. Mr. Long has a grotesque case of psoriasis, and his knuckles and forearms are covered with scaly red flaking patches. The skin of his hands is leathery and mottled, and their unexplained, constant tremble is communicated to the sheet of paper he holds. I have read the poem already in class, and my fellow classmates have complimented me on it. The haven't suggested any changes; they've only given empty compliments. His eyebrows raise as he hands the poem back to me, and he shakes his head slightly and smiles. "This is a hell of a poem," he says. Then he begins talking to me about publication, about where I should send my poem, how I should prepare it. He is serious. Behind him, through the window of his third story office, I see the plush green campus lawn and the few residential streets and houses that border it; beyond these, miles of wheatfields blaze toward the horizon, where towering gray walls of cumulonimbus cloud are built. I try to focus on Mr. Long's words to stop the sensation of falling, and to detract my attention from the overwhelming clarity of the tableau outside that window, where something seems to have fallen away and my future opens before me. I have never thought of writing as a profession before. Coming from anybody else, it would seem absurd. I feel somehow that the thought of writing professionally, which seems an almost devious idea to me, has been presented to me for the first time.

I am twenty-seven years old. I teach writing. My students are gathered into groups of three and four, editing each other's papers as I sit at my desk, half pretending to read. They have devised constitutions for this purpose. They seem at ease. Doan and Blakely, obviously sidetracked, are laughing. Andrea, who strikes me as a born leader, holds a pen in her right hand as she speaks to her group members, punching her most salient points with it, conducting the symphony of her thought. Angelique nods. Steve seems disinterested, slumped down in his chair, his legs crossed at the ankles. In group four, Jason is hunched over his desk, peering around the classroom. Krystl is talking loudly, and although I can hear her voice above the other snippets of discussion that leap out at me, I have no idea what she is talking about, except that it seems to have nothing to do with writing. Sandra, who graduated high school twenty years ago, is the only member of the class who seems uncomfortable. Her pale blue eyes seem to have become fiercer, faceted with desperation. Her forehead is shiny, and her cheeks are blotched with tones of peach and scarlet. Although she is older than me, she comes closer to being a member of my generation than any of my other students. When she looks up, sighing, and catches me watching her, I raise my eyebrows and look away. *Sorry.* I have suddenly closed my mouth to prevent the word from escaping.

Why should I be sorry? I am thinking I know why Sandra is uncomfortable with peer editing. She is a woman approaching middle age, and she feels foolish among these children. Furthermore, the subject of her essay is delicate. She is writing about a murder which was committed by one of her best friends many years ago. The friend had confessed to Sandra—only to her. Sandra had gone to the police, turned in her best friend, and had sat there at the trial almost a year later as her friend was sentenced to life in prison without the possibility of parole. Sandra told me she felt *she* had taken a life, just as her friend had. "For years," she said, "I've tried to forget about this. I don't know why I want to dredge it up again now, after all the therapy and putting it behind me, but I do. It just seems necessary."

"Then it is," I said. We had this discussion in the privacy of my office. Now when she looks at me in class, I feel I have somehow let her down, that I have violated her trust. I feel this way because of my belief that although writing should seek to be universal, the process of writing is intensely personal. I know I don't like to share my drafts with anyone, especially when writing about myself and my life. I have a few friends I'll let read my drafts—not my best friends necessarily, but the ones whose opinions on writing I respect.

Ashli waits for me at the door after class. Ashli strikes me as diametrically opposed to Sandra in many ways. She is young and attractive, a tall willowy blonde; whereas, Sandra is pudgy, with epicene features further androgenized by a careless mop of a haircut. The only thing they seem to have in common is that they are both good writers, though for different reasons. Ashli has real talent—language aptitude, literary instinct, and a poet's sense of the aesthetic moment, a penchant for producing the shimmering turn of phrase. Her writing has an almost intangible, serendipitous quality. Sandra, though, possesses the other necessary quality common to all good writers: real sincerity in regard to writing. She is a good writer because her subject—her life—demands it, because she feels it is incumbent upon her—"necessary," she had said—to do it justice.

Ashli is asking about her proposed topic for the next essay. I tell her it's fine. Then I ask her about peer editing.

"It's okay," she says. "I just don't think my other group members are helping me much."

"Are you helping them?" I ask.

"Well," she says, "I think I am. We usually spend a lot of time working on their papers, and not much on mine."

"Why?" I ask, thinking I know the answer.

"I think," she begins, "it's because they don't want to talk about my writing." I finish for her. "They don't feel their criticism is justified?"

"Maybe," she says.

I tell her that peer editing should be seen as a chance to help each other, not hurt each other. Then I say something that will badger me for the rest of the day. "Peer editing is just that way," I tell her. "The people who are really talented and who come to class with a polished essay aren't going to get as much out of it, but the people who need the most help are going to benefit from your insight and ability."

At this, Ashli gives me a weary look. I can tell she appreciates the compliment, but I also think I see confusion creeping into her face, or maybe I'm just searching her features for a hint, some expression that will tell me how I'm supposed to feel about what I just said.

It is two weeks later. Ashli and Sandra have spoken to me in conference, and their papers have improved, and they know how impressed I am with their writing. We talked about the peer editing process. Sandra still seemed a little dismayed with it. Ashli seemed tolerant, but they both seemed resigned to it. Now, they no longer seem lost.

Last night, there was a lunar eclipse. The moon glowed an eerie blood-red behind a dark gauze of clouds. I took it as a sign of providence when, rummaging through the wreckage of my bedroom, I found a computer disk filled with old poems and essays I had written as an undergraduate years ago. I slid the disk into my computer, and read myself as my teachers must have read me then, equally impressed and frustrated. I was also embarrassed, literally. I actually blushed, there in my bedroom, alone. The words glowing on that computer screen, the person who had written them, tugged at some old forgotten blood inside me, pulling it warm and pulsing into my face, the way the earth's gravitational field, on rare occasions, seems to flush the moon with blood. Reading my juvenalia, I realized that everything I have ever written that I care about—every poem, every essay, every story—was written with the explicit goal of pleasing someone I perceived at that time to be my literary superior. I also realized that I've always viewed this mentor/student relationship as a very secretive one requiring the same kind of confidence an analyst affords her patient, or that a confessor would expect from a priest.

As a creative writing student, I have been told repeatedly that the most important relationship is between the writer and his writing, that the writer must write for himself. This is safe advice usually, but the thought behind it is entirely too simple. I've never written anything well that wasn't a thinly veiled plea for affirmation as a writer from someone whose opinion I respected, and I'm not generous with that kind of respect. I've always written primarily for my teachers, not my colleagues.

Peer editing, I think, is a very useful classroom exercise. It emphasized revision. It can help students find their critical voices. It fosters essay writing as the communication of meaningful thought and emotion, not just sentences strung together in support of a thesis. In spite of these positive aspects, I am wary of peer editing, just as I am wary of other exercises that have been introduced into writing courses during the shift from product-oriented methods of teaching composition to process-oriented instruction.

I am discomforted by such strategies as collaborative learning, free writing, and peer editing, and not just because I sometimes feel useless as an instructor while they're going on. I don't know how the fragmentation of literary theory over the past thirty years—the advent of gender theory and reader response in particular—has affected methods of teaching composition. Nor is it possible to measure the effects of the great proliferation of creative writing programs in American universities over the last few decades. But I do know that composition classes are becoming more and more like writing workshops, in which the teacher has become more of a moderator who helps the students help themselves and each other. In writing workshops, the channels of energy do not go from student to professor and back to student; the class is seen as a community of writers working with each other under the leadership of a senior writer.

In conferences, I hear myself telling students to be more creative. "Show, don't tell," I say. "Use more dialogue. Begin with narration." I tell them to write from personal experience, to be honest and sincere. I find myself, in my comments, referring to essays as "poetic," "good stories," or to essay writers as "good storytellers." I tell them they can make things up. I especially like to tell them that they don't have to try to plug their own thoughts and ideas, which are unique to them, into a formulated five paragraph paradigm. I hear my colleagues saying similar things to their students. I am happy for all of this, and I think my students are too.

Yet I fear, when recognizing this trend, that the teaching of composition is in danger of going down the long, sad slide to "workshopping." As a creative writing student, I have been privy to many workshops. I've taken fiction and poetry workshops as both an undergraduate and graduate student. I've written short stories, "creative" essays, formal poetry, free verse, "flash fiction," "prose poetry," and one lamentable screenplay. If ever there was a product of the workshop system, I'm it, but I know that the quality of my output in every workshop I've ever taken was directly proportional to my perception of the instructor's critical or literary abilities. In some workshops, the instructors let so much of the burden of criticism fall on the students and fostered such a relativistic, "anything goes" attitude, that my work suffered despite my best efforts. The classes didn't require my best efforts.

Teachers of composition, I think, are becoming less authoritative in the classroom, perhaps because the criterion for good writing, the conception of what is good, of what will suffice, has been changed so much by critical theory in recent decades. There's no longer a strong consensus. Composition classrooms are becoming more and more like workshops, where the burdens of criticism are dispersed throughout the class, where students' possibilities for becoming successful writers are more interrelated than ever before. This is a hopeful trend, but I also see an inherent danger in it. It probably raises the general level of writing among composition students. The worst students get better, the best students, the ones with real talent and conviction as writers, are the ones who suffer. As a young student of writing, I recoiled at professors who gave me a model, a paradigm of what was "good," and required me to write that way. I applaud efforts to focus on the process of writing, to demystify it and share its laboriousness and frustration.. But let's not throw the baby out with the bathwater. One positive aspect of that old method of teaching writing was that it fostered a mentor/student relationship and placed a great deal of emphasis on the professor's opinion. When we decenter the classroom, we necessarily dilute power, and what is "good" may become the subject of a debate which is beneath us.

As I teach process, I sometimes feel envious of those instructors of my past who expected a polished product from me and who judged that product based on what it was, not what I might become. I also wonder, remembering those teachers, why writing, the actual business of it, the process, seems always to have been such a closely guarded secret. I'm not sure I know why, but I think I have an idea. When I write, I shut myself up in my room, and turn the lights down, and sometimes unplug the telephone, and what I do during that time is secret, and I am almost ashamed of it. I am ashamed because the words, as they come, are not good enough for the teachers whose affirmation I still need, though they may be good enough for my peers.

I want each student in my class to feel like the most important student, like their writing is worth the meticulous scrutiny and experienced opinion that I, above all their peers, can give them. I'd like to be to them what my mentors have been to me: an authority figure capable of approving or disapproving of their writing. I want my opinion to matter more than the grades I give. And I want my students to understand that the act of writing is a secret, often lonely act, that first drafts are dreadful secrets, things to keep hidden, and that these feelings, which strike me as a curious mixture of shame and pride, and necessary to great writing.

Postmodernism and Composition:
The Persuasion

First Draft

Tom Connelly

Tom Connelly   **First Draft**

Postmodernism and Composition: The Persuasion

> See to it no one takes you captive through philosophy and
> empty deception, according to the tradition of men, according
> to the elementary principles of the world. (Colosians, 2:8)

> Curriculum isn't just learning out of a textbook; curriculum is
> those kinds of community-involved life experiences that hap-
> pen from the time a child wakes up in the morning until the
> time they go to bed. (Michael Charney, Trustee Cleveland
> Teachers Union.)[1]

During one of my classes as a graduate student, a professor related the following anecdote. He was teaching English at a southern university and it was the
first day of the semester. Students filed into his classroom with nervous anticipation, unsure what his class would be like and what was expected of them. He, of
course, was aware of all this and began to drone on about the syllabus and the
course in general. Throughout his opening remarks he was calm and composed,
if not boring. His students, likewise, began to suspect that this was going to be
the dullest experience of their lives. Then something startling occurred. A
strange man stormed into the room, pointed to him exclaiming—"Williams,
you're fired!"—and left, slamming the door behind him. The students were in a
state of shock, trying to process what was going on. He, still calm and composed,
turned toward them and said—"Write what you just saw. Class dismissed." Not
surprisingly, each student came back with a different version of what happened.

I like this exercise. It creates a startling first impression of what a writing
course can be about—varied experiences as opposed to textbook scenarios. It
also effectively questions the nature of perception and reality. The papers that
the students wrote and later read to each other were each valid; they were
"true" accounts of what happened during the first five minutes of class. But they
were also, at times, contradictory, since each account was shaped by the personal experiences and prejudices of each writer. Students, hopefully, left the exercise with an awareness of two things: 1) that they each have a personal voice (a
point of view that is separate from everyone else in the classroom) that is capable of contributing something original; 2) that there is no all-encompassing
"truth" about what actually happened—all that is available are versions.

As a composition teacher I find such an exercise compelling. I believe it is
important to empower writers, to instill a confidence that will enable them to
give voice to their own experiences. I also feel that the exercise is dramatic, original, and easy to use. My fear, though, is that composition teachers will utilize
such exercises for their novelty—their shock value, without ever considering the
effect on their students.

In the preceding exercise, for example, the focus was on a simple event—
staging a drama and asking a room of eyewitnesses to report what they saw. The

effect of the exercise, however, was anything but simple. It raised several postmodern issues concerning truth and experience. There was no master narrative at work in that classroom; rather, knowledge was shown to be pluralized and fluid. The subjects involved left knowing that their experience, thought it may be shared through language, could never be "known" by another. They realized that they each live in isolation, however empowering that may be.

Due to what I believe to be the long-term effect of this exercise—isolation—I am reluctant to stage the event in my classroom. It would be incredibly shortsighted of me to use postmodern theory as a tool of empowerment without ever dealing with its nihilistic associations. Other writers seem less concerned. W. Ross Winterowd, for example, uses postmodern ideologies in his reexamination of the student essay.[2] He questions the traditional modes of formal and informal writing and posits exploratory discourse as a viable model for composition production. Writers, using this model, would engage in a discovery process, ignoring conclusion and hopefully invigorating their writing. Paul Northam similarly contends that post-structuralist practices will inspire young writers. Such practices will lead students to "the cultivation of a sense of playful intellectual joy in interpretation and a competence in their [abilities]."[3] In both examples the writers use postmodern/post-structuralist ideas to enliven the writing process. They each are attracted to the notion of empowerment, but neglect to consider the ramifications of such power. Is exploratory discourse necessarily a good thing? What if the discourse becomes unhinged, degenerating into confusion? When does the "joy" of interpretation become bitter disillusionment? The optimism of these theories of composition does not seem to allow room for such speculation or concern.

Many would argue that my concerns are belated. We already live in a postmodern world and it is not a teacher's responsibility to try to convince students otherwise. I would agree, but only in part. My students are required to keep a journal throughout the semester to catalog their thoughts about being college freshman. After reading them, I would agree that my student's experiences are influenced by postmodernism. They each have varied lives; they each come from different ethnic and economic backgrounds. One is dealing with the death of a friend who committed suicide, another the death of a friend who was involved in a car accident. I have a student who is an alcoholic. I have a student whose friend is in a gang. I have a student who is a jazz musician. I have students who write about their husbands, their fiancees, even their unborn children. They come from fractured homes and they view their futures with uncertainty and confusion. Their language consists of sound bites from movies and radio. I see all these differences as potential sites for excavation and I would be stupid not to encourage my students to draw on these experiences in their writing. Exploratory writing could be rewarding, but up to a point.

Let me explain. I have a student who spent some time during high school in a Christian school in north Dallas. After transferring to a public high school his sophomore year he realized how inadequately he had been trained. The teachers at his former school did not have any background in education; they were selected from the church congregation, sometimes lacking the knowledge to even take the course they taught (my student complained that this algebra teacher didn't know how to do it). Using postmodernism in the composition classroom would necessitate a restructuring of the teacher/student relationship. In each of the above examples, the teacher disappears into the background. In the anecdote, the teacher becomes a performer, another eyewitness with a version of the "truth." Northam and Winterowd both offer strategies that distance the teacher from the writer. As my student illustrates, however, such distancing doesn't work. He still needed an authority figure to guide him through the course, just as I believe writers need guides to help them make sense of their own writing.

What I am arguing for is not the abandonment of postmodernism strategies in the classroom. Postmodernism, rather, needs to be confronted and dealt with critically. Teachers need to recognize when they are being drawn into "the spectacle" of theory, the exciting and shocking exercises that transform traditional classroom experiences into something original. The classroom should indeed be the site of originality, but not at the detriment of the student.

Notes

[1] *Children in American Schools*, written and directed by Jeffrey Hayden, The Saint/Hayden Company, 1996

[2] W. Ross Winterowd, "Rediscovering the Essay," *Composition Theory for the Postmodern Classroom*, ed. Gary Olson and Sidney I. Dobrin (Albany: State U of New York P, 1994) 121.

[3] Paul Northam, "Heuristics and Beyond: Deconstruction/Inspiration and the Teaching of Writing Invention," *Writing and Reading Differently*, ed. G. Douglas Atkins and Michael L. Johnson (U P of Kansas, 1985) 126.

Postmodernism and Composition:
The Persuasion

Rewrite

Tom Connelly

Tom Connelly   **Rewrite**

Postmodernism and Composition: The Persuasion

> See to it no one takes you captive through philosophy and
> empty deception, according to the tradition of men, according
> to the elementary principles of the world. (Colosians, 2:8)

> Curriculum isn't just learning out of a textbook; curriculum is
> those kinds of community-involved life experiences that hap-
> pen from the time a child wakes up in the morning until the
> time they go to bed. (Michael Charney, Trustee Cleveland
> Teachers Union.)[1]

During one of my graduate classes, a professor related the following anecdote. He was teaching English at a southern university, and it was the first day of
the semester. Students filed into his classroom with nervous anticipation, unsure
what his class would be like and what was expected of them. He, of course, was
aware of all this and began to drone on about the syllabus and the course in general. Throughout his opening remarks he was calm and composed, if not boring.
His students, likewise, began to suspect that this was going to be the dullest experience of their lives. Then something startling occurred. A stranger stormed into
the room, pointed at him exclaiming—"You're fired!"—then left, slamming the
door behind him. He then turned toward his dismayed class and said—"Write
what you just saw. Class dismissed." Not surprisingly, each student came back
with a different version of the shocking, yet calculated, event.

I like this exercise. It creates a startling first impression of what a writing
course can be about—varied experiences as opposed to textbook scenarios. It
also effectively questions the nature of perception and reality. The papers that
the students wrote and later read to each other were each valid; they were
"true" accounts of what happened during the first five minutes of class. But they
were also, at times, contradictory, since the personal experiences and prejudices
of each writer shaped each account. According to my professor, the aim of the
exercise was to highlight such inconsistencies. Students hopefully realized that
the "truths" they cling to were ultimately arbitrary—dependent not on any objective reality, but rather, on something more subjective.

As a composition teacher I find such an exercise compelling. I believe an
awareness of varied "truths" can empower students' writing. It could show students how they each have a personal voice, a point of view that is separate and
original from everyone else's in the classroom. This would hopefully instill a confidence that would enable them to give voice to their own experiences in later
papers. I also feel that the exercise is dramatic, original, and easy to use. My fear,
though, is that composition teachers will use such exercises for their novelty—
their shock value, without ever considering the effect on their students.

In the preceding exercise, for example, the focus was on a simple event—
staging a drama and asking a room of eyewitnesses to report what they saw. The

effect of the exercise, however, was anything but simple. My professor wished to demonstrate the pluralized and fluid nature of knowledge; he wanted to show how no master narrative was at work in that classroom. But once that awareness is achieved, the meaning of the exercise itself becomes fluid. Students' may become empowered by learning that their experience, though shared through language, can never be "known" by another. But they could just as easily become disempowered by the realization that they each live in isolation. An exercise that deconstructs master narratives may be exciting and shocking, but it isn't necessarily a good thing.

Due to what I believe to be a possible effect of this exercise—isolation, I am reluctant to stage the event in my classroom. It would be incredibly shortsighted if I used postmodern theory as a tool of empowerment without ever dealing with its nihilistic associations. Other writers seem less concerned. W. Ross Winterowd, for example, uses postmodern ideologies in his reexamination of the student essay.[2] He questions the traditional modes of formal and informal writing and posits exploratory discourse as a viable model for composition production. Teachers, he argues, should encourage writing used as a discovery process. They should not focus so much on the form of paper (the premises and thesis of an argument, for example), but instead on what the student is able to learn from his or her ideas. Paul Northam similarly contends that post-structuralist practices will inspire young writers. Deconstructive reading, or reading against the grain, will lead students to "the cultivation of a sense of playful intellectual joy in interpretation and a competence in their [abilities]."[3] Both writers use postmodern/post-structuralist ideas to enliven the writing process. They are attracted to the notion of empowerment, but neglect to consider the consequences of such power. Is exploratory discourse necessarily a good thing? What if the discourse becomes unhinged, degenerating into confusion? When does the "joy" of interpretation become bitter disillusionment? The optimism of these theories of composition does not seem to allow room for such speculation or concern.

Many would argue that my concerns are belated. We already live in a postmodern world, and it is not a teacher's responsibility to try to convince students otherwise. I would agree, but only in part. My students are required to keep a journal throughout the semester to catalog their thoughts about their first year of college. After reading them, I would agree that postmodernism influences my student's experiences. They each have varied lives; they each come from different ethnic and economic backgrounds. One is dealing with the death of a friend who committed suicide, another the death of a friend who was involved in a car accident. I have a student who is an alcoholic. I have a student whose friend is in a gang. I have a student who is a jazz musician. I have students who write about their husbands, their fiancees, even their unborn children. They come from fractured homes, and they view their futures with uncertainty and confusion. Their language consists of sound bites from movies and radio. I see all these differences as potential sites for excavation and I would be stupid not to encourage my students to draw on these experiences in their writing. Exploratory writing could be rewarding, but up to a point.

Let me explain. I have a student who spent some time during high school in a Christian school in north Dallas. After transferring to a public high school his sophomore year he realized how inadequately he had been trained. The teachers at his former school did not have any background in education; they were selected from the church congregation, sometimes lacking the knowledge to even take the course they taught (my student complained that his algebra teacher was competent in the subject). Ironically, my experience with postmodernism in the composition classroom suggests that this would be the ideal teaching environment. The "teacher" should disappear into the background, allowing students to develop their own writing style. But as my student illustrates, such distancing doesn't work. He needed an authority figure to guide him through the course; he needed to be sure that his calculations were sound—not just the product of exploratory exercise. I believe that students of composition require the same kind of security. They need guides to help them make sense of their own writing.

What I am arguing for is not the abandonment of postmodernism strategies in the classroom. Postmodernism, rather, needs to be confronted and dealt with critically. Teachers need to recognize when they are being drawn into "the spectacle" of theory, the exciting and shocking exercises that transform traditional classroom experiences into something original. The classroom should indeed be the site of originality, but not at the detriment of the student.

Notes

[1] *Children in American Schools*, written and directed by Jeffrey Hayden, The Saint/Hayden Company, 1996

[2] W. Ross Winterowd, "Rediscovering the Essay," *Composition Theory for the Postmodern Classroom*, ed. Gary Olson and Sidney I. Dobrin (Albany: State U of New York P, 1994) 121.

[3] Paul Northam, "Heuristics and Beyond: Deconstruction/Inspiration and the Teaching of Writing Invention," *Writing and Reading Differently*, ed. G. Douglas Atkins and Michael L. Johnson (U P of Kansas, 1985) 126.

Part III
Bibliography

Camp, G. *Teaching Writing: Essays from the Bay Area Writing Project.* Upper Montclair, NJ: Boynton/Cook, 1982.

Clifford, John, and John Schilb, eds. *Writing Theory and Critical Theory.* New York: MLA, 1994.

Coles, William E., Jr. *Teaching Composition.* Upper Montclair, NJ: Boynton/Cook, 1974.

———. *The Plural I: The Teaching of Writing.* New York: Holt, Reinhart and Winston, 1978; rpt. Upper Montclair, NJ: Boynton/Cook, 1988.

Deen, Rosemary, and Marie Ponsot. *Beat Not the Poor Desk: Writing: What to Teach, How to Teach It, and Why.* Upper Montclair, NJ: Boynton/Cook, 1982.

Faigley, Lester. *Fragments of Rationality: Postmodernity and the Subject of Composition.* Pittsburgh: U of Pittsburgh P, 1992.

Fulwiler, Toby. *Teaching with Writing.* Portsmouth, NH: Heinemann-Boynton/Cook, 1987.

Greenblatt, Stephen, and Giles Gunn, eds. *Redrawing the Boundaries: The Transformation of English and American Studies.* New York: MLA, 1992.

Irmscher, William. F. *Teaching Expository Writing.* New York: Holt, Rinehart and Winston, 1979.

Lindemann, Erica. *A Rhetoric for Writing Teachers.* 3rd ed. New York: Oxford U P, 1995.

McQuade, D. *The Territory of Language: Linguistics, Stylistics, and the Teaching of Composition.* 2nd ed. Carbondale, IL: Southern Illinois U P, 1986.

Moffett, James. *Teaching the Universe of Discourse.* Boston: Houghton Mifflin, 1968.

Murray, Donald. *Learning by Teaching: Selected Articles on Writing and Teaching.* Portsmouth, NH: Heinemann-Boynton/Cook, 1982.

———. *A Writer Teaches Writing.* 2nd ed. Boston: Houghton Mifflin, 1985.

Neel, Jasper. *Plato, Derrida, and Writing.* Carbondale, IL: Southern Illinois U P, 1988.

Russell, Christina G., and Robert L. McDonald, eds. *Teaching Composition in the 90s: Sites of Contention.* New York: HarperCollins, 1994.

Shaughnessy, Mina. *Errors and Expectations: A Guide for the Teacher of Basic Writing.* New York: Oxford U P, 1977.

Sheridan, Jean, ed. *Writing across the Curriculum and the Academic Library: A Guide for Librarians, Instructors, and Writing Program Directors.* Westport, CT: Greenwood, 1995.

Tate, Gary, and Edward P.J. Corbett. *Teaching Freshman Composition.* New York: Oxford U P, 1967.

———. *Teaching Composition: Twelve Bibliographic Essays.* Fort Worth: Texas Christian U P, 1976.

Tate, Gary, and Edward P.J. Corbett, eds. *The Writing Teacher's Sourcebook.* New York: Oxford U P, 1981.

White, Edward M. *Assigning, Responding, Evaluating: A Writing Teacher's Guide (Including Diagnostic Tests).* 2nd ed. New York: St. Martin's P, 1992.

Witte, Stephen, Neil Nakadate, and Roger D. Cherry, eds. *A Rhetoric of Doing: Essays on Written Discourse in Honor of James L. Kinneavy.* Carbondale, IL: Southern Illinois U P, 1992.

Writing Assignments

Bain, Alexander. *English Composition and Rhetoric.* London: Longmans, 1877.

Bartholomae, Donald. "Writing Assignments: Where Writing Begins." In *Forum: Essays on Theory and Practice in the Teaching of Writing.* Ed. P. Stock. Upper Montclair, NJ: Boynton/Cook, 1983. 300–312.

Coles, William E., Jr. *The Plural I: The Teaching of Writing.* New York: Holt, 1978.

———. "The Sense of Nonsense As a Design for Sequential Writing Assignments." *College Composition and Communication* 21 (1970): 27–34.

Farrell, Edmund J. "The Beginning Begets: Making Composition Assignments." *Rhetoric and Composition: A Sourcebook for Teachers.* Ed. Richard L. Graves. Rochelle Park, NJ: Hayden, 1976. 220–224.

Hillocks, George, Jr. *Research on Written Composition: New Directions for Teaching.* Urbana, IL: National Council of Teachers of English, 1986.

Irmscher, William F. *Teaching Expository Writing.* New York: Holt, 1972.

Kinneavy, James L. *A Theory of Discourse.* New York: Norton, 1980.

Larson, Richard. "Teaching Before We Judge: Planning Assignments in Composition." *Teaching High School Composition.* Eds. Gary Tate and Edward P.J. Corbett. New York: Oxford U P, 1970. 207–218.

Lunsford, Andrea. "Assignments for Basic Writers: Unresolved Issues and Needed Research." *Journal of Basic Writing* 5 (1986): 87–99.

MacDonald, S.P. "Problem Definition in Academic Writing." *College English* 49.3 (1987): 315–331.

Moffett, James. *Teaching the Universe of Discourse.* Boston: Houghton, 1968.

Polanyi, Michael. *Personal Knowledge: Towards a Post–Critical Philosophy.* New York: Harper, 1964.

Using Readings

Corcoran, William, and E. Evans, eds. *Readers, Texts, Teachers.* Upper Montclair, NJ: Boynton/Cook, 1987.

Ewald, Helen Rothschild. "What We Could Tell Advanced Student Writers about Audience." *JAC: A Journal of Composition Theory* 11.1 (1991): 147–158.

Fish, Stanley. *Is There a Text in This Class? The Authority of Interpretive Communities.* Cambridge, MA: Harvard U P, 1980.

Flynn, Elizabeth A. "The Classroom As Interpretive Community: Teaching Reader-Response Theory and Composition Theory to Preprofessional Undergraduates." In *Reorientations: Critical Theories and Pedagogies.* Eds. Bruce Heinricksen and Thais E. Morgan. Urbana, IL: U of Illinois P, 1990. 193–215.

Gamer, Michael. "Fictionalizing the Disciplines: Literature and the Boundaries of Knowledge." *College English* 57.3 (1995): 281–286.

Gould, C., and K. Gould. "College Anthologies of Readings and Assumptions about Literacy." *College Composition and Communication* 37 (1987): 204–211.

Green, Stuart. "Mining Texts in Reading to Write." *JAC: A Journal of Composition Theory* 12.1 (1992): 151–170.

Hayhoe, M., and S. Parker, eds. *Reading and Response.* Philadelphia and Buckingham, United Kingdom: Milton Keynes and Open U P, 1990.

Huckin, Thomas, and Linda Flower. "Reading for Points and Purposes." *JAC: A Journal of Composition Theory* 11.2 (1991): 347–362.

McCord, Phyllis Frus. "Reading Nonfiction in Composition Courses: From Theory to Practice."*College English* 47.7 (1985): 747–762.

Nelms, B.F., ed. *Literature in the Classroom: Readers, Texts, and Contexts.* Urbana, IL: National Council of Teachers of English, 1988.

Neverow, Vera. "Reading *A Room of One's Own* as a Model of Composition Theory." In *Virginia Woolf: Emerging Perspectives.* Eds. Mark Hussey and Vera Neverow. New York: Pace U P, 1994. 58–64.

Newkirk, Thomas. *Only Connect: Using Writing and Reading.* Upper Montclair, NJ: Boynton/Cook, 1986.

Nist, S., and D.L. Mealey. "Teacher-Directed Comprehension Strategies." In *Teaching Reading and Study Strategies at the College Level.* Eds. R.F. Flippo and D.C. Caverly. Newark, DE: International Reading Association, 1991. 42–85.

Salvatori, M. "Reading and Writing a Text: Correlations between Reading and Writing Patterns." *College English* 45 (7): 657–666.

Scholes, Robert. *Textual Power: Literary Theory and the Teaching of English.* New Haven, CT: Yale U P, 1985.

Shoos, Diane, Diana George, and Joseph Comprone. "Twin Peaks and the Look of Television: Visual Literacy in the Writing Classroom." *JAC: A Journal of Composition Theory* 13.2 (1993): 459–475.

Sleven, James F. "Reading and Writing in the Classroom and the Profession." In *Writing Theory and Critical Theory.* Eds. John Clifford and John Schilb. New York: MLA, 1994. 53–71.

Tierney, R.J., P.L. Anders, and J.N. Mitchell, eds. *Understanding Readers' Understanding: Theory and Practice.* Hillsdale, NJ: Lawrence Erlbaum, 1987.

Trimbur, John. "Literature and Composition: Separatism or Convergence?" *Journal of Teaching Writing* 3.1 (1984): 109–115.

Welch, Nancy. "One Student's Many Voices: Reading, Writing, and Responding with Bakthin." *JAC: A Journal of Composition Theory* 13.2 (1993): 493–502.

Wiley, Mark. "How to Read a Book: Reflections on the Ethics of Book Reviewing." *JAC: A Journal of Composition Theory* 13.2 (1993): 477–492.

Responding to Student Writing

Anson, Chris M. "The Artificial Art of Evaluating Writing." *Journal of Teaching Writing* 1.2 (1982): 159–170.

Anson, Chris M., ed. *Writing and Response: Theory, Practice and Research.* Urbana, IL: National Council of Teachers of English, 1989.

Berkenkotter, C. "Student Writers and Their Sense of Authority over Texts." *College Composition and Communication* 35.3 (1984): 312–319.

Brannon, Lil, and C.H. Knoblauch. "On Students' Right to Their Own Texts: A Model of Teacher Response." *College Composition and Communication* 33.2 (1982): 157–166.

Cooper, Charles. R., and Lee Odell, eds. *Evaluating Writing: Describing, Measuring, Judging.* Urbana, IL: National Council of Teachers of English, 1977.

Diederich, Paul B. *Measuring Growth in English.* Urbana, IL: National Council of Teachers of English, 1974.

Faigley, Lester, and Stephen Witte. "Analyzing Revision." *College Composition and Communication* 32.4 (1981): 400–414.

Haswell, Richard. "Minimal Marking." *College English* 45 (1983): 600–604.

Larson, Richard. "Training New Teachers of Composition in the Writing of Comments on Themes." *College Composition and Communication* 17 (1966): 152–155.

Lawson, B., S. Sterr Ryan, and W.R. Winterowd, eds. *Encountering Student Texts: Interpretive Issues in Reading Student Writing.* Urbana, IL: National Council of Teachers of English, 1989.

Sommers, Nancy. "Responding to Student Writing." *College Composition and Communication* 33 (1982): 148–156.

Spear, Karen. *Sharing Writing: Peer Response Groups in English Classes.* Portsmouth, NH: Boynton/Cook, 1988.

White, Edward M. "Post-Structural Literary Criticism and the Response to Student Writing." *College Composition and Communication* 35 (1984): 186–195.

———. *Teaching and Assessing Writing.* San Francisco: Jossey-Bass, 1986.

Conferences and Small Groups

Arbur, Rosemarie. "The Student Teacher Conference." *College Composition and Communication* 28 (1977): 338–342.

Beach, Richard. "Showing Students How to Assess: Demonstrating Techniques for Response in the Writing Conference." In *Writing and Response.* Ed. C.M. Anson. Urbana, IL: National Council of Teachers of English, 1989. 127–148.

Beaven, Mary H. "Individualized Goal Setting, Self Evaluation, and Peer Evaluation." In *Evaluating Writing: Describing Measuring, Judging.* Eds. Charles R. Cooper and Lee Odell. Urbana, IL: National Council of Teachers of English, 1977. 135–156.

Brooke, R.E. *Writing and Sense of Self: Identity Negotiation in Writing Workshops.* Urbana, IL: National Council of Teachers of English, 1991.

Bruffee, Kenneth A. "Writing and Reading as Collaborative or Social Acts." In *The Writer's Mind.* Eds. J.N. Hanes, P.A. Roth, J.R. Ramsey, and R.D. Foulke. Urbana, IL: National Council of Teacher of English, 1983. 159–170.

———. "Collaborative Learning and the 'Conversation of Mankind.'" *College English* 46.7 (1984): 635–652.

Carnicelli, T. "The Writing Conference: A One-to-One Conversation." In *Eight Approaches to Teaching Composition.* Eds. Timothy R. Donovan and Ben W. McClelland. Urbana, IL: National Council of Teachers of English, 1980. 101–131.

Flower, Linda, et al. "Detection, Diagnoses, and the Strategies of Revision." *College Composition and Communication* 37.1 (1986): 16–55.

Freedman, S.W., ed. *The Acquisition of Written Language: Response and Revision.* New York: Ablex, 1985.

Garrison, Roger. "One-to-One: Tutorial Instruction in Freshman Composition." *New Directions for Community Colleges* 2 (1974): 55–84.

George, D. "Working with Peer Groups in the Composition Classroom." *College Composition and Communication* 35.3 (1984): 320–326.

Gere, Allison Ruggles. *Writing Groups: History, Theory, and Implications.* Carbondale, IL: Southern Illinois U P, 1987.

Harris, Muriel. 1986. *Teaching One-to-One: The Writing Conference.* Urbana, IL: National Council of Teachers of English, 1986.

Jacobs, S.E., and A. Karlinger. 1977. "Helping Students to Think: The Effect of Speech Roles in Individual Conferences on Quality of Thought in Student Writing." *College English* 38(5): 489–505.

Jones, David. "The Five Minute Writing." *College Composition and Communication* 28 (1977): 194–196.

Murray, Donald. "The Listening Eye: Reflections on the Writing Conference." *College English* 41 (1979): 13–18.

Newkirk, T. "Direction and Misdirection in Peer Response." *College Composition and Communication* 35.3 (1984): 300–311.

——. "How Students Read Student Papers: An Exploratory Study." *Written Communication* 1 (3) 1984: 283–305.

——. "The First Five Minutes: Setting the Agenda in a Writing Conference." In *Writing and Response.* Ed. C.M. Anson. Urbana, IL: National Council of Teachers of English, 1989. 317–331.

Nystrand, M., and D. Brandt. "Response to Writing as a Context for Learning to Write." In *Writing and Response.* Ed. C.M. Anson. Urbana, IL: National Council of Teachers of English, 1989. 209–230.

Polanyi, Michael. *Personal Knowledge: Towards a Post-Critical Philosophy.* New York: Harper, 1964.

Thomas, D., and G. Thomas. "The Use of Rogerian Reflection in Small-Group Writing Conferences." In *Writing and Response.* Ed. C.M. Anson. Urbana, IL: National Council of Teachers of English, 1989. 114–126.

Trimbur, John. "Consensus and Difference in Collaborative Learning." *College English* 51 (6) 1989: 602–616.

Course Designs

Bartholomae, Donald, and Anthony Petrosky. *Facts, Artifacts and Counterfacts: Theory and Method for a Reading and Writing Course.* Upper Montclair, NJ: Boynton/Cook, 1986.

Bishop, Wendy. "Texts and Contexts: A Social-Rhetorical Model for Teaching Writing-with-Literature Courses." *The Writing Instructor* Summer 1986: 190–202.

Carden, P. "Designing a Course." In *Teaching Prose: A Guide for Writing Instructors.* Eds. F.V. Bogel and K.K. Gottschalk. New York: Norton, 1984. 20–45.

Connolly, Paul, and Teresa Vilardi, eds. *New Methods in College Writing Programs.* New York: MLA, 1986.

Donovan, Timothy R., and Ben W. McClelland, eds. *Eight Approaches to Teaching Composition.* Urbana, IL: National Council of Teacher of English, 1980.

Kail, Harvey. "Narratives of Knowledge: Story and Pedagogy in Four Composition Texts." *Rhetoric Review* 6.2 (1988): 179–191.

Klaus, Carl H., and Nancy Jones, eds. *Courses for Change in Writing: A Selection from the NEH/Iowa Institute.* Upper Montclair, NJ: Boynton/Cook, 1984.

Rose, Mike. "Remedial Writing Courses: A Critique and a Proposal." *College English* 45.2 (1983): 109–128.

Sherman, S.W. "Inventing an Elephant: History as Composition." In *Only Connect: Uniting Reading and Writing.* Ed. T. Newkirk. Upper Montclair, NJ: Boynton/Cook, 1986. 211– 226.

Welch, Kathleen. "Ideology and Freshman Textbook Production: The Place of Writing Theory in Writing Pedagogy." *College Composition and Communication* 38.3 (1987): 269–282.

Teaching Writing As Process
Abercrombie, M.L.J. *Anatomy of Judgement.* Harmondsworth: Penguin, 1960.
Bartholomae, Donald. "The Study of Error." *College Composition and Communication* 31 (1980): 253–269.
Beach, Richard. "Self-Evaluation Strategies of Extensive Revisers and Non-Revisers." *College Composition and Communication* 27 (1976): 160–164.
Berthoff, Ann. "The Problem with Problem Solving." *College Composition and Communication* 22 (1971): 237–242.
Bilsky, Manuel, McCrae Hazlitt, Robert E. Streeter, and Richard M. Weaver. "Looking for an Argument." *College English* 14 (1953): 210–216.
Briggs, John C. "Peter Elbow, Kenneth Burke, and the Idea of Magic." *JAC: A Journal of Composition Theory* 11.2 (1991): 363–375.
Britton, James, Tony Burgess, Nancy Martin, Alex McLeod, and Harold Rosen. *The Development of Writing Abilities.* Basingstoke: Macmillan Education, 1975.
Bruffee, Kenneth. "Writing and Reading As a Collaborative or Social Act." In *The Writer's Mind: Writing As a Mode of Thinking.* Eds. Janice Hays, Phyllis Roth, Jon Ramsey, and Robert Foulke. Urbana, IL: National Council of Teachers of English, 1983. 159–170.
——. *A Short Course in Writing.* 3rd ed. Boston: Little, Brown, 1985.
——. "Social Construction, Language, and the Authority of Knowledge." *College English* 48 (1986): 773–790.
Burke, Kenneth. *Counter-Statement.* Los Altos, CA: Hermes, 1931.
——. *A Rhetoric of Motives.* Englewood Cliffs, NJ: Prentice-Hall, 1950.
——. *A Grammar of Motives.* Englewood Cliffs, NJ: Prentice-Hall, 1952.
Corbett, Edward P.J. "Toward a Methodology of Heuristic Procedures." *College Composition and Communication* 30 (1979): 268–269.
Daly, John. "Writing Apprehension and Writing Competency." *Journal of Educational Research* 72 (1978): 10–14.
Daniell, Beth. "Theory, Theory Talk, and Composition." In *Writing Theory and Critical Theory.* Eds. John Clifford and John Schilb. New York: MLA, 1994. 127–140.
Dyer, Patricia M. "What Composition Theory Offers the Writing Teacher." In *Language Proficiency: Defining, Teaching, and Testing.* Ed. Louis A. Arena. New York: Plenum, 1990. 99–106.
Ede, Lisa. "What is Social about Writing As a Social Process?" CCCC paper. (1987): ERIC ED293151.
Elbow, Peter. *Writing without Teachers.* New York: Oxford U P, 1973.
——. *Writing with Power.* New York: Oxford U P, 1981.
——. *Embracing Contraries.* New York: Oxford U P, 1986.
——. "Reflections on Academic Discourse." *College English* 53 (1991): 135–155.
English, Hubert M., Jr. "Linguistic Theory as an Aid to Invention." *College Composition and Communication* 15 (1964): 136–140.
Faigley, Lester. "Competing Theories of Process: A Critique and a Proposal." *College English* 48 (1986): 527–542.
Flower, Linda. *Problem-Solving Strategies in Writing.* New York: Harcourt, Brace, and Jovanovich, 1981.

———. "The Construction of Purpose in Writing and Reading." *College English* 50 (1988): 528–550.

Flower, Linda, and John Hayes. "Problem-Solving Strategies and the Writing Process." *College English* 39 (1977): 449–462.

———. "Identifying the Organization of Writing Processes." In *Cognitive Processes in Writing: An Interdisciplinary Approach.* Eds. Lee Gregg and Erwin Sternberg. Hillsdale, NJ: Lawrence Erlbaum, 1980. 3–30.

———. "A Cognitive Process Theory of Writing." *College Composition and Communication* 32 (1981): 365–387.

———. "The Pregnant Pause: An Inquiry into the Nature of Planning." *Research in the Teaching of English* 15 (1981): 229–244.

———. "Interpretive Acts: Cognition and the Construction of Discourse." *Poetics* 16 (1987).

George, Diana. "The Politics of Social Construction and the Teaching of Writing." *Journal of Teaching Writing* 8 (1989): 1–10.

Glassner, Benjamin. "Discovering Audience/Inventing Purpose." CCCC paper (1983): ERIC ED227513.

Hairston, Maxine. "The Winds of Change: Thomas Kuhn and the Revolution in the Teaching of Writing." *College Composition and Communication* 33 (1982): 76–86.

Harrington, Elbert W. *Rhetoric and the Scientific Method of Inquiry: A Study of Invention.* Boulder: U of Colorado P, 1948.

Hassett, Michael. "Increasing Response-Ability through Mortification: A Burkean Perspective on Teaching Writing." *JAC: A Journal of Composition Theory* 15.3 (1995): 471–488.

Kantor, Kenneth. "Classroom Contexts and the Development of Writing Intuitions." In *New Directions in Composition Research.* Eds. Richard Beach and Lillian Bridwell. New York: Guilford, 1984.

Kaufer, David S., and Geisler, Cheryl. "A Scheme for Representing Written Argument." *JAC: A Journal of Composition Theory* 11.1 (1991): 107–122.

Knoblauch, C.H. and Lil Brannon. *Rhetorical Traditions and the Teaching of Writing.* Upper Montclair, NJ: Boynton/Cook, 1984.

LaBaugh, Ross. "Talking the Discourse: Composition Theory." In *Writing across the Curriculum and the Academic Library.* Ed. Jean Sheridan. Westport, CT: Greenwood, 1995. 23–31.

LeFevre, Karen Burke. *Invention As a Social Act.* Carbondale, IL: Southern Illinois U P, 1987.

Macrorie, Ken. *Writing to Be Read.* Rochelle, NJ: Hayden, 1968.

Matsuhashi, Ann. "Pausing and Planning: The Tempo of Written Discourse Production." *Research in the Teaching of English* 15 (1981): 113–134.

Minock, Mary. "Toward a Postmodern Pedagogy of Imitation." *JAC: A Journal of Composition Theory* 15.3 (1995): 289–509.

Moffett, James. *Teaching the Universe of Discourse.* Boston: Houghton Mifflin, 1968.

———. *Active Voice: A Writing Program across the Curriculum.* Portsmouth, NH: Boynton/Cook, 1981.

Newkirk, Thomas. "Anatomy of a Breakthrough: Case Study of a College Freshman Writer." In *New Directions in Composition Research.* Eds. Richard Beach and Lillian Bridwell. New York: Guilford, 1984.

Olson, Gary. "Social Construction and Composition Theory; A Conversation with Richard Rorty." *Journal of Advanced Composition* 9 (1989): 1–9.

Perl, Sondra. "The Composing Process of Unskilled College Writers." *Research in the Teaching of English* 13 (1979): 317–336.

Pianko, Sharon. "A Description of the Composing Process of College Freshmen Writers." *Research in the Teaching of English* 13 (1979): 5–22.

Pullman, George L. "Rhetoric and Hermeneutics: Composition, Invention, and Literature." *JAC: A Journal of Composition Theory* 14.2 (1994): 367–387.

Reither, James. "Academic Discourse Communities, Invention, and Learning to Write." CCCC paper (1986).

Roberts, Patricia, and Virginia Pompei-Jones. "Imagining Reasons: The Role of Imagination in Argumentation." *JAC: A Journal of Composition Theory* 15.3 (1995): 527–541.

Rohman, D. Gordon. "Pre-Writing: The Stage of Discovery in the Writing Process." *College Composition and Communication* 16 (1965): 106–112.

Rose, Mike. "Rigid Rules, Inflexible Plans, and the Stifling of Language: A Cognitive Analysis of Writer's Block." *College Composition and Communication* 39.4 (1980): 389–400.

——. *When a Writer Can't Write: Studies in Writer's Block and Other Composing Problems.* New York: Guilford, 1985.

——. "Narrowing the Mind and the Page." *College Composition and Communication* 39 (1988): 267–302.

Scardamalia, Marlene, Carl Bereiter, and Hillel Goelman. "The Role of Production Factors in Writing Ability." In *What Writers Know: The Language, Process, and Structures of Academic Discourse.* Ed. Mark Nystrand. New York: Academic, 1982. 173–210.

Schiappa, Edward. "Burkean Tropes and Kuhnian Science: A Social Constructionist Perspective on Language and Reality." *JAC: A Journal of Composition Theory* 13.2 (1993): 401–422.

Selzer, Jack. "Exploring Options in Composing." *College Composition and Communication* 35 (1984): 276–284.

Smith, Michael. *Reducing Writing Apprehension.* Urbana, IL: National Council of Teachers of English, 1984.

Sommers, Nancy. "Revision Strategies of Student Writers and Experienced Adult Writers." *College Composition and Communication* 31 (1980): 378–388.

Sosnoski, James J. "Postmodern Teachers in Their Postmodern Classrooms: Socrates Begone!" In *Contending with Words: Composition and Rhetoric in a Postmodern Age.* Eds. Patricia Harkin and John Schilb. New York: MLA, 1991. 198–219.

Sotirou, Peter. "Articulating a Hermeneutic Pedagogy: The Philosophy of Interpretation." *JAC: A Journal of Composition Theory* 13.2 (1993): 356–380.

Stallard, Charles. "An Analysis of the Writing Behaviors of Good Student Writers." *Research in the Teaching of English* 8 (1974): 206–218.

Walters, Frank D. "Isocrates and the Epistemic Return: Individuality and Community in Classical and Modern Rhetoric." *JAC: A Journal of Composition Theory* 13.1 (1993): 155–172.

Witte, Stephen. "Pre-Text and Composing." *College Composition and Communication* 38 (1987): 379–425.

Collaboration

Bizzell, Patricia. "Academic Discourse: Taxonomy of Conventions or Collaborative Practice?" CCCC paper (1986): ERIC ED270806.

Bruffee, Kenneth. "Writing and Reading As Collaborative or Social Act." In *The Writer's Mind: Writing As a Mode of Thinking.* Eds. Janice Hays, Phyllis Roth, Jon Ramsey, and Robert Foulke. Urbana: National Council of Teachers of English, 1983. 159–170.

Carey, Julia. "Not-Teaching Writing: Discovering the Writing Process through Collaboration." *Carleton Papers in Applied Linguistics* 3 (1983): 47–76.

Corder, Jim W. "Tribes and Displaced Persons: Some Observations on Collaboration." In *Theory and Practice in the Teaching of Writing: Rethinking the Discipline.* Ed. Lee Odell. Carbondale, IL: Southern Illinois U P, 1993. 271–288.

DeCiccio, Albert. "Social Constructionism and Collaborative Learning: Recommendations for Teaching Writing." CCCC paper (1988): ERIC ED294201.

Ede, Lisa. "The Case for Collaboration." CCCC paper. (1987): ERIC ED282212.

George, Diana. "Working with Peer Groups in the Composition Classroom." *College Composition and Communication* 35 (1984): 320–326.

Gere, Anne Ruggles. *Writing Groups.* Carbondale, IL: Southern Illinois U P, 1987.

Hermann, Andrea. "Teaching Writing with Peer Response Groups." ERIC ED307616.

Inge, M. Thomas. "The Art of Collaboration in Popular Culture." In *Eye on the Future: Popular Culture Scholarship into the Twenty-First Century.* Eds. Marilyn Motz, John Nachbar, et al. Bowling Green, OH: Popular, 1994. 31–42.

Lunsford, Andrea, and Lisa Ede. "Why Write . . . Together." *Rhetoric Review* 1 (1983): 157.

Mason, Edwin. *Collaborative Learning.* London: Ward Lock, 1970.

Nystrand, Martin. "A Social-Interactive Model of Writing." *Written Communication* 6 (1989): 66–85.

Smith, David. "Some Difficulties with Collaborative Learning." *Journal of Advanced Composition* 9 (1989): 45–57.

Spellmeyer, Kurt. "On Conventions and Collaboration: The Open Road and the Iron Cage." In *Writing Theory and Critical Theory.* Eds. John Clifford and John Schilb. New York: MLA, 1994.

Stewart, Donald. "Collaborative Learning and Composition: Boon or Bane?" *Rhetoric Review* 7 (1988): 58–83.

Trimbur, John. "Collaborative Learning and Teaching Writing." In *Perspectives on Research and Scholarship in Composition.* Eds. Ben McClelland and Tim Donovan. New York: MLA, 1985.

Winkelmann, Carol L. "Electronic Literacy, Critical Pedagogy, and Collaboration: A Case for Cyborg Writing." *Computers and the Humanities* 29.6 (1995): 431–448.

Teaching Grammar and Style

Baron, Dennis E. *Grammar and Good Taste: Reforming the American Language.* New Haven: Yale U P, 1982.

Bartholomae, Donald. "The Study of Error." *College Composition and Communication* 31 (1980): 253–269.

Christensen, Francis. "A Generative Rhetoric of the Sentence." *College Composition and Communication* 14 (1963): 155–161.

———. "A Generative Rhetoric of the Paragraph." *College Composition and Communication* 16 (1965): 146–156.

Corbett, Edward P.J. "Approaches to the Study of Style." In *Teaching Composition: Twelve Bibliographic Essays.* Ed. Gary Tate. Fort Worth: Texas Christian U P, 1987.

Crew, Louie. "Rhetorical Beginnings: Professional and Amateur." *College Composition and Communication* 38 (1987): 346–350.

D'Eloia, Sarah. "The Uses—and Limits—of Grammar." In *A Sourcebook for Basic Writing Teachers.* Ed. Theresa Enos. New York: Random House, 1987.

Faigley, Lester. "Names in Search of a Concept: Maturity, Fluency, Complexity, and Growth in Written Syntax." *College Composition and Communication* 31 (1980): 291–300.

Harris, Muriel, and Katherine R. Rowan. "Explaining Grammatical Concepts." *Journal of Basic Writing* 6 (1989): 21–41.

Haswell, R.H. "Error and Change in College Student Writing." *Written Communication* 5.9 (1988): 479–499.

Horning, Alice. "Readable Writing: The Role of Cohesion and Redundancy." *JAC: A Journal of Composition Theory* 11.1 (1991): 135–145.

Kolln, M. *Understanding English Grammar.* 3rd ed. New York: Macmillan, 1990.

——. *Rhetorical Grammar.* New York: Macmillan, 1991.

Lanham, Richard. *Analyzing Prose.* New York: Scribner's, 1983.

O'Hare, Frank. *Sentence Combining: Improving Student Writing without Formal Grammar Instruction.* Urbana, IL: National Council of Teachers of English, 1973.

Shaughnessy, Mina. *Errors and Expectations: A Guide for the Teacher of Basic Writing.* New York: Oxford U P, 1977.